PUBLIC DEBT AND THE BIRTH OF THE DEMOCRATIC STATE

FRANCE AND GREAT BRITAIN, 1688–1789

Does establishing representative democracy increase commitment to repay public debt? This book develops a new theory about the link between debt and democracy and applies it to a classic historical comparison: Great Britain in the eighteenth century, which had strong representative institutions and sound public finance, versus ancien regime France, which had neither. The book argues that whether representative institutions improve commitment depends on the opportunities for government creditors to form new coalitions with other social groups, which is more likely to occur when a society is divided across multiple political cleavages. It then presents historical evidence to show that improved access to finance in Great Britain after 1688 had as much to do with the development of the Whig Party as with constitutional changes. In France, the balance of partisan forces made it unlikely that an early adoption of "English-style" institutions would have improved credibility. Given the importance of government credibility for different issues, the arguments developed here will be relevant for a wide range of scholars.

David Stasavage is a Lecturer in the Department of International Relations at the London School of Economics. His research focuses on the political economy of money and finance and on comparative political economy more generally. He holds a Ph.D. from the Department of Government at Harvard University and has published in a number of political science and economics journals.

T0370636

POLITICAL ECONOMY OF INSTITUTIONS AND DECISIONS

Series Editors

Randall Calvert, Washington University, St. Louis
Thrainn Eggertsson, Max Planck Institute, Germany, and University of Iceland

Founding Editors

James E. Alt, Harvard University
Douglass C. North, Washington University, St. Louis

Other Books in the Series

Continued on page following index

PUBLIC DEBT AND THE BIRTH OF THE DEMOCRATIC STATE

France and Great Britain, 1688–1789

DAVID STASAVAGE

London School of Economics

CAMBRIDGE
UNIVERSITY PRESS

CAMBRIDGE UNIVERSITY PRESS
Cambridge, New York, Melbourne, Madrid, Cape Town, Singapore, São Paulo

Cambridge University Press
The Edinburgh Building, Cambridge CB2 8RU, UK

Published in the United States of America by Cambridge University Press, New York

www.cambridge.org
Information on this title: www.cambridge.org/9780521809672

First published 2003
This digitally printed version 2008

A catalogue record for this publication is available from the British Library

Library of Congress Cataloguing in Publication data

Stasavage, David.
Public debt and the birth of the democratic state : France and Great Britain,
1688–1789 / David Stasavage.
    p.   cm. – (Political economy of institutions and decisions)
Includes bibliographical references and index.
ISBN 0-521-80967-3
    1. Debts, Public – Europe – History.   2. Europe – Politics and government –
1648–1789. I. Title.   II. Series.

HJ8615 .S85   2003
336.41′09′033 – dc21   2002031583

ISBN 978-0-521-80967-2 hardback
ISBN 978-0-521-07127-7 paperback

For Emmanuelle

Contents

Acknowledgments

When I first began work on this book I was interested in exploring whether the eighteenth-century experiences of France and Great Britain could provide general lessons about the link between representative democracy and policy credibility. Like many other scholars, I had been influenced by an article published by Douglass North and Barry Weingast in 1989 that argued that the constitutional changes associated with the Glorious Revolution of 1688 had allowed the British state to commit to repaying its debt and thus to gain unprecedented access to finance. Their argument also seemed well supported by the experience of ancien régime France, where the monarchy had near absolute authority, yet it struggled to find deficit finance and regularly resorted to default. While fascinated by the comparison, I was struck by several unanswered questions; most importantly, why would granting greater authority to Parliament in the United Kingdom result in commitment to repay debt when government creditors at this time had only limited representation in the House of Commons? I was also surprised to discover that many historians of eighteenth-century Britain considered that the emergence of cohesive political parties after 1688 was as significant a development as the constitutional changes following the Glorious Revolution. To confront these issues, in this book I have sought to develop new theoretical propositions about public debt and democratic politics and then evaluate them using historical evidence from France and Great Britain during the eighteenth century. In doing so I have been helped by a great number of people, all of whom have proved open to a research project which is necessarily interdisciplinary. A number of people read and commented on several preliminary papers that laid the basis for the final book, including Lawrence Broz, Keith Dowding, Macartan Humphreys, Phil Keefer, Gilat Levy, Richard Mash, Ken Scheve, Ken Shepsle, Barry Weingast, and Stewart Wood. I was also fortunate to receive comments from participants at seminars organized at Harvard (by Jeff Frieden), New York University (by Bill Clark and Mike Gilligan), Washington University in St. Louis (by Randall Calvert), Yale (by Ken Scheve), Trinity College, Dublin (by Ken Benoit), the London School of Economics (LSE) (by Cheryl Schonhardt-Bailey), and Oxford (by Iain McLean and Stewart Wood). The following people graciously gave comments on the book manuscript: Michael Behrent, Randall Calvert, Jeff Frieden, David Hayton, Phil Hoffman, Iain McLean, Andy Rutten, and Norman Schofield. Two anonymous readers for Cambridge University Press also gave useful comments and suggestions, and Stephanie Sakson provided editorial advice on the final version of the manuscript. Andrew Hanham and David Hayton also kindly allowed me to read material from the History of Parliament Trust's forthcoming *The House of Commons: 1690–1715*, and Michel Troper suggested several readings on the separation of powers that I would not have otherwise discovered. I especially thank the series editor, Randall Calvert, for the advice he offered from beginning to end, and Lewis Bateman at Cambridge University Press, who also provided much advice that improved the project. In terms of funding, the Suntory-Toyota International Centre for Economics and Related Disciplines at the LSE provided a grant that allowed me the time to complete the manuscript. Finally, I thank Emmanuelle Ertel for her support and patience. This book is dedicated to her.

I

Introduction

1. Credibility and Public Debt

Like many areas of economic policy, public borrowing is subject to a credibility problem. Borrowing on capital markets is advantageous, because it gives governments a means of deferring part of the cost of financing public goods. A state that has access to credit can expand public investment without a sharp and immediate increase in taxation. The problem is that once a government has borrowed, it may face incentives to defer repayment or even to default on its obligations, in order to reduce the burden of taxation on those who contribute to repay debts. Default was a common occurrence that hindered the development of public borrowing in early modern Europe. Today, default may no longer be a worry for those who are considering investing in bonds issued by OECD governments, but it is a major issue for governments in developing and transition economies that seek to offer assurances about debt repayment. If prospective lenders anticipate that a government may default, they will invest only if they are given a high rate of return that compensates for this risk. In extreme cases, they will refrain from lending at all.

This book investigates the link between public debt and representative democracy. In it I develop three theoretical arguments about the effect of constitutional checks and balances, political parties, and bureaucratic delegation on government credibility, and I then confront these propositions with historical evidence from England and France during the eighteenth century. In a concluding chapter I consider broader implications of my findings, focusing on links between democracy and economic performance and on the study of institutions. The theoretical sections of the book use basic game-theoretic models to examine how different institutional features of representative government influence the possibility for states to commit to repaying their debts. While there are now a number of studies that investigate how representative institutions may allow governments to solve commitment problems, some authors have argued that this literature often fails to explicitly consider partisan motivations on the part of political actors.[1] Alternatively, those models of commitment problems in debt and taxation that do take partisan motivations into account often pay only limited attention to institutional features of decision making.[2] The theoretical and empirical analysis here attempts to fill this gap by drawing simultaneously on political economy theories that emphasize partisan pressures on economic policy, as well as analyses that show how the rules of democratic decision making may influence economic policy choices.

I pay particular attention to three features of representative political institutions that may improve a government's ability to make credible commitments. The first emphasizes constitutional checks and balances (multiple veto points in current terminology). According to one view, which extends back to theorists such as Madison and Montesquieu, representative institutions improve commitment when they involve features such as a division of power between legislature and executive or between multiple houses of a legislature. My first main argument suggests that while constitutional checks and balances can improve possibilities for credible commitment, they are neither a necessary nor a sufficient condition for this to occur. They are not a necessary condition, because interests opposed to default may gain influence even in the absence of checks and balances. They are not a sufficient condition, because those opposed to default may fail to gain influence even in a country where the constitution provides for checks and balances. The implications of this argument for credible commitment have not been previously examined.

A second potential credibility-enhancing feature of representative institutions involves party formation in a plural society. When governments borrow, a division is likely to emerge between those who own public debt and those who pay the taxes to service public debt. This raises the

---

[1] See Przeworksi and Limongi (1993) and Elster (2000). The most frequently cited piece in the literature on representative institutions and credible commitment is North and Weingast (1989). See also Bates (1996), De Long and Shleifer (1993), Firmin-Sellers (1994), Levy and Spiller (1996), North (1981, 1990), Olson (1993, 2000), Shepsle (1991), Tsebelis (2002), and Weingast (1995, 1997).

[2] A good example here is the model in Persson and Tabellini (1994).

question of how society could commit to repaying debt if creditors are a minority of the population. My second main argument suggests that in societies where there are multiple dimensions of political conflict, even if government creditors are a small minority, other groups can face incentives to support timely repayment of debts in order to gain the support of government creditors on issues such as religion, foreign policy, or constitutional questions. As a result, careful attention should be paid to whether political conflict is in fact multidimensional and to whether government creditors are able to form durable coalitions with other social groups. This second argument implies that democratic compromise may provide commitment even in the absence of constitutional checks and balances.[3]

A third feature of representative government that may enhance credibility involves the possibility for rulers and politicians to delegate authority to individuals who are committed to pursuing a particular policy, whether it be repaying debt, maintaining low inflation, or regulating industries in a socially desirable manner. In the area of public borrowing it was common for rulers in early modern Europe to delegate authority with the express intent of improving their credibility. So, for example, a ruler might give a group of officials the right to manage public revenues so as to ensure full debt repayment. My third main argument suggests that bureaucratic delegation can reduce default risk, but it will be ineffectual in doing so unless creditor interests have power within a representative assembly, either as an outright majority or as part of a majority coalition. The reason is that when government creditors lack such political influence, rulers will find it easy to alter unilaterally agreements with individuals to whom they have delegated.

In exploring the politics of debt repayment, this book also asks when the institutions or practices that reduce the risk of default are consistent with basic democratic principles. The key question here is, When does commitment occur as a result of democratic politics pushing policies toward "moderate" outcomes? and alternatively, When is the problem solved only at the expense of democracy, by giving government creditors a privileged position in society? As a result, this study should be relevant not only to theoretical debates about credibility, but also to debates about the "structural power of capital" and economic policy making in an era of global finance.

---

[3] The effect of multi-issue conflict on economic policy choices has also been considered recently by Besley and Coate (2001) and Roemer (1998, 1999, 2001).

2. Historical Setting and Scope of the Study

My empirical focus on Britain and France is motivated by the fact that it has become popular to contrast the financial experiences of these two countries during the eighteenth century. Great Britain has been portrayed as the first state to establish a modern system of public finance, while France has been viewed more frequently as an example of failed reform.[4] For some authors, understanding the development of state finance in the two countries has been the end objective of study, while for others, state finance has proved of interest because of the possible link with other developments including economic growth and international rivalries.[5] In this book I pursue the former approach. As a result, I do not directly consider whether state finances must be sound before private financial markets can develop.[6] Nor do I seek to ask whether the Glorious Revolution in Great Britain coincided with increased protection of property rights in the economy more generally.[7] My objective is instead to consider Great Britain and France as fascinating cases that can be used to develop more general inferences about the link between representative government and credible commitment. In so doing I hope to add to other recent work that considers the link between political institutions and state finance in early modern Europe.[8] I also hope to show that it is possible to use game theoretic models of politics combined with historical analysis in the style of "comparative historical institutionalism."[9] Finally, while I draw extensively on research in the fields of economic history and political history, as well as primary sources in selected areas, it is worth emphasizing that this book is primarily a work of political science. My goal for the empirical

---

[4] Several classic contributions on the development of state finance in Britain include Clapham's study on the Bank of England (1958), Dickson (1967), Roseveare (1969, 1991), and, more recently, Brewer (1989) and Jones (1988). Knowledge about state finance in eighteenth-century France has been significantly expanded by Hoffman, Postel-Vinay, and Rosenthal (2000), Lüthy (1959–61), Marion (1919), Riley (1987), and Velde and Weir (1992). Comparative studies on state finance include Bonney (1999) and Mathias and O'Brien (1976).

[5] See Schultz and Weingast (1996).

[6] This is a claim made by North and Weingast (1989) but contested by Hoffman et al. (2000). See also Rousseau and Sylla (2001) for a more general discussion on the historical link between financial development and growth.

[7] Clark (1996) has argued that security of property rights was a feature of the British economy well before 1688.

[8] See Carruthers (1996), Ertman (1997), Hoffman and Norberg (1994), Potter (1997, 2000), Potter and Rosenthal (1997), and Root (1994).

[9] See Thelen (1999) on this point.

chapters is to draw on historical work on England and France in order to gain new perspectives on enduring questions posed by political scientists and economists. Likewise, I hope that historians may find this book of interest to the extent that it draws links between partisan politics, political institutions, and state finance in a way that existing work may not have emphasized.

The British historical background to this study involves the dramatic set of changes that took place in English government finance after the Glorious Revolution of 1688. When faced with the need to borrow, English monarchs before 1688 had resorted largely to ad hoc methods; default on these loans had always been a possibility; and as a result the Crown had often been unable to gain access to credit at anything less than exorbitant rates of interest. After the Glorious Revolution this picture changed dramatically. Methods for borrowing were regularized, Parliament gained substantial prerogatives in the area of public finance, the Bank of England was created, and the Crown found itself able to borrow larger amounts at lower rates of interest than ever before. Many of these changes were directly inspired by earlier institutional reforms in the Netherlands, a subject I explore in Chapter 3. It was the simultaneous nature of these developments in Great Britain that prompted North and Weingast (1989) in their seminal article to suggest there was a causal link between the establishment of a limited monarchy in the United Kingdom and improved access to credit.

Chapter 4 presents evidence to show that interest rates on British government debt did indeed take a downward trend after 1688. However, what North and Weingast's argument seems less able to explain is why it took over thirty years after 1688 before the British government could borrow as cheaply as could the government of Holland, which was universally recognized at the time for its creditworthiness. Moreover, despite the long-term trend toward lower costs of borrowing, there was very significant volatility in interest rates during the reigns of King William III (1689–1702) and of Queen Anne (1702–14), as well as periodic runs on Bank of England shares. At times during these years the British Crown actually found itself borrowing at rates as high as those that had prevailed before 1688, and as high as those paid by the French monarchy. These observations raise questions about how debt politics evolved over time in the United Kingdom. Was this post-1688 volatility related to political events, such as changes in the partisan control of government? What were the factors that allowed the British government after 1715 to borrow as cheaply as the Dutch government? While economic historians have extensively documented the development of British government borrowing after 1688, the possibility that post-1688 trends in interest rates were correlated with political trends has not been thoroughly investigated.

I argue that the improvement in the British Crown's access to finance cannot be understood unless one recognizes that apart from the establishment of a limited monarchy, the last decade of the seventeenth century also witnessed another major change: the development of cohesive political parties.[10] Politics in Great Britain between 1688 and 1742 was characterized by conflict between two parties, the Whigs and the Tories, that took differing stances on a range of issues including religion, the succession to the throne, foreign policy, and state finance. The Whigs in particular were a party founded on a compromise among several different groups with diverse interests, including government creditors, Protestant dissenters seeking religious freedom, and landed aristocrats who sought, among other objectives, to increase Parliament's constitutional prerogatives. Because those landowners who participated in the Whig coalition differed with government creditors over questions of taxation and finance, it was crucial for the success of the coalition that both groups nonetheless had similar preferences on a number of other issues in British politics. From the 1720s, as issues such as religion became less salient in British politics, the Whig coalition under Robert Walpole was increasingly held together by patronage, though patronage alone never sufficed for Walpole to maintain a majority.

In Chapters 4 and 5, I show that trends in interest rates on U.K. government debt after 1688 can be better understood when one considers that government creditors were active members of the Whig party, whereas the Tory party was much more closely aligned with those landed interests who chafed at the tax payments necessary to repay public debt on schedule. Chapter 4 presents several basic econometric tests to show that interest rates on U.K. government debt tended to be lower when the Whig party had firmer control of Parliament. Given that the shareholders of the Bank of England were the most prominent of the government's new creditors during this period, it is not surprising that the split between Whigs

---

[10] In emphasizing the importance of political parties, I draw on extensive work by historians of eighteenth-century Britain, as well as recent work by Carruthers (1990, 1996). Historical work on political parties in early eighteenth-century Britain is discussed extensively in Chapter 6 and includes studies by De Krey (1985), Hayton (1984, 2002), Holmes (1967, 1993), Holmes and Speck (1967), Jones (1991, 1997), Plumb (1967), Richards (1972), Sedgwick (1970), Speck (1970, 1977, 1981), and Walcott (1956).

and Tories over state finance was also reflected in Bank of England share prices. These suffered a precipitous crash after a Tory electoral victory in 1710.[11]

While the British government after 1688 gained access to larger quantities of credit at lower rates of interest, no such change took place in France, and the French Crown would continue for the duration of the eighteenth century to face greater difficulty than its British counterpart in borrowing. This has prompted a number of authors to suggest that the French Crown's difficulties were attributable to the failure to adopt British-style institutions. Painstaking work by economic historians has provided evidence consistent with this argument. Throughout the eighteenth century the French monarchy was forced to borrow at significantly higher interest rates than did the British government.[12]

While discussions of state finance in eighteenth-century France have often focused on "missed opportunities" for institutional reform, I argue that even if France had adopted British-style institutions, this would have been unlikely to improve the monarchy's credibility as a borrower. To support this claim I focus on three specific episodes of abortive reform. The first occurred following the death of Louis XIV in 1715. In the midst of a major financial crisis, several senior figures in the French court proposed reinvigorating France's national representative institution, the Estates General, which had not met since 1614. Two authors have recently argued that the failure of the Regent of France to follow England's example at this time represented a missed opportunity for the French monarch to establish credibility for its financial commitments. In doing so, however, Sargent and Velde (1995) do not consider which partisan forces would have been represented within the Estates. Chapter 6 presents evidence from contemporary eighteenth-century observers that the result of calling the Estates General would in fact have been to trigger a default on debt, rather than to avoid one. Evidence on the political divisions in French society during this period supports the conjecture that within the Estates

---

[11] This conclusion that default risk on government debt was lower under the Whigs represents a difference between my own interpretation of events and the argument about partisan politics presented by Carruthers (1990, 1996). Carruthers emphasizes the link between religion, party, and state finance, but he does not focus on credibility of debt repayment, nor does his work give as much emphasis to the role of political parties as heterogeneous coalitions.

[12] See in particular the study by Velde and Weir (1992), which is described in greater detail in Chapter 4. Hoffman et al. (2000) demonstrate that in spite of the French Crown's lack of credibility as a debtor, private financial markets developed quite rapidly in France during the latter half of the eighteenth century.

General, government creditors would have been poorly represented. As a result, the establishment of representative political institutions may well have been insufficient to solve the French Crown's borrowing problems.

A second episode of failed institutional reform in France involved the national bank created by the Scottish financier John Law in 1716. The Regent who governed France agreed to Law's plan for a public bank that would issue a paper currency and that would aid the monarchy in retiring its stock of debt. The plan was inspired in part by the success of the Bank of England, which had been founded in 1694. Law's bank failed soon after its creation, however, due in large part to an excess issue of bank notes. His project was one of a series of attempts by French rulers during the eighteenth century to borrow indirectly from the public via corporate groups or public banks in order to obtain better access to credit. The failure of these institutional innovations to establish credibility shows that as long as they retain the right to alter agreements unilaterally with officials to whom they have delegated authority, then absolute monarchs and other unconstrained rulers will find it impossible to reduce default risk through delegation.

After the period of financial crises following the death of Louis XIV and the failure of Law's bank, there was a gradual transformation of French public borrowing during the eighteenth century. The monarchy relied increasingly on the sale of bonds purchased by a broad cross-section of the French population. As a result, it would be inaccurate to say that there was no evolution of French financial institutions during this period.[13] No reduction in default risk accompanied these changes, however, as studies have shown that the French government continued to pay a premium on its loans, and in fact there were two further defaults in 1759 and in 1770.

With this background of repeated crises of public finance, the deputies of the new French Constituent Assembly in 1789 (now the chief lawmaking body in France) faced several options including proposals to default, to raise new taxes, and/or to create a national central bank. In the end, a majority opposed the proposal to create a national bank similar to the Bank of England, but the assembly did vote to create a new currency, the *assignat*, backed by funds generated from the confiscation of church lands. Subsequently, excess issues of *assignats* led to massive price inflation in France. Some authors have seen this episode as another missed opportunity for the French government to adopt the sort of financial institutions that would have improved its access to finance (Sargent and Velde 1995).

---

[13] See Hoffman et al. (2000).

Chapter 6 presents evidence that supports a different interpretation. The difficulties of the new revolutionary government were due not only to a failure to adopt certain institutional innovations. More fundamentally, they reflected an underlying distribution of political forces in France that was unfavorable to government creditors. Unlike the Glorious Revolution of 1688 in England, the transfer of significant prerogatives to a legislative assembly in France in 1789 was not accompanied by the development of a cohesive majority coalition within which government creditors played a significant role.

3. Theories of Representative Government and Credible Commitment

Theoretical arguments about representative government and commitment focus on the idea that there is less risk of a sudden reversal of policy when decisions are made by a legislature, rather than by an unconstrained executive such as an absolute monarch or a dictator. While this claim is an appealing one, existing work has not fully addressed the question of why those who control representative institutions should necessarily oppose actions such as defaulting on public debts. One possibility may be that devolving power to a legislative assembly will improve credibility if those who represent government creditors constitute a majority within the legislature. On the other hand, one could just as easily imagine a scenario where creditors would be in the minority, and thus a legislative majority would have an incentive to default on debt, because this would allow a reduction in future taxes. This would seem all the more likely given that in many historical contexts ownership of government debt has been concentrated within a narrow segment of the population.[14] Theoretical work in the field of political economy has not considered this issue in detail.[15]

To consider the link between representative government and public debt, then, one needs to allow for the possibility that legislators may represent government creditors, but they may also represent those who pay the taxes to service debt. When a legislature is given decision-making

---

[14] In their discussion of England after 1688, North and Weingast (1989) do not directly confront this issue, apart from suggesting that the "commercially minded Whig ruling coalition" would have found it anathema to default.

[15] One interesting exception here is an article by Dixit and Londregan (2000) that suggests that those who expect to hold power in the future will be more likely to purchase government debt. Their article, however, does not specifically consider decision making within a legislative assembly.

power over issues of debt and taxation, this should only reduce default risk if the legislative majority takes the interest of government creditors into account when making policy. In some legislatures, government creditors may actually form a majority, in which case the analysis is straightforward. This seems to be a fair description of the Estates of Holland during the sixteenth century, an early example of borrowing by a legislature that is considered in Chapter 3. More frequently, though, government creditors will be in the minority. Within the British Parliament during the eighteenth century, in fact, the overwhelming majority of legislators were landholders, as were their constituents. Given that landowners paid a significant share of the taxes that went to service government debt during this period, this raises the question of why granting more power to Parliament after 1688 should have necessarily reduced the risk of a default. More generally, how could a legislature commit to repaying debts if those who represent government creditors make up only a small percentage of its members?

Constitutional Checks and Balances

One way to refine the argument about political representation and public debt is to suggest that what actually matters for credibility is the number of constitutionally determined veto points in a political system.[16] The greater the number of veto points, the greater the likelihood that those favorable to repaying debt will be able to block attempts to default. This follows the classic defense given by James Madison in *The Federalist* No. 51 for checks and balances in government; oppression of a minority by the majority will be less likely to occur when the legislature is divided into different branches, and when there is a separate executive and legislature

---

[16] A "veto point" can be defined as a political institution, the holder of which has the power to block a proposed change in policy. Throughout this study when I refer to "veto points" or "veto players" I am referring to what Tsebelis (2002) calls "institutional" veto players, those specified by a country's constitution. Tsebelis distinguishes "institutional" veto players who have veto power because a country's constitution grants them this authority, and "partisan" veto players, who are individual member parties or factions in a ruling coalition. The latter may have veto power because they can threaten to exit a coalition if a bill they find unfavorable is passed. As a result, Tsebelis's "partisan" veto players are similar to the individual groups I consider that combine to form political parties. The key difference is that in Chapter 2, I provide an explicit model of the process of party formation rather than assuming that each group within a party is a veto player. For a comprehensive discussion of veto points and policy making, see Tsebelis (2002).

so that they can balance against each other. Madison himself followed earlier thinkers, and notably Montesquieu, who also saw the separation of powers as a means of protecting minority rights.[17] Following on this idea, we might suggest that establishing representative government will increase credibility to the extent that it involves an increase in the number of veto points in a political system. North and Weingast suggest something close to this in the conclusion to their 1989 article, highlighting the importance of the "balance between Parliament and the monarchy" in Great Britain after 1688 and of the presence of multiple veto points.[18] So, for example, if an absolute monarchy or a dictatorship (where there is only one constitutional veto point) is replaced with a unicameral legislature, then credibility may not be enhanced. If, on the other hand, an absolute monarchy is transformed into a limited monarchy where both king and Parliament have the right to veto policy proposals, then opportunities for commitment may be enhanced by the fact that the Parliament places a check on the authority of the monarch, while the monarch simultaneously places a check on the authority of Parliament.

A key question about constitutional checks and balances is whether the mere existence of institutions such as bicameralism, or a separation of power between legislature and executive, is sufficient to ensure that a given political group – such as government creditors – controls a veto point. Alternatively, one might argue that checks and balances will only ensure commitment if there is some mechanism that makes it virtually certain that a given group will control a specific institution, such as the upper chamber of a legislature. Modern critics of the separation of powers system have long suggested that in practice it is intended to stack the deck of the political game so that certain groups are ensured veto power. Charles Beard (1913) made a famous critique of the U.S. Constitution as an attempt by owners of property to reduce the risk that republican government might be controlled by debtors and small farmers. Subsequent work has pointed out weaknesses in Beard's account, but the underlying question remains. Among the founding fathers in the United States, Alexander Hamilton was the most explicit supporter of giving owners of property a privileged position in government, as illustrated by

---

[17] *De L'Esprit des Lois*, book XI.
[18] Referring to the constitutional changes introduced after 1688: "Increasing the number of veto players implied that a larger set of constituencies could protect themselves against political assault, thus markedly reducing the circumstances under which opportunistic behavior by the government could take place" (1989: 829).

the following statement made to the Federal Convention of 1787:

All communities divide themselves into the few and the many. The first are the rich and well born, the other the mass of the people. The voice of the people has been said to be the voice of God: and however generally this maxim has been quoted and believed, it is not true in fact. The people are turbulent and changing; they seldom judge or determine right. Give therefore to the first class a distinct, permanent share in government. They will check the unsteadiness of the second, and as they cannot receive any advantage by a change, they therefore will ever maintain good government.[19]

There have been critiques of Montesquieu's support for the separation of powers that parallel Beard's critique of the U.S. Constitution. Althusser (1959) suggested that Montesquieu's advocacy of the separation of powers was motivated by a desire to ensure that the nobility would retain a privileged position in French society.[20] Montesquieu in *The Spirit of the Laws* does in fact make quite explicit his preference for a bicameral legislature with the upper chamber reserved for the nobility.[21] It is interesting to note in this regard that Montesquieu's idea of the separation of powers as a check on majority rule drew on earlier visions going back to Aristotle of a "mixed constitution" that would provide *guaranteed* representation for each segment of society.[22] In contemporary terms, one reason why federal systems may be particularly effective at protecting minority rights is precisely because they give guaranteed representation to certain groups (based on geographic location). One might make the same observation of the power-sharing arrangements that are sometimes created after civil wars; these too are characterized by guaranteed representation for each party.

Existing formal treatments of the effect of veto points have not asked whether multiple veto points alone are sufficient to ensure credible commitment, or alternatively whether credibility can be achieved only if, in addition to creating multiple veto points, there is some mechanism that

---

[19] Max Farrand, ed., *The Records of the Federal Convention of 1787* (New Haven, 1911), vol. 1, p. 299. On this subject, see also the discussion in Manin (1997).

[20] Althusser himself relies heavily on earlier work by Eisenmann (1933).

[21] As an illustration of the importance of having different legislative chambers controlled by different social groups, Montesquieu cites the example of the Venetian Republic, which had constitutional checks and balances that meant little in practice, because all veto points were controlled by the same social group. *De L'Esprit des Lois*, book XI, chap. 6.

[22] On this point, see the discussion in Raynaud (1993), and Manin's consideration of how modern forms of representative government have retained certain "aristocratic" elements (1997).

ensures that government creditors will control one of these veto points in the future.[23] In practical terms, if one assumes that control of one veto point by government creditors is sufficient to avoid a default, then those deciding whether to invest in government debt will need to develop some expectation about the likelihood that those who oppose default will have veto power. If it is thought that there is a very high probability that owners of public debt will control at least one veto point, then people will be more willing to lend to the government. In other cases, however, outcomes may be sufficiently uncertain that individuals would be dissuaded from purchasing government debt. The legislative bargaining model developed in Chapter 2 of this book considers the effect of multiple veto points under two different scenarios: when the future identity of veto players is known and when future control of veto points is random. In the case where government creditors are certain to have control of a veto point, not surprisingly, there is less risk of opportunistic actions such as default on debt. When future control of veto points is random, however, the effect is much less significant. In other words, constitutional checks and balances may have little effect on credibility unless there is some mechanism that ensures that government creditors are the ones to enjoy veto power.

Beyond uncertainty about future control, a further problem with multiple veto points as a commitment device is that even if government creditors have veto power over policy, this may be insufficient to ensure that public debt is repaid. The reason here is that default frequently occurs in situations where there is no agreement on the alternative (raising taxes and/or cutting spending). A government that aims to repay its debt needs to maintain a tax rate that generates sufficient revenue to meet its debt-servicing obligations. In an economy with a constant rate of growth and no shocks to economic activity, debt servicing could be assured with a stable tax rate. Under these conditions, as long as government creditors controlled one veto point, they could successfully oppose any attempts to change this rate. In practice, governments may need periodically to adjust tax rates and levels of spending to respond to revenue shortfalls.

---

[23] Tsebelis (2002) fully acknowledges that policies may not be stable even when there are multiple veto points, if veto points are controlled by players with similar preferences, but to my knowledge this implication has not been considered in discussions of multiple veto points and credible commitment. McCarty (2000) has developed general propositions about the effect of veto power on outcomes, but for a bargaining context where preferences are homogeneous. Londregan (2001) has considered the effect of veto points when the future bargaining context is uncertain, but not when future control of veto points is subject to uncertainty.

As a consequence, when revenues are unstable and unpredictable, holding veto power may be insufficient to guarantee full repayment of debt.

The above discussion leads to my first principal argument. *Constitutional measures establishing multiple veto points may reduce default risk, but they are neither a necessary nor a sufficient condition for this outcome.* They are not always necessary, because in some representative assemblies creditor interests may have an outright majority. At the same time checks and balances may be insufficient to ensure debt repayment if there is substantial uncertainty whether government creditors will hold veto power in the future, or if revenues are unstable and unpredictable.

Party Government in a Plural Society

Rather than establishing commitment through constitutional checks and balances, an alternative possibility I consider is that credible commitment in a democracy results from the compromises necessary to form a durable majority in a legislature that represents a diverse society. Even if owners of government debt are a small minority within the legislature, if they participate in a broader majority coalition, bargaining within this coalition may result in "moderate" policies with regard to debt and taxation. If wealth holders anticipate this outcome, they will be more likely to invest in government bonds.

In a frequently cited work, Schattschneider (1942) argued that in societies where there is conflict over multiple issues and where the dividing lines in each conflict do not coincide, then any legislative majority that votes cohesively on multiple issues will need to be held together by compromises and concessions that lead to moderate policies. For Schattschneider, political parties were the primary means in a representative democracy of cementing such compromises. He also suggests that the moderating effect of creating a legislative majority is a clear implication of James Madison's claim in Federalist No. 10 that the diversity of interests in a large republic makes it less likely that any one individual interest will dominate. In Schattschneider's opinion, Madison failed to foresee that if bargaining to construct a legislative majority necessarily leads to compromise, this might actually obviate the need for constitutional checks and balances in order to guard against tyranny of the majority.[24] Schattschneider's argument is also related to the well-known

---

[24] (1942: 9). See also Hofstadter (1969) on this point. Kernell (2001) and McLean (2001) provide recent discussions of the contradictions between Madison's writings in Federalist No. 10 and Federalist No. 51.

comparative politics literature on "cross-cutting cleavages" that suggests that when social divisions tend to cross-cut each other, policies are likely to be more moderate. As an example, this would be the case in a society divided between "rich" and "poor" as well as Catholic and Protestant, but where not all "rich" are Protestant and not all "poor" are Catholic.[25] It is also related to work in the field of American politics and in the field of international relations.[26]

This vision of political party formation is strikingly close to that presented in a number of recent game-theoretic models of parties. Voting in legislatures presents a collective dilemma in which there are strong incentives for a majority party to form in order to improve on the expected outcome of voting in the absence of parties. One can illustrate this possibility using the example of a three-member legislature facing three proposed bills, each of which would provide a positive payoff to two members while providing a negative payoff to a third member (with the third member differing in each case). If a bill is not approved, players receive zero utility. In this sort of a game, Aldrich (1995) and Schwartz (1989) have emphasized that two players can improve their payoff if they could commit to a party platform of only voting in favor of the one bill that provides them both with a positive payoff. One can extend this model of political party formation and legislative bargaining to a more general setting, using a legislative bargaining model first developed by Baron and Ferejohn (1989).[27] In Chapter 2, I present a game-theoretic model that demonstrates how the politics of public debt can be affected by cross-issue deals and by formation of political parties. In doing so I make sure to take account of the critique made by Krehbiel (1993), who argued that

---

[25] See Almond (1956), Lipset (1960), and Lipset and Rokkan (1967).

[26] See Aldrich (1995), Key (1964), and Stokes (1999) for accounts from the field of American politics on parties as collections of heterogeneous groups. Work in the field of international relations has also emphasized the implications for credibility of the multi-issue nature of political debate. See Frieden (1994), Martin (1994), and Stasavage and Guillaume (2002).

[27] In doing so I draw on work by Calvert and Fox (2000) and Jackson and Moselle (2002). Alternative models of parties as solutions to collective dilemmas faced by legislators have been developed by Cox and McCubbins (1993) and Snyder and Ting (2000). Roemer (1998, 1999, 2001) constructs a model where the presence of an ideological dimension influences choice of policies on a second, economic dimension. His model differs from that developed here in that, rather than focusing on a political party as a means for actors with different policy preferences in a legislature to commit to a common platform, he models a game where, in an electoral context, party members differ over the extent to which they prefer to win an election even if this implies a compromise on policy.

observed party cohesion may reflect similarities in preferences rather than an independent effect of parties on outcomes.

As with the argument about constitutional checks and balances, my argument about party formation and credibility is based on a number of assumptions that may not always hold. First, if government creditors are in the minority, then party formation can improve credibility only if there are multiple dimensions of social conflict. This is an observable implication of the argument that I consider at length in the following chapters. In societies where all conflicts can be distilled into a single dimension and where preferences across this dimension are highly polarized, a legislative majority is unlikely to be moderate.[28] A second requirement is that there must be means to ensure party cohesion; individual legislators must be able to commit to voting the party platform, even in cases where their short-term interest would be better served by voting otherwise. So, in the case relevant to this book, legislators whose constituents do not own debt must be prepared to support debt repayment in order to gain the support of creditors on other issues. Real-world political parties have evolved a number of mechanisms to ensure cohesion, such as the possibility of sanctioning members who deviate from the party line. I show that party members can benefit from the repeated character of legislative bargaining in order to enforce cooperation.[29] The empirical chapters of this book will investigate the actual mechanisms developed by political parties in eighteenth-century England and France to enforce internal cohesion.

The argument that party formation in a plural society can improve credibility is further complicated by the possibility of electoral volatility. Take the case where a legislature contains a majority party of which government creditors are a part. To the extent they think this party may not retain its majority in future elections, wealth holders will invest in government debt only if they are paid a higher rate of return that includes a default premium. As a result, we should expect trends in default premia on debt to be correlated with anticipations about the partisan composition

---

[28] This possibility was explicitly recognized by Schattschneider (1942). If there is only one dimension of conflict, but preferences are not highly polarized, then this may also clearly lead to a moderate outcome.

[29] See Calvert and Fox (2000). More generally, my arguments here follow the approach proposed by Calvert (1995a, b) to model a social institution (such as a political party) as an equilibrium outcome of an underlying repeated game. My model is also closely related to Bawn (1999), where players subscribe to an ideology that is defined as the equilibrium strategy profile of a repeated game.

of future legislatures. This is a key observable implication of the theory that I consider in subsequent chapters.

The above discussion leads to my second main argument: *In societies with multiple dimensions of conflict, the process of party formation will reduce default risk provided that government creditors are members of the majority coalition.* Default premia will also be lower to the extent that this coalition is expected to retain power. While this argument implies that party government may lead to credible commitment even in the absence of constitutional checks and balances, these two alternative arguments are not necessarily exclusive. In some cases, credibility may depend on both the process of party formation and the presence of multiple constitutional veto points. This would be the case if government creditors were a small faction of a larger party that controlled one veto point in a political system with multiple veto points.

This argument about party formation may seem surprising, given the implications from social choice theory that policy instability is likely to occur when there are multiple issue dimensions (in the absence of a structure-induced equilibrium of the sort identified by Shepsle 1979). While social choice theory in the context of legislative bargaining assumes that all alternatives are considered simultaneously, in Chapter 2, I adopt the assumption that legislative proposals are considered sequentially, and that if a proposal receives a requisite majority it is implemented for some amount of time. This plausible assumption yields equilibrium outcomes even for cases of multidimensional bargaining where social choice theory would predict that there would be no stable outcome.[30] While sequential choice theories of bargaining do not require institutions such as a committee structure to generate stability, when there are multiple dimensions of policy, creating institutions such as a political party may nonetheless allow legislators to realize significant gains. It is also worth noting here that even under social choice assumptions, it has been recognized that there are strong incentives for individuals to form coalitions, and these coalitions can imply trade-offs across issue dimensions, leading to moderate policies.[31]

One final implication of party government worth considering is that it is a fundamentally democratic means of achieving credibility. Commitment in this case is supported by a majority, rather than depending on according

---

[30] For a thoughtful discussion of the reasons for preferring either the sequential choice or the social choice assumptions, see Baron (1994).
[31] See Laver and Schofield (1990) and Schofield (1993).

some special status or privileges to owners of government bonds. To the extent that party formation is accompanied by creation of an ideology, then this ideology will also need to focus on ideas that resonate with a majority of the population, and thus it will need to emphasize some project that goes beyond the simple need to please government bond holders.[32]

Bureaucratic Delegation

A third feature of representative democracy that may influence commitment involves granting authority to unelected officials or intermediaries. There are reasons to believe that delegation of management of government debt to an independent agency, like a central bank, can increase credibility of debt repayment. This claim parallels more general arguments about the potential for bureaucratic delegation to change economic policy outcomes.[33] The literature on public finance in eighteenth-century Britain has suggested that the Bank of England (created in 1694) played a critical role in the modernization of British state finance.[34] While the Bank of England did not yet set monetary policy as does a modern central bank, it did arguably fulfill several functions that made it more costly for the British government to default on its debts. For one, because government revenues were increasingly channeled through the bank, some have argued that any decision to default would have quickly led to a halt in payments from the bank to the government.[35] In addition, as the largest lender to government during this period, in the event of a suspension of payments on debt, the bank might have organized a creditor cartel that would refuse to make any future loans to government.[36]

In strong contrast with Great Britain, France during the eighteenth century did not succeed in establishing a national bank. Some have argued that the French government's difficulties in obtaining access to cheap credit during this period were directly linked to this absence of institutional reform. Others have argued that despite its failure to create

---

[32] This argument would still be consistent with a rational choice approach if one referred to ideology as a rule for sharing benefits between different members of a coalition, as modeled by Bawn (1999).

[33] While bureaucratic delegation is relevant for a large number of areas of economic policy, the best-known example involves delegating monetary policy to an independent central bank. See Cukierman (1992) for an extensive survey.

[34] See, e.g., Broz (1998), North and Weingast (1989), and Root (1994).

[35] This is suggested by North and Weingast, following an earlier argument by Macaulay (1861).

[36] See Weingast (1997b).

a national bank, the French monarchy before 1789 was able to make at least a partial commitment to repaying its debts by borrowing indirectly through corporate bodies and local assemblies.[37] As discussed in Chapters 4 and 6, this indirect borrowing can also be seen as a form of bureaucratic delegation to the extent that it removed debt servicing from day-to-day management by the Crown.

My third principal argument suggests that *bureaucratic delegation will improve credibility only if government creditors already have influence within a representative assembly*. Much theoretical work on delegation and commitment makes the simplifying assumption that once a decision has been made to delegate, it can be reversed only at great cost. More recent work on the politics of delegation has demonstrated that this assumption is not always tenable in practice and that nominally independent government agencies often respond to pressures from partisan political principals. In some political systems, politicians who delegate to nominally independent bureaucrats actually retain substantial room to influence future decisions. One way in which this can occur is through the implicit or explicit threat of revising a bureaucratic agency's statute. Such threats will be more menacing in political systems where power is concentrated in the hands of a single individual, such as a monarch or dictator. In contrast, if government creditors have political influence within a representative assembly, then they may be able to block any attempts to revise an agency's statute.[38] Interestingly, this argument also corresponds closely with eighteenth-century views about the feasibility of establishing a national bank in an authoritarian system. Kaiser (1991) was the first to highlight the fact that contemporary observers in eighteenth-century France thought that a national bank could have little authority in an absolute monarchy. As far as credibility is concerned, then, bureaucratic delegation is at best a complement, but not a substitute, for having representative political institutions.

When Are Representative Institutions Stable?

One possible objection to my arguments about representative institutions and commitment is that they rest on the assumption that actors

---

[37] Sargent and Velde (1995) have focused on the absence of a national bank in France. Bien (1989), Potter (1997, 2000), Potter and Rosenthal (1997), and Root (1989, 1994) have considered the practice of borrowing through intermediaries.

[38] A point made by several authors, including Epstein and O'Halloran (1999) and McCubbins, Noll, and Weingast (1989); see also Keefer and Stasavage (2001, 2002).

who feel disadvantaged by policy decisions have no option but to respect them. This is not a plausible assumption for eighteenth-century France, nor for Great Britain, nor would it be justified in many countries today. Chapter 7 considers whether the theoretical propositions about representative government developed in Chapter 2 can hold even in a context where parliamentary groups have an "outside option" of resorting to political unrest.[39] Chapter 7's extension to the theoretical model developed in Chapter 2 relies on the basic idea that actors will be more likely to resort to rebellion the more they dislike the policies adopted by majority vote in the legislature. As a result, "moderate" policies are less likely to trigger extraconstitutional action by the minority. Some theorists such as Kelsen (1932) have suggested that the threat that the minority might exercise an outside option can be a force leading to more moderate policies.

Two main conclusions appear from Chapter 7. First, the process of party formation in a plural society can lead to credible commitment even when there is a threat of unrest. Second, the mere threat of the minority exercising an outside option will not necessarily be sufficient to prompt the majority to adopt a more moderate policy. I then argue that even if members of the majority do not have an incentive to compromise in order to reduce the risk of an outside option being used, when there are multiple political cleavages in society, the process of forming a legislative majority may nonetheless lead both to moderate policy choices and to a reduced likelihood of extraconstitutional action. Chapter 7 then considers this possibility using historical evidence from France and Great Britain.

The discussion about the stability of representative institutions also raises a further question: Would credible commitment through political bargaining be possible even outside the framework of democratic institutions? When there are multiple cleavages it might be possible for political bargaining to result in moderate politics even in an autocracy. While this is entirely plausible, it would need to be shown what institutional mechanisms in autocracies allow heterogeneous interests to make commitments over time in the same way that political parties allow diverse groups to commit to a common policy platform in representative democracies.

---

[39] In previous work, Ellman and Wantchekon (2000) have considered how the existence of this sort of outside option might influence electoral outcomes. Powell (1996, 1999) has considered the effect of outside options (the ability to resort to force) in interstate bargaining.

4. Alternative Routes to Credibility

While different features of representative government might reduce risk of default, there are also alternative forces that could have this same effect. These involve the risk of capital flight, the possibility for government creditors to serve as a lobby, and the effect of restrictions on political participation.[40] While each of these factors might allow commitment, the latter solution achieves this outcome through means that observers today would characterize as being fundamentally undemocratic.

Capital Mobility

When capital is mobile, governments may be more wary of taxing it heavily, so as to avoid a massive flight of funds from their countries. This might be true both with regard to taxes on capital, as well as for default, which can be seen as a one-off tax on holders of government bonds. Studies of globalization have made much of this idea recently, and it can be seen as a more general manifestation of Lindblom's (1982) conception of "the market as prison" or other arguments about the "structural power of capital."[41] The implication for public debt may be that rather than studying commitment problems, one might better study the question of how to reduce the preponderant influence of government creditors on policy choices. In the extreme case, if it were possible for owners of capital to shift their assets costlessly and instantaneously in anticipation of government actions, then credibility problems involving debt and capital taxation would disappear altogether.[42]

There are a number of reasons to believe that in the case of government borrowing, capital mobility is unlikely to serve as a full solution to commitment problems.[43] The most basic reason involves the fact that by lending to a sovereign government, individuals actually cede control over their capital. This means that in the case of default, in the absence

---

[40] Chapter 2 also considers the issue of reputation as a source of commitment.

[41] On this latter issue, see Przeworski and Wallerstein (1988). Arguing that capital mobility can actually help promote democracy, Bates and Lien (1985) have investigated the implications of capital mobility in the historical context of eighteenth-century France and Great Britain.

[42] This possibility has been formally modeled by Kehoe (1989).

[43] Arguments about the structural power of capital often also overlook the significant costs that capitalists face in reversing other types of investment decisions. In recent years economists have recognized that many investment choices, such as the choice to build a factory in a particular country, are essentially irreversible once made (see Dixit and Pindyck 1993).

of some third-party enforcement, the only way creditors can sanction a government is by refusing to lend in the future and investing their funds elsewhere. This is the key intuition behind a model developed by Bulow and Rogoff (1989), who show that fear of high future borrowing costs may be insufficient to dissuade many governments from defaulting.[44] It is true that a government may suffer from an immediate increase in borrowing costs if it is even feared that default is likely, but this does not alter the basic argument that capital mobility may be insufficient to guarantee commitment to repay debt. Finally, this argument is also supported empirically by the fact that today, in a context where capital is much more mobile than in the eighteenth century, many emerging market countries still pay very high risk premia on their debt issues. If capital mobility could guarantee commitment, one would expect emerging market countries to be able to borrow at interest rates similar to those paid by OECD governments.

Financial Sector Lobbying

Rather than trying to influence policy through representation in a legislature or participation in a political party, an alternative route for government creditors to gain influence on economic policy is to act as a lobby. The advantage of this strategy is that it may necessitate less compromise, and it may allow government creditors to retain their influence regardless of which political party has majority control. For lobbying to be successful, representatives must not be fully accountable to their electors. Otherwise, those who represent the non-debt-holding majority will be obliged to follow the majority's ex post facto preferences to default. Under these circumstances, even if government creditors are in the minority within a legislature, they may nonetheless be assured of repayment of government debt if their lobbying influence is sufficiently strong. Lobbying can involve campaign finance contributions (to legislators who value remaining in office regardless of the policies they choose), patronage, or bribes. In cases where ownership of financial capital is concentrated in a narrow group of wealthy individuals, while ownership of other factors of production is spread more widely, then lobbying will lead to outcomes that are less democratic to the extent that some individuals will have greater lobbying resources than others. While evidence that financial sector interests lobby governments is plentiful, as with the argument about capital mobility,

---

[44] I discuss this model in greater detail in Chapter 2.

one should not immediately assume that this provides an irresistible force in all countries obligating governments to repay their debt. Otherwise it would be difficult to explain why many governments continue to pay very high risk premia on their debt issues.

Restrictions on Political Participation

Rather than rely on the ability of government creditors to buy influence, in many countries historically, credibility of public debt has been reinforced by fundamentally undemocratic means: restricting the access of certain groups to the political system. This can involve formal restrictions on the suffrage as well as requirements for serving as a representative. While laws of this type controvert what most people today would see as a fundamental democratic principle, it is important to recognize that in the eighteenth century it was commonly seen as being legitimate to restrict political participation in this manner. There was broad support in eighteenth-century Britain for the idea that only those who owned property should be eligible to vote and to hold elected office, and despite controversy, this principle remained a feature of politics in both the early American republic and in France in the years after its revolution (Manin 1997). Restrictions on political participation undoubtedly provided the principal explanation for the weak representation of labor in the British Parliament after 1688 as well as in the French National Assembly after 1789. As a result, this book makes the simplifying assumption that labor was essentially absent from politics.

5. Observable Implications of My Arguments

My goal for the empirical sections of this book is to adopt a methodological approach that is eclectic yet rigorous. The phenomenon I seek to explain is government credibility, defined as the perceived likelihood that a government will honor debt contracts. Chapter 4 presents a number of different measures of credibility for the French and British governments over the course of the eighteenth century. I then examine relevant observable implications for my three arguments concerning constitutional checks and balances, party formation, and bureaucratic delegation. Some observable implications can be tested quantitatively using time-series evidence. More frequently, I rely on historical evidence.

My first argument suggests that constitutional checks and balances can improve credibility, but they are neither a necessary nor a sufficient condition for doing so. This is obviously quite a general statement, and so, based on available evidence from France and Great Britain, I restrict myself to one main implication of the theory: Credibility may not be assured even when there are multiple veto points. For Great Britain I consider to what extent there was substantial variation in the perceived likelihood of a default after 1688. As argued above, the existence of significant volatility in interest rates on government debt after the Glorious Revolution is a potential indication that the constitutional changes of 1688 were not sufficient to establish credibility for U.K. government borrowing. For France, the evidence is necessarily more speculative for the period before 1789. Existing work has assumed that the Estates General, if convened, would have taken actions in order to repay debts. I consider whether there is evidence to support an alternative interpretation; given the balance of political forces in France at the time, a default would have occurred even if the Estates had been called. I perform a similar exercise for the case of the French Constituent Assembly in 1789.

My second argument suggests that in countries where there are multiple dimensions of political conflict, the process of forming a majority will lead to commitment, provided that government creditors are members of the coalition. One observable implication here is that trends in partisan control should be correlated with trends in credibility, and this can be tested with time-series evidence on partisan control of government, interest rates on government debt, and prices for assets such as Bank of England stock. One should expect to observe that government creditors were members of the party that tended to be associated with low default premia when it was in power. I also examine to what extent contemporary observers saw changes in the partisan control of government as significant for financial markets. There are further observable implications of this second argument. If credibility was high we should expect to see that multiple dimensions of conflict existed, and that members of coalitions had the necessary mechanisms to enforce agreements over time. Both of these implications can be evaluated using historical evidence on the functioning of political parties in the British Parliament after 1688. I do the same for the French Constituent Assembly after 1789.

My third argument involves the claim that bureaucratic delegation will only improve credibility in cases where government creditors already have political veto power. This issue can be addressed by comparing British and French experiences in this area. Both the British and French governments made attempts during the course of the eighteenth century to improve their access to credit by creating national banks or by borrowing through intermediaries, yet only in the British case did government creditors actually enjoy significant power within a representative assembly. In Britain the principal innovation in this area involved the creation of the Bank of England in 1694 and subsequent decisions to increase the role that it played in government finance. In France monarchs also attempted to use bureaucratic institutions to improve their access to credit. These involved the creation of John Law's bank (1716–20) and a number of initiatives to borrow through bureaucratic intermediaries. If the evidence here is consistent with the argument, then one would expect to observe that the failure of bureaucratic institutions to improve credibility in France was directly attributable to the monarchy's penchant for unilaterally revising contracts with agents of the Crown. In Great Britain the argument would imply that the performance of the Bank of England was closely linked to the political fortunes of the Whig coalition in Parliament that continually supported the bank. In the absence of Whig support, my argument would imply that the bank would have been subject to the same sort of interference as occurred with bureaucratic arrangements in France.

6. Plan of the Book

Chapter 2 of this book presents the credibility problem in government borrowing in greater detail, and it builds a game-theoretic model that I use to support my three arguments about checks and balances, political parties, and bureaucratic delegation. Chapter 3 then presents historical background material by reviewing the development of public borrowing in early modern Europe. This includes a discussion of the emergence of modern institutions for public borrowing in the Netherlands during the sixteenth century, followed by England after 1688. Chapter 4 reviews the experience of public borrowing in Great Britain and in France between 1688 and 1789, relying on data covering rates of interest on government loans and episodes of default in order to measure trends in credibility. The goal here is to make comparisons both between the two countries and over time within each country. Chapters 5 and 6 continue the investigation by examining to what extent observed trends in credibility can be accounted for by partisan politics and by the structure of political institutions. Chapter 7 then considers the stability of representative institutions. Chapter 8 presents a summary and conclusion.

2

A Model of Credible Commitment
under Representative Government

1. Introduction

In the first chapter I presented three arguments about the credibility-enhancing effects of constitutional checks and balances, political parties, and bureaucratic delegation. This chapter derives and develops each of these arguments more formally, using a game-theoretic model of bargaining among legislators. I construct a simple model where legislators must set taxes on land and capital in order to meet an exogenous budget constraint. Partisan preferences are included explicitly by allowing legislators to represent districts that derive variable amounts of income from land and from capital. This division fits an eighteenth-century political context. This political model of capital taxation, which is adapted from Persson and Tabellini (1994), can also be applied to the politics of public debt, because a default on debt represents a one-off tax on owners of this type of capital (government bonds).

A primary implication of the model is that landowning majorities can face a credibility problem. Once owners of capital have made investment decisions (such as purchasing government debt), a landowning majority will have an ex post facto incentive to raise all revenues from income on capital. Anticipating this outcome, capital owners will fail to invest, and in equilibrium, all groups will be worse off compared with a situation where the majority could commit to a moderate tax rate on capital. I next show that if legislators also bargain over a second issue dimension, such as the degree of religious toleration, and if landowner preferences are split over this issue, then more liberally minded landowners may moderate their demands with respect to taxation in order to acquire support of capitalists on the issue of religious toleration. As a result, in cases where legislators bargain over multiple issues, credible commitment can emerge as a byproduct of partisan political bargaining. I use the specific example of religious toleration here, but the model could be used to fit the patterns observed in a number of societies, which are divided along an economic cleavage, as well as a second, sociopolitical cleavage.

As a next step, I expand the model to consider the effect of political parties. In the legislative bargaining context I consider, there is a strong incentive for individual legislators to form durable coalitions so as to increase their likelihood of being in the majority, even if this necessitates compromising with respect to policy.[1] I show that under certain specific conditions, formation of a party will lead to lower expected capital taxation. This supports the argument I made in Chapter 1 that the process of party formation may lead to credible commitment if a society is divided by multiple cleavages. Given this fact, I also establish why we would expect credibility to vary with trends in partisan control of government.

The next section provides formal support for my argument about constitutional checks and balances. To do this I show that unless there is some mechanism ensuring that government creditors have veto power, then the mere fact of having constitutional provisions such as bicameralism will do little to improve credibility. As a tractable way of modeling the effect of having a bicameral legislature, I expand the legislative bargaining model by allowing for the possibility that one member of the legislature has veto power over policy decisions. I consider two scenarios. In the first scenario the future identity of the veto player is known. In this case the model predicts, not surprisingly, a lower expected rate of capital taxation when capital owners have veto power and the reverse when landowners have veto power. I next consider how expected taxation is affected if the future control of veto points is allocated randomly and capital owners do not know the identity of veto players at the time they make investment decisions. Under these conditions the expected effect of veto power on credibility is much less significant.

The final section of the chapter provides support for my third argument that bureaucratic delegation will fail to improve credibility under autocracy, or under any other system where government creditors lack influence within a representative assembly. I consider the effect of giving

---

[1] This motivation for the formation of political parties draws on ideas developed by Aldrich (1995) and Schwartz (1989). To formalize party formation within a legislative bargaining model, I draw on work by Jackson and Moselle (2002), as well as by Calvert and Fox (2000).

an independent agency the right to manage debt and to make decisions such as prioritizing debt repayment over other expenditures in the event of a revenue shortfall. Following recent literature on the politics of delegation, I then assume that this decision to delegate can be reversed by the legislature. I argue that under these conditions, bureaucratic delegation will be meaningless in cases where capital owners are neither in the majority nor part of a broader coalition, because the landed majority will have an ex post facto incentive to reverse its decision to delegate. Delegation can be effective only in cases where owners of capital expect to be part of a future majority coalition, so that they can block any decision to reverse delegation.

2. Distributional Politics and Capital Taxation

While early models of credibility problems in taxation and borrowing assumed away partisan motivations on the part of governments, researchers have provided strong theoretical and empirical reasons to believe that government policies in this area respond to partisan pressures.[2] Persson and Tabellini (1994) have developed a partisan model of capital taxation that allows for individual heterogeneity in ownership of assets. The results of this model can also apply directly to the case of government borrowing, to the extent that government debt is one type of capital investment, and default on debt represents a one-off tax on owners of government bonds.[3] To reflect the groups that held political influence in the eighteenth century, and in particular the exclusion of labor from the political process, I present a model where individuals hold variable endowments of land and capital.

A Political Model of Capital Taxation

I assume that a legislature is made up of three players, each of whom has an exogenous endowment, e, which reflects the relative importance of land income and income from capital as a share of their constituents' total income. Individuals for whom $e > 0$ own more land than the average member of society, and individuals with $e < 0$ own more capital

---

[2] For a review of theoretical contributions on partisanship and public debt, see Drazen (2000) and Persson and Tabellini (2000).

[3] See Persson and Tabellini (2000) and Prescott (1977). Including a fully specified model of government borrowing here would require several modifications but would not change the basic results.

than the average member of society. The quantity of capital income and land income of the ith individual in this economy is determined by the following equations where k_1 and l denote the average per capita quantities of capital income and land income, with the subscript "1" denoting the first period, and the subscript "i" an individual's share. Since the stock of land is fixed, I suppress the time subscript for this variable.

$$k_{i1} = k_1 - e \tag{2.1}$$

$$l_i = l + e \tag{2.2}$$

The game has two periods. In the first period players choose whether to save or to consume their exogenous endowment of capital income; they gain utility from any consumption $U(c_{i1}) = c_{i1}$; and players are assumed to be risk neutral. Land income cannot be consumed in period 1.[4]

In the second period, tax rates on land and capital are chosen subject to a government budget constraint g (expressed in per capita terms in Eq. 2.4), and the players consume any after-tax income from capital and land. The government budget constraint might be taken to represent essential expenditure for national defense. Capital saved from period 1 is assumed to earn an exogenous rate of return r as indicated in Equation 2.3. Thus capital owners may have an incentive to save. Second period utility $U(c_{i2}) = c_{i2}$ can be expressed as a linear function of both types of income and the tax rates (where θ is the tax rate on capital income, and τ is the tax rate on land income).

$$k_{i2} = (k_{i1} - c_{i1})(1 + r) \tag{2.3}$$

$$g = \tau l + \theta k_2 \tag{2.4}$$

$$U(c_{i2}) = (1 - \theta)k_{i2} + (1 - \tau)l_i \tag{2.5}$$

Using Equations 2.1 and 2.2, Equation 2.5 can be rewritten as expressed in Equation 2.6 to show that a player's second period utility is a linear function of the player's idiosyncratic endowment, e. As a result, while the policy problem of how much to tax capital and how much to tax land is a two-dimensional one, given the utility functions and the government budget constraint defined above, the problem can be reduced to a unidimensional one where players must choose a policy defined as the

---

[4] This assumption does not alter the results. An alternative would be to specify a game with one period where capital owners are required to make their investment/consumption decision in advance of tax rates being set.

difference between the tax rate on capital and the tax rate on land $(\theta - \tau)$.[5]

$$U(c_{i2}) = (1 - \theta)k_2 + (1 - \tau)l + e_i(\theta - \tau) \qquad (2.6)$$

Given Equations 2.4 and 2.6, individuals will save all of their period 1 capital as long as expected taxation is low enough to make this worthwhile, or if $(1 - \theta^e) > 1/(1 + r)$. The expected tax rate on capital, θ^e, will depend on expectations about bargaining between the three legislators. In the case where two of the three legislators represent landowners $(e > 0)$, a credibility problem is likely to exist (I leave formal specification of the equilibria for the next subsection). Landowners would prefer owners of capital not to consume all of their capital in the first period. Otherwise, the government budget constraint must be satisfied exclusively with taxes on land income. The problem is that in period 2, if capital owners decide to save, then a landowning majority would have an incentive to increase taxes on capital ex post, setting θ equal to g/k_2. Owners of capital will anticipate this incentive, and as a consequence, they will consume their entire endowment of capital in period 1. The public good will then need to be financed exclusively by taxes on land income at a rate of g/l. This is an undesirable outcome for all concerned.

A key implication of the above model is that a landowning majority would benefit from the ability to commit to choosing a rate of taxation lower than g/k_2. Persson and Tabellini (1994) argue that a society with a majority that has a commitment problem might have an incentive to elect a legislator with a personal interest in taxing capital lightly. This raises questions, however, about how such an arrangement could be sustained, in particular if there are reelection concerns. In practice, eighteenth-century European political institutions tended to bias policies in favor of landowners who were concerned about their possessions being expropriated by those without property. These restrictions on political participation might have credibly committed the poor to not expropriating the property of the rich (through undemocratic means), but they did little to solve the credibility problem landowners suffered with respect to capital taxation.

Another frequently evoked solution to credibility problems involves reputation. Governments may refrain from opportunistic behavior because of the negative future consequences that such decisions might have. If a government has made ex post facto changes in capital taxes in the past, it may be less likely to enjoy significant capital investment in the

---

[5] Persson and Tabellini (1994) establish this result following Grandmont (1978).

future. Likewise, a government that defaults on its debts may find it difficult to attract new lenders in the future, or it will be forced to pay a default premium on its debt issues. While it is well known from the theory of repeated games that actors who do not discount the future too heavily may be able to sustain equilibria in a repeated context that would not be sustainable in a one-shot game, it is also well known that this solution is by no means guaranteed.[6]

In the case of government debt, the likelihood of obtaining a reputational solution may be even less plausible than with capital taxation. Bulow and Rogoff (1989) show that reputational forces will be insufficient to guarantee debt repayment in equilibrium as long as a government can continue to hold assets abroad after it defaults.[7] These foreign assets can be used to insure against future negative economic shocks. Following the Bulow and Rogoff model, debt repayment can be ensured only if creditors are able to impose additional costs on defaulters, such as seizure of assets or restrictions on trade.[8]

Multi-Issue Bargaining and Credible Commitment

While political economy models of macroeconomic policy frequently consider only one dimension of social conflict, such as rich versus poor, labor versus capital, or creditors versus debtors, in practice economic policies are set by legislators who bargain simultaneously over multiple additional issues including foreign policy, religion, and social policy. It has long been known that this legislative context opens up the possibility that politicians might compromise on one dimension of policy in order to receive legislative support on another issue. Likewise, the comparative politics literature on "cross-cutting cleavages" has explored how heterogeneity of

---

[6] Fear of future consequences here could involve either the anticipation that lenders will resort to some sort of punishment strategy or, alternatively, that a default will have a major impact on lenders belief about a borrower's "type." See Tomz (1999, 2001) for a discussion of reputation and public borrowing. He argues that reputational models with incomplete information, where investors learn about a borrower's commitment to repay, provide a better fit with empirical observations than do complete information models where lenders follow trigger strategies in order to sanction defaults.

[7] They show this in the context of an infinite horizon game where revenues are stochastic in each period.

[8] A different conclusion is reached by Chari and Kehoe (1993), who assume that after default a government does not have the option of holding assets abroad in order to insure against future shocks.

preferences across two dimensions can lead to compromise policy choices. In this subsection I explore formally whether the presence of a second issue dimension over which landowner preferences are split can increase possibilities for credible commitment to moderate rates of capital taxation.

My analysis follows the frequently used model of legislative bargaining developed by Baron and Ferejohn (1989). They extend the Rubinstein model of alternating offers bargaining to a situation where there are more than two players and decisions are carried by a majority. In their model the sequential nature of the bargaining process allows one to establish equilibria where the social choice literature frequently would predict instability, in the absence of a structure-induced equilibrium of the type identified by Shepsle (1979). This bargaining model has been extended by Baron (1991) to cover bargaining over multiple issues where preferences are heterogeneous.

As in the previous section, I assume that there are three players: A, B, and C. Each player has preferences over the issue of taxing land versus capital, and in addition, each also has preferences over the degree of religious toleration. While I incorporate religious toleration as the second issue here in order to fit the historical context considered later in the book, in practice the second issue could involve any other policy over which landowners are divided. Preferences are separable across the two dimensions. As previously, preferences over taxation depend on an individual's idiosyncratic endowment, e, except I now assume e to be bounded by the interval $[-1, 1]$. To increase tractability of the model without altering basic results, I also assume that the government budget constraint can be met by a 100 percent tax on either land or initial capital income, and I normalize each of these parameters to 1 ($g = k_1 = l = 1$). These assumptions imply that any legislator whose constituents own more land than capital ($e > 0$) will prefer to set $\theta = 1$ and $\tau = 0$, and any legislator whose constituents own primarily capital ($e < 0$) will prefer the reverse. It is important to note, however, that for a legislator with $e > 0$, the utility loss of setting $(\theta - \tau) < 1$ will be increasing in e.[9]

I also assume that legislators have preferences over a second issue dimension, the degree of religious toleration ρ, with $\rho = 1$ implying full toleration and $\rho = -1$ implying no toleration. The second period utility

[9] Given the distributions of preferences that I subsequently consider for the three players, this normalization also implies that average capital income in the legislature may differ from average incomes in society. This is a useful simplifying assumption that does not alter the basic results.

functions for player i can be written in terms of $(\theta - \tau)$ and ρ as in Equation 2.7. In these equations z is an exogenous parameter analogous to e (and also bounded $[-1, 1]$). For coherence, I have specified utility with respect to religious toleration in a similar manner to utility with regard to taxation. Any individual with $z > 0$ will prefer full toleration, and the reverse will be true for any individual with $z < 0$. The utility loss from setting ρ away from an individual's ideal point will be determined by the magnitude of z. As a result, z and e determine the relative weight that players place on each dimension in their utility function, or in a sense, the "salience" of each issue.

$$U_{i2} = (1 + e_i(\theta - \tau)) + (1 + z_i\rho) \qquad (2.7)$$

As a final specification, players also share a common discount factor δ. The discount factor might be less than 1 for standard time-preference reasons. Existing literature has also suggested that discounting could reflect the possibility that a legislator would not be reelected if bargaining continues to the next round.[10] An additional reason for discounting in the context of this game could involve an increasing possibility that failing to satisfy the government budget constraint for one period will result in invasion (in which case legislators would be replaced), or in some other unfavorable outcome.

The game proceeds in the following sequence.

1. Players receive their exogenous endowments e and z, and they choose whether to consume their capital endowment or to save it.
2. One of the three players is chosen at random to propose a set of policies ($\theta - \tau$ and ρ), which is then voted on, without possibility for amendment, under majority rule. If two players vote in favor of the proposal, the policy is implemented and the game ends.
3. If two players do not support the proposal, stage 2 is repeated, potentially an infinite number of times.

To identify the possible subgame perfect equilibria of this legislative bargaining game, I first make the assumption that players can adopt only stationary strategies, that is, strategies where actions chosen do not depend on the history of the game. I later relax the assumption of stationary strategies. Finally, I also restrict my attention to pure strategy equilibria.

The subgame perfect equilibria of this legislative bargaining game can be identified as follows. A subgame perfect equilibrium must satisfy the

---

[10] This follows Baron (1989) and Baron and Ferejohn (1989).

condition that when proposing policies, each player maximizes his or her own utility subject to the constraint of offering another player at least his or her expected utility from continuing the game. In addition, players must not be able to improve on their utility by unilaterally deviating and offering to an alternative player.

While the literature on legislative bargaining is concerned with deriving general propositions about government policy choices, my goal here is to develop a more specific proposition, that multi-issue bargaining may lead to government commitment in the area of capital taxation even when a majority of members of the legislature represent landowners. To illustrate this possibility I consider four specific configurations of preferences for the three-legislator game and solve for the subgame perfect equilibria. The other reason for using specific examples is that attempts to establish general properties of equilibria in this game with multiple policy dimensions have proved difficult (Baron 1991). The appendix presents all calculations.

Example 1: Single Issue Bargaining. As a benchmark for comparison, I first consider an example where players care only about tax policy (that is, $z_a = z_b = z_c = 0$) and where there is a landowning majority. Player A owns only capital, and players B and C own only land. The two subgame perfect equilibria of this simple case are particularly straightforward. In both cases player B proposes $(\theta = 1, \tau = 0)$ to C and C proposes the same policies to B. In the first equilibrium player A will propose $\theta - \tau = (8\delta - 6)/(3 - \delta)$ to B, while in the second equilibrium he or she will make an identical proposal to C. A can successfully propose a tax of capital of less than 100 percent to B and C as long as they discount the future. The expected rate of capital taxation (which is identical in each of these equilibria) is the simple average of these three possibilities. It ranges from 1 (when $\delta = 1$, so there is no discounting) to 0.66 when $\delta = 0$.

Example 2: Multi-Issue Bargaining. Bargaining outcomes change significantly when one introduces a second issue dimension. This helps to establish one of the main observable implications of my argument about party formation: When capital owners are in the minority, multi-issue bargaining may nonetheless lead to credible commitment if landowners are split over a second issue. Figure 2.1 depicts a situation where society is composed of a landowning majority but where landowners are divided in terms of their attitudes toward religious toleration. Player C is a conservative landowner who opposes toleration, player B is a liberal landowner who favors toleration, and player A is a capitalist who also favors religious

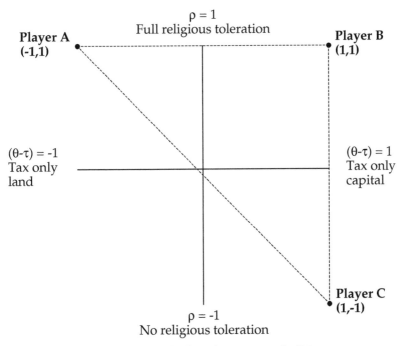

Figure 2.1. Preferred policies for taxation and religion.

toleration. Figure 2.1 can be taken as a stylized representation of politics in many countries in early modern Europe where landowners made up the majority in political assemblies, but where holders of financial capital were also present, and where landowners were themselves split over policies such as religion, foreign policy, and individual rights.

In Example 2, I assume that players own exclusively land or exclusively capital (so $e_a = -1, e_b = 1, e_c = 1$) and the following parameters determine their utility gain from religious toleration ($z_a = 1, z_b = 1, z_c = -1$). Equations 2.8a–c represent the second period utility functions for the three players.

$$U_{a2} = 2 - (\theta - \tau) + \rho \qquad (2.8a)$$

$$U_{b2} = 2 + (\theta - \tau) + \rho \qquad (2.8b)$$

$$U_{c2} = 2 + (\theta - \tau) - \rho \qquad (2.8c)$$

Given the above configuration of preferences, there are two subgame perfect equilibria, and in each of these the expected rate of capital taxation is substantially lower than in the single-issue case. In the first equilibrium, player A offers to B, B offers to A, and C offers to B. In the second equilibrium player A offers to B, B offers to C, and C offers to B. Each of these two subgame perfect equilibria exist for all values of the discount factor δ.

Equations 2.9a–c show the proposals for each player in the first equilibrium. Player B proposes his or her own ideal point, regardless of how heavily players discount the future, and A votes in favor based on the gains he or she receives in terms of religious toleration. This strong bargaining position reflects the centrality of player B's preferences with respect to the other two players. For low discount factors ($\delta < 0.75$), player A also proposes his or her ideal point, although when players discount the future less heavily, A is obliged to moderate his or her proposed tax policy in order for B to accept. Likewise, for high discount factors player C moderates his or her proposal with respect to religious toleration. The equilibrium proposals are as follows.

$$(\theta - \tau)_a = \frac{9 - 10\delta}{2\delta - 3}, \qquad \rho_a = 1 \tag{2.9a}$$

$$(\theta - \tau)_b = 1, \qquad \rho_b = 1 \tag{2.9b}$$

$$(\theta - \tau)_c = 1, \qquad \rho_c = \frac{9 - 10\delta}{2\delta - 3} \tag{2.9c}$$

In Example 2 with the exception of cases where there is no discounting or where the discount factor is extremely low (so all players propose their ideal point in equilibrium), the expected rate of taxation is lower than the case where players bargain only over taxation (as shown in Fig. 2.2). The appendix demonstrates that this result holds more generally as long as the three players place equal weight on the religious toleration dimension. While the equilibrium tax proposals by B and C are the same as in the single issue example, player A now can attract player B's support with a proposal for a more moderate rate of capital taxation, combined with full religious toleration.[11]

Example 3: Multiple Issues When Player B Has a Mixed Income. I next consider how the equilibrium proposals of the three players change when player B, the liberal landowner, earns part of his or her income from capital, instead of earning income exclusively from land. Under these conditions there is a subgame perfect equilibrium in pure strategies where

---

[11] In the second equilibrium, the expected rate of capital taxation is identical to that in the first equilibrium, and so it is not reported.

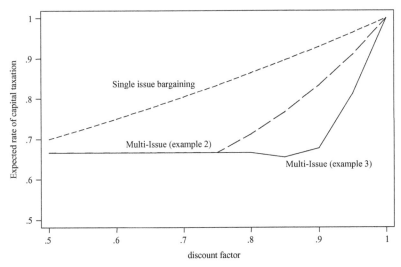

Figure 2.2. Expected capital taxation: single versus multi-issue bargaining. Example 1: $z_a = z_b = z_c = 0$; $e_a = -1$, $e_b = 1$, $e_c = 1$. Example 2: $e_a = -1$, $e_b = 1$, $e_c = 1$, $z_a = 1$, $z_b = 1$, $z_c = -1$. Example 3: $e_a = -1$, $e_b = 0.5$, $e_c = 1$, $z_a = 1$, $z_b = 1$, $z_c = -1$.

player A offers to B, B offers to A, and C offers to B. The equilibrium tax proposals of A and B now change significantly, as one might expect, leading to a significant decrease in the expected rate of capital taxation. This reflects the fact that as the share of his or her income owned from land decreases, player B loses less utility from any proposal for a capital tax rate lower than unity. Figure 2.2 illustrates this result using an example where player B earns 25 percent of his or her before-tax income from capital. The appendix establishes a more general result showing that expected capital taxation decreases as the share of player B's income derived from land decreases.

Example 4: Multiple Issues When Religion Is Less Salient for Player A. As a final variation, I consider how expected taxation changes as the weight that player A places on religious toleration z_a decreases. There is once again a subgame perfect equilibrium in pure strategies where player A offers to B, B offers to A, and C offers to B. As discussed in the appendix, this equilibrium result holds for all except extremely high discount factors. Example 4 is not illustrated in Figure 2.2, though it is considered in greater detail in the next section.

In sum, these results show under several different scenarios how bargaining between legislators over multiple issues will lead to lower rates of taxation on capital than would prevail if players bargained only over taxation. To the extent that cross-issue bargaining leads to expected rates of capital taxation that are sufficiently low that owners of capital will save and invest (i.e., if $1 - \theta^e > 1/(1+r)$), then we can say that it improves possibilities for credible commitment.

Robustness of the Results

It is worth considering to what extent the results presented above depend on key assumptions in the legislative bargaining model. First, to what extent is it reasonable to assume that players discount the future and, similarly, that time periods have length greater than zero? In the context of legislative bargaining the argument of lengthy periods seems to make sense, given the time it usually takes to reintroduce a bill. One could also ask to what extent my results depend on the assumption that there is not an exogenously defined status quo. In practice, similar results might be obtained if there was an exogenous status quo and all players received the same utility from this set of policies. A status quo closer to a particular player's ideal point would, predictably, result in a bargaining outcome closer to that player's ideal point. As a result, my basic results here are unlikely to depend on the status quo assumption. Finally, what about the assumption that players vote without possibility for amendment? One possibility would have been to consider an "open rule" of the type described by Baron and Ferejohn (1989) where, subsequent to any proposal, another legislator is chosen at random to propose an amendment. This would have the effect of moving the bargaining outcome toward the ideal point of player B (the liberal landowner), but the core result about multi-issue bargaining leading to more moderate taxation would still hold.

One possible further extension to the model would be to consider how bargaining outcomes are affected if owners of capital or owners of land were able to lobby legislators. This could be done by using part of their income to make payments in return for favorable votes.[12] If this possibility were introduced into the game presented here, then one could add an extra term to each player's utility function to reflect utility gained from any lobbying payments. This would entail relaxing the assumption that legislators are perfect agents of the groups they represent. One likely implication would be that even if capital owners are in the minority and there

---

[12] Helpman and Persson (1998) have considered this possibility in the context of a legislative bargaining game where players have homogeneous preferences.

is no ideological dimension of policy over which landowners are split, then capital owners might nonetheless be able to make side-payments in order to form a coalition with one of the two landowning legislators.[13]

3. Party Government and Credible Commitment

Now that I have laid out the basic model and considered the effect of cross-issue bargaining, the next step is explicitly to consider party formation. In this section I show how party formation can lead to credible commitment when players bargain over multiple dimensions of policy. In the examples I have presented two players might be able to significantly improve on their expected utility if they could commit support to a common policy platform that represented a compromise between each party member's ideal set of policies. This is the rationale for party formation established by Schattschneider (1942) and more recently by Schwartz (1989) and Aldrich (1995). As an example, if capitalists and liberal landowners could agree to form a political party, and thus exclude the conservative landowners from any majority, then they are likely to choose a party platform that combines religious toleration with a policy of moderate capital taxation. The result would be for commitment to moderate capital taxation to emerge as a byproduct of coalition bargaining between heterogeneous interests. I first consider a model of parties proposed by Jackson and Moselle where one assumes players can commit support to a party platform. I then relax this assumption and pursue an alternative provided by Calvert and Fox (2000), who model parties as the outcome of a repeated game.

Parties as Commitments to a Platform

Following Jackson and Moselle (2002), the game proceeds in the same sequence of stages as in the previous section, except that at the outset, a group of players may enter into a cooperative agreement to propose a specific set of policies if recognized and to vote to approve such a proposal if another member of the party is recognized. If a player outside the party is recognized, then party members vote to reject any proposal. This in effect ensures that the party platform is implemented as policy. This specification can be taken as implicitly assuming that membership in a political party is an underlying repeated game in which players can commit support to

---

[13] Jackson and Moselle (2002) produce an analogous result.

a common party line, but for reasons of tractability one does not make this intraparty bargaining more explicit.

The next relevant question is what exact set of policies members of a party will adopt. Jackson and Moselle (2002) model party members as adopting the Nash bargaining solution, with the reservation payoffs determined by expected utility from the noncooperative bargaining game when there are no parties. So, for example, the vector of policies x chosen by a party of player A and player B would maximize the following expression.[14]

$$\arg\max_{x} \left(U_{a2}^x - U_{a2}^{nc}\right)\left(U_{b2}^x - U_{b2}^{nc}\right) \tag{2.10}$$

One important feature of the way I model parties here is that this method distinguishes between "significant" party behavior, which involves voting behavior that would not be observed in the absence of a cooperative agreement, and "party-like" behavior, where party cohesion is attributable merely to similarities in preferences between players. As a result, it responds to Krehbiel's (1993) critique that voting cohesion alone is not sufficient to demonstrate that parties matter.

As in the previous section, I consider several specific preference configurations, but in this case showing how outcomes can change if players form a political party. If players A and B are able to sign a binding agreement to support a party platform, then they will agree to full religious toleration ($\rho = 1$), and they will then adopt a compromise tax policy that maximizes the product of their utility gains, as in Equation 2.11.

$$\arg\max_{(\theta - \tau)} \left(2 + e_a(\theta - \tau) + z_a - U_{a2}^{nc}\right)\left(2 + e_b(\theta - \tau) + z_b - U_{b2}^{nc}\right) \tag{2.11}$$

It should be noted, however, that it may also be possible for B and C to both improve on their expected utility by forming a party, in which case the expected rate of taxation would be 1.[15] As a consequence, credibility of taxation will depend crucially on whether the party that has control of the legislature is a landowning party (formed by B and C) or a party that includes both landowners and capitalists (formed by A and B). While the model presented here does not allow for the majority party to change due

[14] A logical alternative for modeling intraparty bargaining would be to make it noncooperative by specifying an alternating offers bargaining game between party members. But to the extent that time periods for intraparty bargaining are short, the equilibrium result would converge to the Nash bargaining solution.
[15] It is not possible in any of the examples for A and C to improve on their expected utility by forming a party.

to electoral shifts, we can nonetheless draw a clear observable implication for empirical work: Perceived credibility of debt repayment will be correlated with partisan shifts in control of the legislature. This is an observable implication of the theory that I consider at length in Chapters 4, 5, and 6.

Example 1: Single Issue Bargaining. The results of Example 1, where players bargain only about taxation, are straightforward. It is impossible for A to form a party with either B or C, but B and C can improve on their expected utility by forming a party. This provides an important observable implication for the empirical chapters: Parties will not improve commitment to moderate capital taxation if society is divided along a single political cleavage.

Example 2: Multi-Issue Bargaining. When players bargain over multiple issues it is possible for them to improve on their expected utility by forming a party, and this process of party formation can lead to moderate capital taxation in equilibrium. In Example 2, as before, player A owns only capital and favors religious toleration, player B owns only land and favors toleration, and player C owns only land and opposes toleration. While policy in terms of religious toleration is altered when compared with the noncooperative equilibrium, the expected rate of capital taxation produced by Nash bargaining between A and B is in fact identical to the expected outcome of the noncooperative equilibrium. This result reflects two things. First, B would lose less than would A from a breakdown in intraparty bargaining. This then influences the outcome of Nash bargaining between A and B. In addition, due to their identical preferences with regard to religious toleration, A realizes a substantial utility gain from forming a party with B, even if the expected capital tax is unchanged. Finally, it should also be noted that it would be possible for B and C to form a party given these parameter assumptions.

Example 3: Multiple Issues When Player B Has a Mixed Income. As previously, Example 3 examines the effect of a decrease in e_b, so that player B is now assumed to derive part of his or her income from capital. In Example 3 for all discount factors the expected rate of capital taxation with a party of A and B is lower than in the noncooperative equilibrium (see Fig. 2.3). This result reflects the fact that B suffers less of a utility loss from compromising on the taxation dimension and that his or her preferences with respect to religious toleration are identical to those of player A.

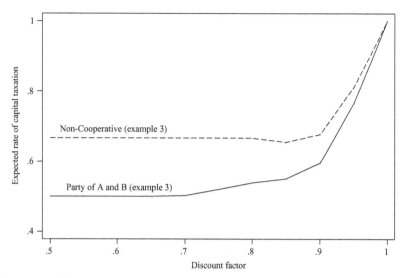

Figure 2.3. Effect of party formation on capital taxation (Example 3). $e_a = -1, e_b = 0.5, e_c = 1, z_a = 1, z_b = 1, z_c = -1.$

Example 4: Multiple Issues When Religion Is Less Salient for Player A. This example demonstrates how taxation is affected when player A places less weight on the issue of religious toleration than on that of taxation. Nash bargaining between A and B now produces an expected rate of capital taxation that for all discount factors is lower than the tax rate in the noncooperative equilibrium.

Parties as Equilibria

The major unaddressed issue with parties as I have modeled them so far involves the assumption that once they form a party, individual members can commit to proposing only the agreed set of policies if recognized and to voting only in favor of identical proposals. Modern political parties have evolved a number of different disciplinary devices that can help solve this problem. So, for example, party leaders frequently have the prerogative to select and deselect candidates who wish to run on the party's ticket.[16] Calvert and Fox (2000) have made a significant advance toward incorporating mechanisms of party discipline within a legislative bargaining

---

[16] A second possibility, modeled by Diermeier and Feddersen (1998) and Huber (1996), is that legislative prerogatives, such as the ability for a prime minister to call a vote of confidence, can also promote party discipline.

model that they extend to a repeated game (in this case one that does not end once an initial set of policies is chosen). In their model party members can pursue nonstationary strategies that involve sanctioning any member who deviates from an agreed party platform. The sanctioned member thus goes into "bad standing," implying exclusion from benefits shared by the party. The punishment strategy used is limited in the sense that a player remains in "bad standing" only for a finite number of periods.[17]

The model developed by Calvert and Fox (2000) is clearly appealing in that it more explicitly models how real-world political parties function. It also involves additional complexity, though, in terms of extending the Baron-Ferejohn framework to a repeated game context. They deal with this problem in part by restricting their attention to a game where preferences are homogeneous and legislators bargain over how to divide a fixed sum of benefits. To consider how parties influence the credibility of capital taxation, however, it is necessary to assume heterogeneity of preferences between owners of land and capital.

I briefly consider here whether players who form a party can enforce cooperation by the use of trigger strategies.[18] I do this to demonstrate how a party could be sustained as an equilibrium strategy profile of a repeated game, while recognizing that constructing a fully satisfying model in a context of heterogeneous preferences remains a subject for future research. In Example 2, if player B formed a party with player A, he or she might subsequently defect by proposing his or her own ideal point rather than the agreed party platform, but A could respond by reverting to his or her equilibrium strategy from the one-shot noncooperative game. If one retains the assumption that players receive zero utility in each period where a majority does not vote in favor of that period's proposal, then it is straightforward to show that as long as their discount factor is not too low, A and B can sustain party cooperation based on the knowledge that defections will be punished by the other player reverting to noncooperative behavior.[19]

---

[17] This follows Carruba and Volden (2000). Jackson and Moselle propose an alternative definition of a "stable" party as being the party that provides each member with greater utility than could be obtained from any other potential party.

[18] One should note that while authors such as Tomz (2001) have pointed out that trigger strategies may be implausible in many financial market contexts, in a legislature with a smaller number of players, such strategies are more plausible. Chapter 5 provides direct evidence of behavior of this type within British political parties.

[19] My assumption that the reversion payoff is 0 may not be innocuous. In the purely distributional game modeled by Calvert and Fox (2000), it makes sense to suggest that the reversion outcome is a payoff of 0 for all players, since in each period there is a fixed sum of resources to be divided. When one considers issues such as taxation

If players A and B follow a strategy of cooperating unless a defection occurs, and subsequently reverting to noncooperative behavior for the rest of the game, then the following inequality needs to be satisfied in order for player B to not have an incentive to defect from a party with A in equilibrium.[20] It is possible to satisfy this inequality for some range of discount factors.[21]

$$U_{b2}^{party}/(1 - \delta) > 4 + \delta\left(U_{b2}^{nc}\right)/(1 - \delta) \qquad (2.12)$$

Satisfying the above inequality demonstrates that a party of A and B *could* be sustained as an equilibrium set of strategies in an infinitely repeated game, but this does not of course demonstrate that party cooperation *will* be sustained. Moreover, it is also possible for B and C to sustain a party for some range of discount factors. As a result, while modeling parties as equilibrium strategy profiles in a repeated game allows one to demonstrate possibilities for party formation, this cannot predict unambiguously which party will form. Finally, if a party is modeled as a nonstationary strategy profile in a repeated bargaining game, then it is also important to note that there are multiple party platforms that could be sustained for either a party AB or a party BC.[22]

---

and religious toleration, however, the reversion payoff may not be equal to 0. It may be the payoff that players derive from the policy that received majority support in the previous period. Given the configuration of preferences in Examples 2 to 4, this could decrease possibilities for A and B to sustain a political party based on trigger strategies. Take an example when the reversion point was the policy agreed to in the previous period, and B defects from a party with A by proposing its own ideal point to C, who accepts. For subsequent periods there is no point that would offer both A and C a higher payoff. However, any policy that lies on the diagonal between $(1, 1)$ and $(-1, -1)$ would offer both A and C an equivalent payoff. This raises the possibility that A could respond to B by proposing one of these policies. This seems plausible, but it adds a further degree of complexity, since it implies modeling a dynamic game where each period is not identical. Baron and Herron (1999) have examined bargaining under these conditions in a finitely repeated game, finding that the game is "remarkably poorly behaved."

[20] Given that 4 would be the one-period payoff for player B if he or she is recognized and defects by offering a proposal of full religious toleration and a capital tax of 1 to player C.

[21] And the range of discount factors for which the inequality can be satisfied is consistently larger than the range of discount factors for which A, B, and C could sustain a moderate rate of capital taxation in a repeated game where taxation was the only issue considered. As such, the presence of a second issue dimension expands opportunities for commitment beyond those described in a more simple reputational equilibrium in a game where it is not possible to form parties.

[22] This corresponds closely to the result in Bawn (1999) where different divisions of payoffs between two members of a coalition correspond to different "ideologies."

4. Constitutional Checks and Balances

Rather than emphasizing party formation and political compromise, an alternative reason why representative institutions might reduce the risk of default is if they involve constitutional checks and balances, such as the sharing of power between a democratically elected executive and a legislature. In Chapter 1, I argued that constitutional provisions establishing multiple veto points were neither a necessary nor a sufficient condition for credible commitment. In what follows I provide formal support for this claim. I show expected capital taxation is reduced considerably if capital owners control a veto point, but multiple veto points have little effect on credibility if future control of veto points is uncertain. One tractable way of modeling the effect of multiple veto points is to consider how expected levels of capital taxation change when one of the three players in the game presented above is given the right to veto any proposal. This veto right might be taken as serving as a proxy for a player's enjoying majority control within a second legislative chamber.

I first consider a case where it is specified in advance that the capital owner (player A) has veto power. In Example 1, where players care only about the tax dimension of policy, if player A can veto any proposal, then B and C must make an offer that will satisfy A's continuation constraint, and as a result, at high discount factors expected capital taxation is significantly lower than in the case where A does not enjoy veto power (Fig. 2.4).[23] In Example 2 where players have preferences over both the issue of taxation and religious toleration, the effect of granting A veto power is again very significant, as expected capital taxation tends toward 0 as $\delta \rightarrow 1$ (Fig. 2.5).

As a next step, I consider how expected equilibrium capital taxation is affected if veto power is randomly assigned to one of the three players, and capital owners must make their investment decision before veto power is assigned. One reason for considering this random case is that in many instances future control of veto points may be uncertain. Another reason for considering the random case is that as the number of veto points in a political system increases, then unless one group is given

---

[23] This result concurs with McCarty (2000), who demonstrates that veto power has a greater effect on policies when time horizons are long. The results are unchanged in Example 1 if B or C have veto power, when compared with the case without a veto player. This is because they have identical preferences, and even in the absence of veto rights, a majority cannot be formed without the agreement of either B or C.

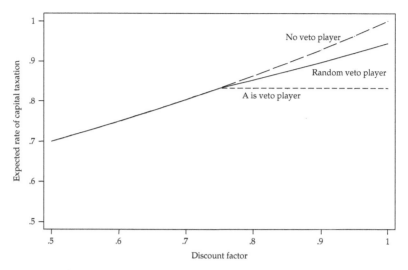

Figure 2.4. Effect of veto power on capital taxation (single-issue bargaining). $z_a = z_b = z_c = 0; e_a = -1, e_b = 1, e_c = 1$.

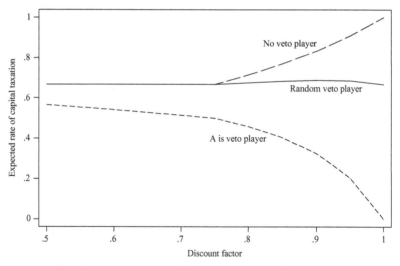

Figure 2.5. Effect of veto power on capital taxation (multi-issue bargaining). $e_a = -1, e_b = 1, e_c = 1, z_a = 1, z_b = 1, z_c = -1$.

privileged representation, we might expect each equally sized social group to have an equal chance of controlling this new veto point. When there is a random veto player, in Example 1 expected taxation is only marginally lower than in the case where there is no veto player (see Fig. 2.4). The effect of a random veto player on capital taxation is more significant in Example 2 (see Fig. 2.5).[24]

The fact that there is often relatively little difference between expected capital taxation with a random veto player and expected capital taxation when there are no veto players lends support to my first main argument: that unless there is some mechanism ensuring that capital owners control a veto point, then establishing multiple veto points may do little improve to credibility. In a more basic sense, the model here makes clear that the effect of constitutional checks and balances is conditional on the partisan composition of a legislature.

5. Bureaucratic Delegation

So far, I have considered the politics of capital taxation in a context where the economic environment is static, and where there is no possibility for delegating any policy functions to bureaucratic authorities. In practice, volatility of revenues may influence credibility of debt repayment to the extent that a sudden revenue shortfall may trigger a default. In this section I explore the possibility that bureaucratic delegation may help to alleviate this problem. I conclude, as suggested in my third main argument from Chapter 1, that delegation will be effective only in cases where government creditors have significant political influence within a legislative assembly. As a result, bureaucratic delegation is a complement rather than a substitute for representative institutions in terms of enhancing credibility. Chapters 4 to 6 consider in depth whether this proposition is supported by empirical evidence.

To consider why delegation may be relevant for credibility of debt, one needs to consider the effect of revenue volatility. My consideration of capital taxation has so far assumed a situation where there are no economic shocks to complicate policy planning. In reality, exogenous events frequently oblige policy makers to make adjustments in policies such as

---

[24] This result might seem surprising. The explanation lies in part in the fact that, relative to the non–veto player equilibrium, A modifies his or her proposed $(\theta - \tau)$ less when C is a veto player than does C when A is a veto player. In addition, relative to the non–veto player equilibrium, B lowers his or her proposed $(\theta - \tau)$ when A is drawn as a veto player, while he or she cannot raise his or her proposed $(\theta - \tau)$ when C is a veto player, because B already proposes $(\theta - \tau) = 1$ in the non–veto player equilibrium. Finally, when drawn as a veto player, C does not raise his or her equilibrium proposal for $(\theta - \tau)$ either, because he or she too already proposes $(\theta - \tau) = 1$ in the non–veto player equilibrium.

the level of taxation. For example, the amount of finance yielded by government taxes on land income and capital income will vary with trends in economic growth. If taxes produce less revenue than projected, then a government will have to decide on new taxes, or cancel certain spending items, or decide to borrow anew to cover the shortfall.

Uncertainty over how much finance a given tax rate will yield has significant implications for the credibility of debt repayment. Take a situation where an actor has purchased a government bond based on the expectation that legislative bargaining will result in a tax rate on capital that is sufficiently low to make the investment profitable at prevailing interest rates. If subsequently a negative economic shock results in a shortfall in revenues, then repaying debts may require a decision on tax increases or new loans. This could undermine the bargaining position of bond holders if they risk going without repayment for one or more periods.

Exogenous shocks to government revenues could be incorporated into the model by adding a stochastic component u to the government budget constraint, as in Equation 2.13, and by having this stochastic component be revealed only after decisions regarding taxation have been made. Any realization of u other than zero will require a new round of bargaining, either to distribute the surplus if u is positive or to levy new taxes if u is negative.

$$g = \tau l + \theta k_2 + u \qquad (2.13)$$

If the realization of u is negative, and government spending g is allocated to both provision of a public good, such as security, and to repayment of debt, then players may face different costs of delay in reaching a new agreement. In particular, if the revenue shortfall leads government bond holders to go unpaid, then the reversion payoff for bond holders if there is no agreement will be lower than otherwise.

One way of reducing the uncertainty provoked by revenue shocks is to establish bureaucratic procedures that ensure that first priority in allocation of revenues is given to servicing of government debt. In the simplest case this could be established in the form of a rule requiring debt repayment to receive priority over other expenditure items. A complementary possibility would be to delegate responsibility for managing government revenue collection. The most common mechanism in early modern Europe for achieving this goal was to grant government creditors the right to collect specific taxes directly. As is described in Chapter 4, after 1688 in Great Britain a number of new institutional steps were taken to ensure that debt repayments received priority allocation of revenues. My argument here could also be extended to other forms of bureaucratic delegation, such as those used in eighteenth-century France, where it was common for the monarchy to borrow indirectly through royal officials.

The potential problem with delegation as a solution to commitment problems is that in practice, a decision to delegate can be reversed. It has been recognized at least since Weingast and Moran (1983) that political principals can use the implicit or explicit threat of revising an agency's statutes in order to influence bureaucratic behavior. Drawing on the sizable political economy literature on bureaucratic delegation, we can make three predictions about the impact of a decision to delegate management of revenues.[25] First, if owners of capital either lack majority control of at least one representative assembly or lack the power to veto a decision to reverse delegation, then bureaucratic delegation will be meaningless, because landowners will find it easy to override any decision made by a nominally independent bureaucratic authority. Second, if owners of capital control all veto points in a political system, then bureaucratic delegation will be superfluous. Capitalists will have the power to block any decision to override a bureaucratic authority, but they would also have the power to protect themselves against opportunistic changes in taxation even in the absence of delegation. Following the logic of this argument, then, the principal circumstance under which bureaucratic delegation can make a difference is if owners of capital lack the power to set tax policy unilaterally, but do have the power to block any attempts to override bureaucratic decisions.

6. Summary

Representative political institutions may improve a government's ability to make credible commitments through several different mechanisms. This chapter has used a formal model of legislative bargaining to provide support for my three main arguments. I first demonstrated that if capital owners are in the minority, then party formation can lead to credible commitment, but only if players bargain over multiple issues. In addition, one can expect the perceived credibility of taxation or borrowing to vary according to the partisan composition of government. Both of these observable implications will be considered in detail in subsequent chapters. I next showed that constitutional checks and balances will have little effect on

---

[25] See Epstein and O'Halloran (1999), Keefer and Stasavage (2001, 2002), and McCubbins, Noll, and Weingast (1989).

credibility unless there is some mechanism ensuring that capital owners control a veto point. This helps support the argument that multiple veto points may in many cases be insufficient to ensure credible commitment. Finally, I developed my argument about bureaucratic delegation, suggesting that it will improve credibility only if capital owners have the political authority to block any attempt to override bureaucratic decisions. This too is an empirical prediction that is considered in subsequent chapters.

3

Historical Background

Sovereign Borrowing in Europe before 1688

1. Introduction

This chapter briefly surveys the development of institutions for sovereign borrowing in early modern Europe, from the first long-term loans contracted in medieval Italian city-states through the innovations introduced in the Netherlands in the sixteenth and seventeenth centuries. I pay particular attention to the precedent set by the Netherlands, because the methods of borrowing used by the Estates of Holland were to become a model for subsequent reforms in England after 1688. In fact, during the reign of King William III in England, newly adopted techniques of long-term borrowing were initially referred to as "Dutch finance." This historical survey reveals a clear trend: There was a connection in many states between the development of sovereign borrowing and the development of representative political institutions. This helps support the claims made by North and Weingast (1989) about representative government and credibility.[1] However, the experience of states such as Holland shows that credibility derived not only from having representative institutions, but equally importantly from the fact that government creditors were well represented within assemblies. Those assemblies in which creditors were well represented tended to be city-states where mercantile groups played a major role (as in Venice, Florence, or Genoa) or states where representation was biased in favor of urban groups (as was the case in the Estates of Holland). This raises the question for later chapters of how devolving power to a representative assembly could improve the credibility of borrowing in a much larger state, such as Great Britain or France, where debt

---

[1] It also parallels the link observed by Hoffman and Norberg (1994), who in a comparative study suggest that representative institutions in early modern Europe were associated with higher levels of taxation.

holders would be a small minority of the population. In Chapters 5 and 6 I suggest that the process of party formation in a society with multiple political cleavages may give creditor interests significant influence even if holders of debt are in the minority.

After the introductory survey, the chapter presents the evolving practices for sovereign borrowing in England and France up to 1688. Post-1688 institutions are considered in Chapter 4. France and England before 1688 did not establish a practice of giving a representative assembly control over public borrowing. In England, while Parliament had control of most tax decisions, it did not retain control over spending, and all public borrowing was left at the discretion of the monarch. In fact, England had no significant system of long-term public borrowing before the Glorious Revolution. Arguably, this absence of preexisting institutions for long-term government borrowing made it easier to introduce reforms after 1688. In France, in contrast, long-term government borrowing developed quite early, but it remained outside the control of France's national representative institution: the Estates General, and the Estates General itself lost power after the fifteenth century. It was not convened at all between 1614 and 1789.

2. Early Developments

For most of Europe in the early modern period, public borrowing was restricted to two forms: short-term advances from bankers and forced loans that represented a one-off levy on wealth holders. More modern forms of finance developed initially in several Italian city-states, based on loans with specific revenues offered as collateral.[2]

Early Examples of Sovereign Borrowing

For medieval princes and monarchs who lacked other access to finance, short-term advances from bankers at high rates of interest were a frequent expedient. In some instances, these loans were contracted with bankers resident outside the jurisdiction of a particular monarch, as with the well-known case of Italian banking houses lending to the English Crown to finance the Hundred Years' War (1337–1453). The principal disadvantage

---

[2] This subsection draws on a number of different secondary accounts, especially Tracy (1985), in addition to Ehrenberg (1928), Fryde and Fryde (1963), Homer and Sylla (1991), Kohn (1999), Munro (2001), Ormrod (1999), and Veitch (1986).

of short-term borrowing was its high cost. There were numerous examples of princes repudiating short-term debt, and as a consequence bankers were willing to engage in this sort of lending only at extremely high rates of interest, sometimes approaching 50 percent per annum.[3]

Instead of relying on foreign creditors, short-term loans could also be contracted with a prince's own subjects, as was frequently true of Italian city-states. Many of the loans "negotiated" in this manner had a strong element of coercion, as all wealth holders were expected to participate. The city of Venice developed a system for forced loans in the thirteenth century when all holders of movable wealth (as determined by a government audit) were required to loan a fixed percentage of their assets to the state.[4] While forced loans, such as those practiced in Venice and other Italian city-states, allowed rulers to avoid paying high rates of interest, these rulers encountered another serious problem. The repeated use of this technique gave citizens an incentive to hide their movable wealth, consume it, or move to another jurisdiction. The other problem with short-term loans was that rulers who sought to repudiate this debt could inevitably find excuses for prosecuting their creditors for some criminal offense. So, for example, the expulsion of the Jews from England by Edward I allowed both confiscation of their property and default on debts contracted with them. Similarly, Philip IV of France in 1307 dissolved the Knights Templar, a monastic order from which the French Crown had borrowed significant sums.[5]

Innovations in Borrowing

Mechanisms for governments to finance themselves by issuing long-term debt backed by tax revenues developed earliest in the Italian city-states. Beginning in the thirteenth century, as it faced increasing difficulty in repaying loans, the Venetian government adopted several new practices that would subsequently be applied elsewhere. In 1262 it announced that a rate of 5 percent interest would be paid on all loans, and the Grand Council of Venice declared that the proceeds from several specific

---

[3] Homer and Sylla (1991) provide a review of interest rates paid by sovereign borrowers during this period.

[4] Waley (1989) suggests that forced loans were pioneered by Venice in 1207, while Homer and Sylla (1991) give a slightly different date of 1171. In most cases these loans appear not to have accrued interest.

[5] Veitch (1986) provides a general discussion of debt repudiation by medieval monarchs.

excise taxes should be earmarked for debt repayment. During the fourteenth century, as the Venetian government took increasingly longer to repay these debts, it allowed a secondary market for its debt to develop. Owners of government debt could sell their loans to third parties at a discount (the rate of discount reflecting the perceived probability of default).[6]

The Genoan government went even further than the Venetian government in attempting to create sound institutions for borrowing. Private investors in Genoa formed a syndicate that made a loan to the state in exchange for the right to manage a new tax, the proceeds of which were to be used exclusively to service the loan (Kohn 1999). One advantage of this system was that it allowed the syndicate to monitor tax collections directly. To the extent it would have been costly for the Genoan government to abolish the new tax, this system also helped to ensure repayment, although ultimately the Genoan authorities retained the right to revise the contract. Waley (1989) observes that similar institutional adaptations occurred in other Italian republics.

While England following the Glorious Revolution has often been seen as the prototypical case where management of government debt was handed over to a representative assembly, it is important to recognize that there were continental precedents for this practice. First, representative assemblies in the Italian city-states were heavily involved in state finance, although membership of these assemblies was limited to a narrow segment of the population.[7] There were also precedents for representative assemblies becoming directly involved in public borrowing in German principalities during the medieval period.[8] It seems clear that on a number of occasions, princes who had accumulated sizable debts felt that in order to continue to service their debt, they had no option but to grant additional powers to representative assemblies.[9]

---

[6] Luzzato (1963), cited in Tracy (1985).

[7] For a discussion of the development of representative assemblies in Italy, see Hyde (1973) and Waley (1989).

[8] See Fryde and Fryde (1963). Tracy (1985) reports that as early as 1356 an assembly of burghers in Bavaria took over from the prince for the management of public debts and revenues. This privilege was short-lived, however, as the assembly administered only debts that had already been accumulated, and the dukes of Bavaria soon began to raise new funds outside the purview of the burghers.

[9] Tracy (1985) gives the example of the Duke of Württemburg, who in 1550 granted all control over revenues and expenditures to a committee of six burghers and two prelates.

The Dutch Precedent

The government of the province of Holland in the Spanish Netherlands was the first to establish a system of legislative control of government borrowing that was recognizably modern. This reform allowed the Estates of Holland by the late sixteenth century to borrow long-term at unprecedentedly low interest rates. In this subsection I describe the reforms undertaken in the Netherlands and in the province of Holland in particular, while also investigating how representative institutions in Holland gave substantial political power to owners of government debt.[10]

The revolution in public borrowing in the Netherlands was driven in part by the Habsburg monarchy's goal of defending its possession against military invasion from France. The Habsburg emperor Charles V from the 1520s through the 1550s engaged in a lengthy conflict with France that necessitated sizable military expenditures. Initially, when revenues proved insufficient to cover expenditures, the Habsburg monarchy borrowed funds on the Antwerp money market at rates that varied widely from 6.25 percent to as much as 15 percent per annum.[11] As the monarchy proved increasingly unreliable as a debtor, however, it soon found itself closed out of this market.

In 1522, seeking an alternative means of finance, Charles V's regent in the Netherlands persuaded several provincial estates to sell government securities backed by specific future tax revenues.[12] Individual cities in the Netherlands had issued long-term securities well before this date, but a significant evolution occurred with the coordination of borrowing at the provincial level (t'Hart 1993; Veenendaal 1994). In addition, instead of being guaranteed by the monarchy, repayment would now be guaranteed by the provincial estates. In the case of the Estates of Holland, the rate established for these loans was very low (6.25 percent), but this is not surprising when one considers that there was initially a significant degree of compulsion in the purchase of these securities. If the loans had been contracted at a market rate, it seems likely that the rates of interest would have been considerably higher.

---

[10] Holland was one of the provinces of the Spanish Netherlands, all of which came under Habsburg control during the fifteenth century.

[11] These are rates reported by Homer and Sylla (1991: 114). This covers rates for loans with a term of at least ten months. For shorter-term loans, rates sometimes went as high as 31 percent.

[12] The estates were the representative assemblies for the Dutch provinces. It is worth noting here that political institutions in the Netherlands were highly decentralized, which helps explain why Charles V dealt with individual provincial estates.

As a result of renewed conflict, in 1542 the Habsburg monarchy made further concessions to the Netherlands estates in exchange for new issues of long-term debt. Instead of relying on taxes administered by the Emperor's officers to provide revenues for repayment, provincial assemblies in the Netherlands now gained full discretion over the levying of their own taxes and their own public expenditures. Furthermore, loans contracted by the estates were now to be repaid not with specific taxes or excises, but with permanent taxes (t'Hart 1993). The underlying idea was that provincial assemblies could be better relied on to generate the revenues necessary to service debts.

Among the provincial estates, the Estates of Holland went the furthest in terms of financial reform. After 1553 the Estates abandoned the practice of compelling wealth holders to purchase public debt.[13] Long-term loans after 1553 were sold on a strictly voluntary basis, and interestingly, they were marketed not only to citizens of the province of Holland, but also to citizens elsewhere in the Netherlands. Prior to 1572 (when the Netherlands provinces revolted against the Habsburgs) the government of Holland scrupulously respected all terms of repayment on its debts. As the perceived likelihood of a government default declined, there was an "explosion of interest" in government debt among wealth holders in Holland.[14]

Figure 3.1 shows the evolution of interest rates on borrowing by the Estates of Holland between the end of forced loans in 1553 and the middle of the seventeenth century. Two clear conclusions can be drawn. First, as early as 1558 the Estates could issue debt for purchase on a voluntary basis at the same rate of 6.25 percent that had long prevailed for compulsory purchases of debt. Second, with the exception of the very high rates that prevailed during the period of the revolt of the Netherlands against the Habsburgs (beginning in 1572), there was a secular decrease in rates paid by the Estates of Holland. As a result of the difficulties caused by the revolt, the Estates of Holland were obliged to briefly suspend debt payments in 1575 (explaining the rise in interest rates at this time), but repayment was soon resumed (Veenendaal 1994).

---

[13] The Habsburg regent had insisted in 1552 that loans continue to be made compulsory "for reasons of equity," but the loan of 1553 showed that investors were willing to purchase debt at the same rate voluntarily (t'Hart 1993).

[14] This increased availability of government finance was also affected by exogenous circumstances, and in particular by economic growth as Amsterdam became an entrepôt for trade with the Baltic, the Mediterranean, and the Americas (t'Hart 1999).

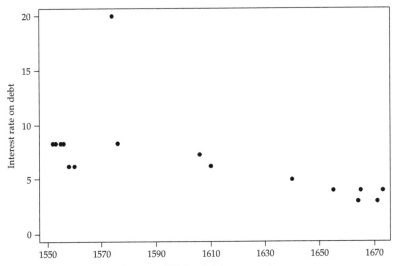

Figure 3.1. Interest rates on Estates of Holland debt, 1553–1673.
Source: t'Hart (1999) and Tracy (1985).

The increased credibility of public loans in Holland was accompanied
by an equally significant increase in levels of per capita taxation in the
province. As noted by t'Hart (1997), by the end of the seventeenth century, contemporary observers recognized that Dutch citizens were taxed
more heavily than their French and British counterparts. Hoffman and
Norberg (1994) suggest that this helps support the idea that there is a link
between representative institutions and ability to raise adequate revenues.
It should be noted, however, that while this increase in taxation was a significant achievement, increased ability to collect revenue does not in itself
provide an explanation of why the Estates of Holland were also able to
borrow at low rates of interest. Borrowing at low rates of interest required
not just maintaining a certain level of current taxes; it also depended on a
commitment to collect sufficient revenues in the future so that debt could
be repaid.

In sum, the experience with public borrowing by the Estates of Holland
shows that a small provincial assembly was able to establish greater credibility as a borrower than was the formidable Habsburg monarchy. Ability
to borrow at low rates of interest was crucial in the political arena, as
the Dutch provinces that rebelled against the Habsburgs were able to
raise substantial funds for military expenditures despite their small economic size. In asking how the Estates of Holland were able to achieve

this outcome, it is useful to consider how the Estates were structured, and who was represented within the institution.[15]

During the fifteenth century the Estates of Holland consisted of seven distinct subrepresentations: one for each of the province's six principal cities and one for a college of nobles from the province, the *ridderschap*. Unlike the Estates of other provinces in the Netherlands, the Estates of Holland did not include a separate representation for members of the church. Rural areas were in theory represented by the college of nobles, but given that half of the population in the province of Holland remained outside the cities, it seems fair to say that rural interests were significantly underrepresented within the Estates. In terms of procedure, as the oldest city in the Netherlands, Dordrecht had right of proposal within the Estates. Normally, decisions on taxation, expenditure, and borrowing could be made by a majority of three cities together with the college of nobles, but Tracy (1985) suggests that individual cities in practice often could block decisions, because if they did not agree with a majority decision, they could simply refuse to participate in collecting funds to repay a loan.

While the Estates of Holland in the early sixteenth century had biased representation in favor of urban areas, it should also be emphasized that their power was circumscribed by the fact that the Estates met only when summoned, and they could not discuss issues such as religion or foreign policy (Israel 1995). With the revolt of the Dutch provinces against the Habsburg monarchy, from 1572 the Estates began meeting more regularly, for lengthier sessions, and it also appears that they became increasingly independent. In addition, membership of the Estates was expanded, first to include fourteen towns (in 1581) and subsequently eighteen towns (by the 1590s). While the group of nobles within the Estates was given right of proposal at all meetings, the *ridderschap* was now outnumbered eighteen to one by urban representatives. Finally, Israel (1995) suggests that the influence of urban interests was further increased after 1585 by a provision stating that any proposal considered by the Estates required a prior debate within the councils of the individual towns that sent representatives to the Estates.

Though it seems clear that the Estates of Holland devolved considerable power to urban interests, it is also important to consider who these urban interests were. It has long been recognized that the magistrates who

---

[15] I focus exclusively on the Estates of Holland here, because Holland was by far the largest province in the Netherlands, and in political terms it exerted a high degree of control over the general government (Israel 1995).

represented each city within the Estates were very frequently merchants or bankers. Tracy (1985) has gone a step further by showing that members of the Estates were disproportionate holders of debt issued by the Estates. Out of a sample of seventy-one purchasers of long-term debt issued by the Estates of Holland between 1542 and 1565, he shows that twenty-three purchasers were magistrates in one of the province's six principal cities, and a further seven were direct relatives of magistrates. After 1572, evidence suggests that ownership of debt issued by the Estates of Holland diversified considerably (t'Hart 1993, 1997), but at the same time, members of the Estates of Holland remained significant purchasers of debt.

The above evidence shows that political institutions in Holland gave urban interests, and in particular government creditors, a very significant degree of control over economic policy. A number of authors, including t'Hart (1993, 1997), Tracy (1985), and Veendendaal (1994), have attributed the financial success of the province at this time to the political power of government creditors. As Tracy argues, "equitable or not, control of fiscal policy by men who themselves had heavy investments in state debt was the real genius of the Netherlands system of public borrowing both in its Habsburg beginnings and in its seventeenth century grandeur" (p. 216).

In sum, the experience of Holland suggests that governments characterized by representative assemblies can establish greater credibility as borrowers than apparently powerful monarchies. However, in explaining the success of the Dutch government in this regard, it would seem equally important to emphasize that the representative institutions that controlled public finance in Holland were dominated by individuals with a direct interest in seeing that government debt was serviced. This raises the question of how the link between representation and debt would operate in a larger republic where financial interests might be in the minority. I turn to this issue in Chapters 5 and 6 after first providing a description of political and financial institutions in England and France before 1688.

3. Political and Financial Institutions in England before 1688

While there were many similarities between state finance in England and state finance in other European countries, from the thirteenth through the seventeenth centuries English institutions in this area had two distinctive characteristics. First, a national representative assembly in the form of the House of Commons and the House of Lords played a virtually continuous role with regard to government decisions on taxation. While

England was not unique in having a representative assembly, and while it is true that Parliament's authority waxed and waned over time, it is difficult to ignore the fact that Parliament did continuously enjoy certain prerogatives. Second, despite the strength of this national representative institution, the English Crown before 1688 did not develop a significant system for long-term borrowing, such as existed in the Italian city-states, in France, or in the Netherlands. As described below, the historical background to the institutional reforms that began in 1688 was a century of conflict between Crown and Parliament over prerogatives and finance.

Weakness of Instruments for Borrowing

While monarchs in medieval England frequently borrowed from bankers and other financiers for short maturities, England was something of an exception among European states in the weakness of its instruments for long-term borrowing. English kings borrowed from both domestic and foreign bankers, and often secured loans by giving their creditors the right to directly collect certain Crown revenues, but they did not regularly issue securities. As noted by Fryde and Fryde (1963), access to short-term loans for English monarchs was greatly facilitated by the fact that from the end of the thirteenth century, Edward I had established a unified system for the collection of customs revenues. Moreover, England had abundant customs revenues thanks to the export of wool to the European continent. Nonetheless, there were some spectacular defaults by English kings, most memorably under Edward III during the Hundred Years' War (Fryde and Fryde 1963; Ormrod 1999).

One potential reason why English monarchs before 1688 did not develop a more regularized system of borrowing was that after the end of the Hundred Years' War in 1453, England faced fewer pressures from external military threats than did its continental neighbors.[16] After the Hundred Years' War (1337–1453), monarchs up to Elizabeth I borrowed frequently, but always through short-term lending, and then often resorted to forced loans from their subjects. In other cases, as with Henry VIII and his seizure of church property, confiscation of the assets of a group of subjects proved a convenient means of avoiding financial crisis.

---

[16] Brewer (1989) emphasizes this absence from major continental wars in explaining the pattern of English financial development. The link between state development and external conflict has also been considered in a comparative context by Ertman (1997) and Tilly (1990).

The Role of Parliament, 1215–1603

The English Parliament developed initially as part of a "Grand Council" of nobles and ecclesiastics that, as stipulated by the Magna Carta agreement, had the authority to accept or refuse demands by the Crown for new taxes. This council soon made a habit of periodically refusing royal demands, and by the early fourteenth century, when a separate House of Lords and House of Commons had developed, Parliament shared a virtual right of colegislation that it was to retain throughout the Hundred Years' War.[17] Parliamentary consent was required for the Crown to levy most types of taxes in England at this time, although customs revenues were generally regarded as a royal preserve. In terms of expenditure and borrowing, however, Parliament had little influence. In addition, Parliament's influence declined somewhat after the end of the Hundred Years' War in 1453, in part because the Crown no longer had as pressing a need to raise finance.

Conflict between Crown and Parliament, 1603–1688

The background to the Glorious Revolution of 1688 was a lengthy period of conflict between Crown and Parliament in which increased royal demands for finance played a significant role. While his predecessor, Elizabeth I, had borrowed little and left a small public debt as part of her legacy, James I significantly increased royal expenditure, in particular by expanding the size of his court. Stone (1965) argues that James, who was Scottish, took these actions in order to gain favor with his new subjects. Given that royal revenues remained stagnant in real terms, the increase in royal expenditures required to maintain the court necessitated some form of financing. Lacking access to long-term borrowing, and faced with a Parliament that was less than eager to consent to new taxes, James I opted for the more expedient technique of selling offices and titles in order to raise funds. This included the sale of knighthoods, baronets, and peerages. In doing so, James was no doubt inspired by the heavy resort to venal office holding by the French monarchy.[18]

---

[17] See Ertman (1997) and Ormrod (1999). Dunham and Wood (1976) review how Parliament's de facto powers during this period even extended to influence over the choice of monarchs.

[18] Rather than the Crown demanding direct payment for these offices, it was much more common for payments to pass via influential intermediaries. In some cases a secondary market in offices actually developed. James also directly auctioned off certain state functions involving monopolies and regulatory authorities, as well as the right to collect certain revenues (Stone 1965: 432–41).

Fiscal pressures for the Crown were exacerbated during the reign of Charles I (1625–49), due in large part to two unsuccessful military conflicts with Spain and with France. The new king responded by continuing the practice of raising revenues through venal practices, combined with short-term loans from bankers.[19] When these sources of funds proved insufficient, a fiscal crisis ultimately forced Charles I to call Parliament. Conflict between Crown and Parliament degenerated into the Civil War, which culminated in the execution of Charles by parliamentary forces in 1649.

In terms of decision making, while English monarchs between 1603 and 1688 made frequent use of royal prerogative to pass bills unilaterally, it is important to recognize that Parliament continuously retained significant authority over tax policy.[20] Parliament vetoed several proposed tax increases under James I (Stone 1965). In the case of Charles I, Parliament proved similarly obstinate. Following the restoration of the Stuart monarchy under Charles II in 1660, despite the presence of a legislative majority that generally sided with the monarchy, Parliament continued to show its independence in matters of taxation. In one notable example, Charles II was forced to put a halt to a military campaign against the Netherlands in 1674 when Parliament refused to levy further taxes to provide supplies and to pay soldiers' wages (Jones 1994).

In strong contrast with the limited royal prerogatives in the area of taxation, the English Crown between 1603 and 1688 continued, as had always been the case, to exercise substantial discretion in its decisions over expenditure and borrowing. In its relations with Parliament, the Crown also had the advantage that it could determine when Parliament sat and when new elections could be called for the Commons. The Cavalier Parliament, which was broadly supportive of Charles II, sat for a lengthy eighteen years between 1661 and 1679. An act had been passed in 1641 calling for a new Parliament every three years, but this act was repealed under Charles II in 1664.

Royal prerogative with regard to expenditure and borrowing before the Glorious Revolution was accompanied by a repeated tendency for

---

[19] Under James I and Charles I, it was also a common practice for the monarchy to borrow by asking its venal officeholders for advances on the revenues that they were due to collect. As was the case in France at the time, this avoided the more costly alternative of turning to bankers for short-term loans, but it proved to be a much less efficient system of government borrowing than the long-term debt issued by the Estates of Holland.

[20] This is true for all types of revenue other than customs taxes, which could be set unilaterally by the Crown.

monarchs to default on the loans they had contracted. This pattern has been previously identified by North and Weingast (1989). The best-known instance of default under the later Stuarts is the Stop the Exchequer of 1671, which was initiated by Charles II. Oddly, the monarchy was not under exceptionally great financial pressure in 1671, but Roseveare (1991) argues that the Stop was decided as a temporary measure to free revenues for an expected military campaign. Most of the £1.3 million in debt that was officially frozen was owed to four families of goldsmiths who served as bankers to the English court during this period. Roseveare (1991) suggests that Charles did not expect this default to have major political ramifications. Charles II was accurate in his assessment to the extent that Parliament did not attempt to defend the bankers, but he failed to anticipate the fact that the Stop would limit his access to credit in the future.

As a final point about English institutions, though monarchs before 1688 continued to default on their loans, there were a number of reforms of state finance implemented between 1660 and 1688. These helped provide greater access to funds and laid the ground for subsequent reforms following the Glorious Revolution. These included above all an increase in the efficiency of tax collection. The practice of tax farming was abandoned, and the Crown instead developed a centralized administrative apparatus for collecting taxes.[21] Authors have emphasized the significance of these administrative reforms, and it seems clear that they explain in part how the British monarchy was able to find the funds to wage several wars of unprecedented expense after 1688. As with the Dutch case, though, one should not presume that reforms that resulted in increased revenue can also explain increased ability to borrow. Access to credit at low rates of interest required not just the ability to collect taxes; it also required a commitment to continue to collect taxes in the future so as to service debt. No such commitment existed in England before 1688.

4. Political and Financial Institutions in France before 1688

French political and financial institutions before 1688 had three main characteristics that are relevant for this study. First, the French monarchy

---

[21] Tax farming was the practice of selling private individuals the right to collect specific royal taxes. These reforms are surveyed in Brewer (1989), Chandaman (1975), and Roseveare (1969, 1991). There were also a number of administrative reforms that improved control over public spending, including, especially, greater Treasury control over other government departments.

moved early to establish a system of long-term loans known as *rentes*. Second, French representative institutions played an important political role during the fourteenth century, but by the middle of the fifteenth century they failed to serve as a check on monarchical power. Finally, given the weakness of these representative institutions, French rulers increasingly relied on venal office holding and on indirect borrowing from royal officials in order to raise funds.[22]

Medieval Institutions

In addition to the common practice of demanding forced loans from their subjects, French monarchs as early as the fourteenth century had established forms of long-term borrowing. Initially, this involved the sale of *rentes*, which consisted of rights to future income from lands owned by the king.[23] In terms of administration, the income derived from the *rentes* continued to be collected by the King's officials, rather than by the creditors themselves as was the case in medieval Genoa or in the Estates of Holland. The consequence of this practice was that creditors remained at the mercy of the king for repayment.

Major (1960) and Wolfe (1972) have suggested that during the century between 1330 and 1430, French monarchs relied increasingly on representative assemblies, and in particular the national representative body, the Estates General, to justify increases in taxes. This paralleled the trend observed in England at this time where Parliament's influence was quite substantial. During the chaos of the 1350s, when the French king was captured by an English army and held for ransom, the Estates General actually briefly seized control of Paris, although this usurpation of power was short-lived. Throughout the next seventy years French monarchs periodically relied on the Estates to seek consent for new taxes to fund military expenditures associated with the Hundred Years' War. The Estates were also repeatedly consulted on other issues, in particular foreign policy, and it was at this time that legal scholars attempted to resuscitate a principal from Roman law: "[T]hat which touches all should be debated and approved by all."[24] As Wolfe (1972) takes pains to emphasize, however,

---

[22] See Hoffman (1994) for a more detailed survey of French state finance during this period.

[23] Technically, the *rentes* did not accrue interest (in order to avoid usury laws), but because the income derived from the *rentes* significantly exceeded the original sale value, government creditors still received an income.

[24] *Quod omnes tangit, ab omnibus tractari et approbari debet.*

the prerogatives of the Estates General were never given a firm legal un-
derpinning. In some cases the King felt compelled to seek the consent of
the Estates for changes in policy, while in other instances tax increases
were announced without any attempt to seek outside consent.[25]

French kings after 1330 ceded part of their power over taxation to
representative bodies, but they did not take the analogous step with regard
to long-term borrowing. Instead of having the Estates General serve as
a sort of guarantor for royal debt, throughout the fourteenth century
kings retained full discretion in terms of decisions regarding the sale of
rentes and the management of revenues designated to pay off this debt.
From the mid-fifteenth century, the French monarchy paid less and less
heed to any idea that representative assemblies should be given decision-
making authority over public finance. As a consequence of this choice,
the Estates General went into a long-term decline from which it would
not recover until 1789. The principal instigator for this change was King
Charles VII (r. 1422–61), who on numerous occasions declined to call the
Estates General and instead opted to establish a practice of levying new
taxes by royal fiat. In addition, Charles VII severely reduced his reliance
on provincial assemblies. By the end of his reign, such institutions were
regularly convened in only a few provinces.

Venality and Indirect Borrowing

As an alternative to borrowing with the support of a representative assembly, French monarchs from the sixteenth century established and expanded other possibilities for raising funds. By the early sixteenth century
renewed military conflict (in this case with the Habsburgs) prompted the
French monarchy to seek new finance. In 1522 the advisers of François
I devised a new borrowing procedure where the king would borrow indirectly through the Paris town hall. The new securities, the *rentes sur*

---

[25] One further aspect of French representative institutions during this period, which
distinguishes them from similar institutions in England, is that they formed a patch-
work of overlapping jurisdictions. The Estates General was the sole assembly with a
claim to being a national representative institution, but it was never clearly defined
what prerogatives the Estates General had in relation to a number of provincial
assemblies. Provincial assemblies were often also consulted by the monarchy before the announcement of new tax measures. Persistence of provincial assemblies
in France is sometimes attributed to the fact that territories such as Languedoc,
which were conquered by the French monarchy, had preexisting local assemblies
that functioned efficiently. In some cases French monarchs subsequently chose not
to abolish these institutions (see Given 1990).

l'Hôtel de Ville, were sold by the monarchy, but repayment would occur through several earmarked taxes that would be administered directly by the officials of the Paris town hall. Interest rates on the *rentes* were set at 8.33 percent. In theory this would make it more difficult for the king to renege on his debts, because an independent body collected the taxes necessary to repay the debts. It can be seen as an example of bureaucratic delegation to the extent that the Crown ceded power over revenue collection.

Initially, François I did not make heavy use of the *rentes sur l'Hôtel de Ville*. Instead, he borrowed heavily from bankers based in Lyon at higher interest rates ranging from 10 to 16 percent per annum (Collins 1988: 58). These bankers were encouraged to form a syndicate, later known as the Grand Parti, which would raise capital for the king, with all loans secured by specific royal tax revenues. Gradually, however, royal payments to the Grand Parti occurred more and more infrequently, and by 1558 the syndicate had gone into default. According to Wolfe (1972), the monarchy would have been willing to continue to service its debts to the Grand Parti, but doing so would have required an increase in taxes in Lyon where the syndicate was based, and this was bitterly opposed locally.[26]

After the failure of the Grand Parti experiment, French monarchs relied increasingly on the sale of *rentes* to raise funds. This included loans contracted not just via the Paris city government, but also with local organizations in provincial cities. In many cases the purchase of these securities was "strongly encouraged" for all wealth holders. In another case, the monarchy actually threatened to withdraw administration of the Paris *rentes* from the officials of the Hôtel de Ville. As recounted by Wolfe (1972: 115), this threat was rescinded after the wealthy citizens of Paris made a sizable "donation" to the royal treasury. The fact that French monarchs resorted to coercive measures to sell *rentes* suggests that the *rentes* had more in common with forced loans than with the securities sold by the Estates of Holland. It undermines the idea that borrowing indirectly through the Hôtel de Ville served as a means of credible commitment for monarchs.

French monarchs during the sixteenth century also dramatically expanded the existing practice of selling venal offices, and subsequently

---

[26] The revenues raised to pay off debts from the Grand Parti came from this one region. Collins (1988) suggests that the failure of the Grand Parti experiment led royal creditors to demand the right to directly collect certain tax revenues in order to ensure debt repayment. So, for example, the monarchy in 1581 gave a syndicate of Italian lenders the right to collect certain taxes in order to secure their debt.

they borrowed funds from those who had purchased offices. As studied in detail by Doyle (1996), French kings had sold offices in exchange for money as early as the thirteenth century. In many cases, offices provided their holder with an annual income, generally derived from the withholding of a portion of the tax revenues that an officeholder was charged with collecting. In other cases offices did not come with the right to collect taxes, but they did provide an annual salary.[27] Kings quickly developed the habit of asking their officeholders to advance certain tax revenues at times of great need. In theory, venal officeholders would have greater assurance of repayment of their debt than would ordinary citizens. The most important reason for this was that in the event the monarchy defaulted, any officeholder with the right to collect taxes could withhold revenues from the king. In practice, however, French monarchs had a number of ways of unilaterally revising contracts with venal officeholders. This issue is considered in greater detail in Chapter 4 for the post-1688 period.

5. Summary

The diffusion of institutions for sovereign borrowing in Europe, beginning with the Italian city-states and culminating with the example set by the Estates of Holland, suggests that long-term loans guaranteed by a representative assembly were an effective means for governments to borrow large sums at low rates of interest. However, this was conditional on government creditors being prominently represented within the assemblies. Neither France nor England followed the Dutch example before 1688, as France had a system of long-term loans but weak representative institutions, and England had a powerful representative assembly but no regular means of long-term borrowing. The next chapter takes a detailed look at borrowing outcomes and institutional innovations in Great Britain and in France after 1688.

---

[27] In other instances offices did not provide access to a regular income, but they brought other benefits, such as immunities from prosecution in certain courts, not to mention social prestige. See Bien (1989) and Doyle (1996) for further discussion.

4

Trends in French and British Sovereign Borrowing, 1689–1789

1. Introduction

In this chapter I examine the institutional context for French and British sovereign borrowing after 1689. I also investigate borrowing outcomes, focusing on market perceptions of default risk. The two subsequent chapters then attempt to explain observed trends in default risk by analyzing partisan politics in each country. Data on government finances and interest rates on public loans for the eighteenth century are limited compared with what is available for today's financial markets, but careful work by economic historians has nonetheless generated a surprising amount of information that can be used to investigate sovereign borrowing in France and Great Britain. In synthesizing existing evidence, I identify three basic trends.

First, the English Crown after 1688 did, on average, pay a lower default premium on its debt than had been the case before the Glorious Revolution. But this basic conclusion masks a more complex reality. Interest rates on government debt remained very volatile during the first thirty years after 1688, and at times during this period, the Crown found itself paying rates that were higher than those that had prevailed before the Glorious Revolution. Interest rates on English government debt did not converge with Dutch interest rates until the early 1720s. The interest rates paid by the Estates of Holland serve as a useful benchmark here, because loans contracted by the Estates were widely seen as carrying very little default risk for the reasons discussed in Chapter 3. Basic econometric tests show that economic factors, such as changes in inflation or in government demand for funds, can only partially explain this post-1688 volatility. In fact, much of the variation is correlated with shifts in partisan control of government between the Whigs and the Tories. This is a finding that is consistent both with my argument that constitutional checks and balances are not a sufficient condition for credibility and with my argument about party formation in a plural society. I consider the effect of partisan trends in greater depth using historical evidence in Chapter 5.

This chapter also compares interest rates between countries, examining English rates in relation to those paid by the French monarchy. As suggested in previous studies, and in particular by Velde and Weir (1992), the evidence shows that the French Crown consistently paid higher interest rates on its debt. What's more, strictly economic factors such as differential rates of inflation cannot explain this gap, and so the higher French rates seem to have been due to the existence of a default premium. This leaves open the question of to what extent higher interest rates in France were attributable to institutional differences (the absence of a representative assembly and a national bank) or, alternatively, to a balance of partisan forces different from that which prevailed in Great Britain at the time. Chapter 6 considers this issue in detail, arguing that an early adoption of English-style institutions in France would have been insufficient to ensure credibility of debt repayment.

A third finding concerns efforts to improve access to credit by bureaucratic delegation. These were less successful in France than in the United Kingdom, but there is also interesting variation to explain within each country. In France, while the Crown was at times able to borrow at lower rates of interest by using officeholders as intermediaries, on many occasions it unilaterally revised these contracts. As a result, indirect borrowing served at best as a weak form of commitment. The interesting exception to this pattern involved indirect royal borrowing through provincial assemblies. Efforts to establish a public bank in France modeled on the Bank of England also failed to improve the monarchy's credibility as a borrower. This was true of John Law's bank (1716–20), the Caisse d'Escompte (created 1776), and the proposal to create a national bank in 1789. Chapter 6 considers the political reasons underlying these failures, and in particular whether they support my third argument, which suggests that attempts to establish credibility through bureaucratic delegation will be ineffective in an absolute monarchy.

With regard to Britain, the monarchy never developed as extensive a system of venal officeholders as was the case in France, and so monarchs after 1688 did not have the option of borrowing indirectly from their officials. The crown did agree to establish a national bank, though, and this institutional reform proved much more successful than any of the French public banks under the ancien régime. This chapter shows, however, that there were several periods after 1694 where it was feared that the bank might be subject to political opportunism, and in these cases the share price for bank stock plummeted. Building on this initial finding, Chapter 5 considers more detailed historical evidence concerning party politics and the Bank of England.

The remainder of the chapter proceeds in four sections, beginning with a consideration of methodological issues in measuring credibility. This is followed by separate sections on French and British government borrowing during the wars at the beginning of the eighteenth century and their aftermath. I consider each country separately because of the poorer quality of French data for this period. A final section then compares French and British borrowing experiences after 1742, a period for which better data are available covering secondary market prices for debt.

2. Methodological Issues in Measuring Default Risk

I present several different types of evidence to gauge default risk. The most direct method involves identifying actual instances where governments either refused to pay their debts or unilaterally revised debt contracts. Another means of measuring this phenomenon is to use data from financial markets to estimate the extent to which purchasers of government debt thought that default was a possibility.

Default Premia

When owners of capital fear that a government may default on its obligations, they will tend to demand a higher interest rate that incorporates a default premium. As a consequence, estimates of how default premia vary over time and across countries are often used as measures of government credibility. Default premia can be estimated by taking yields on government debt and netting out the effect of other determinants, such as expected inflation. Alternatively, default premia can be estimated by comparing the yield on a government's bonds with the yields on bonds from a "safe" issuer. Ideally, data on yields based on secondary market prices of bonds can provide a continuous track record of default risk.[1] Secondary market prices on government debt are available for England and France for the latter half of the eighteenth century. Comprehensive secondary

---

[1] So, for example, default premia on today's dollar-denominated emerging market bonds might be estimated by comparing their yields with yields on U.S. Treasury bills, bonds on which the default risk is considered to be close to zero.

market data are not available for the earlier part of the eighteenth century, but as a second-best method, one can compare initial interest rates on government debt issues. This is predicated on the assumption that governments will accurately estimate the minimum interest rate at which wealth holders are willing to purchase debt.[2]

Quantity Borrowed as a Measure of Credibility

While this chapter focuses above all on the cost of government borrowing as an indicator of credibility, several authors have also used the quantity borrowed to address this question. North and Weingast (1989) present statistics to show that government borrowing in Great Britain expanded dramatically after the Glorious Revolution of 1688. Focusing on quantity borrowed might be justified in two different ways. First, any outward shift in the supply curve for capital due to increased credibility of repayment should result in both a reduction in the equilibrium interest rate and an increase in the quantity borrowed. The potential problem here is that an increase in the quantity borrowed might also be the result of a shift in the government's demand for capital (say, due to war or recession), which would be associated with an increase in interest rates. Without considering how interest rates change over time, it may be impossible to distinguish between these two scenarios.[3]

---

[2] There is one caveat, here, however. When assessing credibility based on initial interest rates, it is important to recognize that there is a potential for selection bias. Governments that have very low levels of credibility may select themselves out of a sample by declining to attempt to issue debt, based on the expectation that they would not be able to obtain any credit.

[3] In some cases there may be reasons for focusing *exclusively* on quantity borrowed as a measure of credibility. Robinson (1998) has raised this possibility for the case of sovereign borrowing in early modern Europe using a simple model where credit rationing takes place. He assumes there is a monarch who is able to borrow from multiple lenders and who has the option of defaulting on debt. Lenders will make an expected profit if the inequality in Equation 4.1 is satisfied, where r is the rate of interest on government debt, R is the rate of return that could be realized on an alternative project, and p is a parameter measuring the probability that government revenues will be sufficiently high for the government to repay its debt. The sovereign will repay debt only if the inequality in Equation 4.2 is satisfied, where L represents the quantity of funds borrowed and C is a political cost suffered by the sovereign if it defaults. Robinson further assumes that competition between lenders drives their expected profits to zero. This implies that the interest rate will be bid down to $r = ((1 + R)/p) - 1$.

$$p(1 + r) \geq (1 + R) \tag{4.1}$$

$$C \geq (1 + r)L \tag{4.2}$$

3. Sovereign Borrowing in England after 1688

Changes in Political Institutions

While this chapter does not seek to give a detailed history of the Glorious Revolution of 1688, it is useful to lay out a few basic facts about the events that led to the replacement of James II by William of Orange. The Glorious Revolution was triggered by policies adopted by James II and by the fear that a Catholic would succeed him as the next king. While Jones (1994) suggests that James II had initially hoped to pursue a liberal course, by the mid-1680s he turned increasingly authoritarian, and in doing so unwittingly succeeded in uniting against him groups that were generally hostile to each other. James II had planned to redraw constituency boundaries for the House of Commons so as to pack Parliament with individuals who would assent to his policies. He also managed to scare both Anglicans and non-Anglican Protestants who feared his Catholicism. Faced with what amounted to a coup d'état supported by the Whigs with the acquiescence of the Tories, James II fled the country and was replaced by William of Orange, who became King William III.

English political institutions underwent a clear transition as a result of the Glorious Revolution.[4] Most importantly for the purposes of this book, the Bill of Rights of 1689 declared illegal any attempt to pass a bill through royal prerogative. This in effect reestablished a practice that had been part of English custom since Magna Carta. The new king also accepted several other innovations: Parliament could audit public expenditures, the maintenance of a standing army by the Crown was to be subject to

---

This model yields different comparative statics for the interest rate r and the quantity borrowed L, depending on whether one assumes that institutional changes that increase government credibility involve an increase in C or an increase in p. Robinson (1998) argues that the Glorious Revolution in England resulted in an increased cost to the sovereign from defaulting, because Parliament could subsequently withhold revenues. In this case, the predicted effect of an increase in C is an increase in the quantity the government can borrow in equilibrium L, while the interest rate remains unchanged. However, rather than increasing exogenous costs of default for a sitting policy maker, a core argument of this book is that the English Glorious Revolution actually stripped the Crown of the opportunity to default on its debt. If this is the case, then the Glorious Revolution is better depicted as a reduction in p, representing a decrease in the likelihood that Parliament would fail to raise sufficient taxes to service debt. The prediction derived from the model would then be a reduction in the interest rate on government debt, combined with an increase in the quantity borrowed in equilibrium.

[4] For surveys of English political institutions during this period, see Harris (1993), Holmes (1993), Kemp (1968), and Stone (1980).

parliamentary consent, and Parliament gained substantial new influence in the area of public borrowing.

Following the Glorious Revolution, the Crown under pressure from Parliament also agreed to a further significant concession. In 1694 the above changes were followed by the passage of the Triennial Act, which stipulated that a new Parliament had to be called at least once every three years. This prevented the Crown from retaining a docile Parliament for a lengthy period of time, as Charles II had done between 1661 and 1679. Finally, through the Act of Settlement of 1701, Parliament established a degree of control over the succession to the monarchy, stipulating that no Catholic could ascend to the throne, and that after the death of Queen Anne (who ruled after the death of William III), the next monarch would be the elector of Hanover. In the eyes of Stone (1980), the Act of Settlement shifted England from a situation where the monarchy had untrammeled sovereignty to one where the King and Parliament shared sovereignty.

Though the above changes were very significant, the Crown did retain substantial formal powers after 1688. It had the authority to dissolve Parliament whenever it saw fit (provided that it called a new election), it retained the right to choose ministers without reference to which party might hold the majority in either the House of Commons or the House of Lords, and it also retained the right to influence the composition of the House of Lords by appointing new peers. Finally, the Crown also retained the legal right to veto legislation by refusing royal assent. However, after 1688 William III used this privilege on only a handful of occasions; Queen Anne did so only once; and King George I, who was crowned in 1715, never vetoed a bill. As a result, while the right to veto legislation was never officially withdrawn from monarchs, authors such as Williams (1939) have argued that after 1688 the practice quickly lost legitimacy.

Changes in Financial Institutions

As argued in Chapter 3, England before 1688 was an outlier among West European monarchies in that it lacked a well-developed system for long-term government borrowing. The British revolution in government finance after 1688 borrowed directly from the example set by the Estates of Holland during the sixteenth century.

The first long-term government loan in England dates from 1693. The impetus for this and the loans to follow was England's declaration of war against France in 1689. Dickson (1967), who remains the most detailed source on the origins of the national debt in England, shows that different proposals for long-term government borrowing had circulated in England for a number of years. The proposal that eventually won the support of Parliament was designed by William Paterson, a Scot who had been studying mechanisms of Dutch government finance. A total of £1 million was to be borrowed at an interest rate of 10 percent per annum, backed by revenues from a new series of excise duties. This was a tontine loan where creditors would receive interest for their own lifetime (or that of a nominee), and in addition, the interest would be paid on a basis where total interest per creditor would increase as some creditors died off. Parliament repeated the exercise in 1694 with a "lottery loan" through which a further £1 million was raised.[5] Those who purchased this loan earned interest on the principal they invested while also earning the right to participate in a lottery.

Specific details of individual government loans during this period varied, but the two most important innovations involved their long-term character and the fact that their repayment was guaranteed by Parliament rather than relying exclusively on the goodwill of King William III. As had been the case in the Habsburg Netherlands, a monarch pursuing foreign policy goals had been prompted to turn fiscal powers over to a representative assembly in order to improve possibilities for long-term finance. This change in decision making was supplemented by several other significant changes in bureaucratic organisation that have been discussed by Brewer (1989). For one, the Department of the Treasury was modernized, making the government's revenue collection more efficient. The government also developed a more effective system for short-term borrowing that helped bridge temporary gaps between payments and receipts.

The final change in financial institutions was the creation of the Bank of England. In 1694, by Act of Parliament, the government launched a £1.2 million loan for which subscribers would receive 8 percent interest (with specific customs revenues offered as collateral). The subscribers would also be allowed to incorporate themselves as "The Governor and Company of the Bank of England" (Andréades 1909). The bank was given the right to issue notes equal to the sum advanced to the government, a valuable privilege that made shareholders willing to lend at lower rates of interest than would otherwise have been the case. In addition, the Bank of England Act contained a provision stating that if the

---

[5] For a description of lottery loans during this period, see Dickson (1967). Tontine loans are considered by Dickson (1967) and in greater detail by Weir (1989).

customs revenues allocated proved insufficient to repay the £1.2 million loan, the Treasury was required, without a further Act of Parliament, to allocate supplementary revenues toward repayment in order to make up the shortfall.[6] This was an important measure that would help protect government creditors against revenue shortfalls. Over time, this system was expanded so that government revenues increasingly passed directly through the Bank of England, and the Bank was authorized to use these revenues to repay public debt without prior authorization by Parliament. This practice was later formalized with the creation of the Consolidated Fund.[7] Channeling revenues through the bank can be seen as a form of bureaucratic delegation that had the potential to increase credibility of debt repayment.[8]

The Bank of England suffered through a difficult first two years as the government borrowed further sums from the bank (forcing its shareholders to borrow on the Amsterdam money market), and its position was jeopardized by the proposed creation by Parliament of another note-issuing bank, the Land Bank, in 1696. The announcement of this scheme prompted a significant drop in the Bank of England's share price, but ultimately the Land Bank failed to find the necessary number of subscribers (Andréades 1909). This conflict between the Bank of England, which was associated with the Whig Party, and the Land Bank, which was more closely associated with the Tory party, is discussed in greater detail in Chapter 5.

In the wake of the Land Bank's failure, the Bank of England was able to extract several further concessions from the government in exchange for an increase in its capital. No other note-issuing bank was to be established by Act of Parliament.[9] The Bank of England was also exempted from taxation, and its charter was extended until 1710 (Andréades 1909). After 1696 as the bank grew in importance as a lender to government, the context of bargaining between the Crown and its creditors also changed significantly. As has been emphasized by Weingast (1997b), instead of facing a multiplicity of small lenders whom it might be possible to play off against one another, given the importance of the bank as a source

[6] Bank of England Act, 1694 (5&6 William & Mary, c. 20).
[7] See Andréades (1909) and Bank of England Act, 1696 (8&9 William III, c. 20). The Consolidated Fund was established in 1787.
[8] North and Weingast (1989) have also emphasized this institutional feature following Macaulay (1861).
[9] In a further extension in 1709 it was prohibited for any corporation of more than six persons, other than the Bank of England, to engage in note issue.

Table 4.1. *British Public Finance, 1689–1742 (in annual terms, million £)*

		Annual spending	Land taxes	Customs and excise	Net borrowing
War of the League of Augsburg	1689–97	5.1	1.4 29%	1.6 33%	1.8 35%
War of Spanish Succession	1702–13	7.8	2.0 28%	3.1 43%	1.8 24%
Relative peace	1714–42	6.0	1.4 23%	4.2 72%	0.5 9%

Note: Figures may not sum to 100 percent, because additional stamp taxes and post office taxes were levied. The sum of greater than 100 percent for 1714–42 is due to a discrepancy in the official statistics.
Source: Mitchell (1988).

of finance, the Crown may well have found it more difficult to pursue a strategy of selective default.[10]

Government Finance, 1689–1742

The British monarchy's efforts to wage war against France between 1689 and 1697 and between 1702 and 1713 led to an unprecedented demand for funds. Table 4.1 shows total British government spending during the course of the War of the League of Augsburg (1689–97), during the War of the Spanish Succession (1702–13), and during the subsequent period of relative peace (1714–42). It also lists the quantity of funds raised from different types of revenue, together with net borrowing.

An unprecedented increase in revenues after 1688 helped fund military expenditures. The two principal revenue sources at this time were customs and excises taxes and a Land Tax, a post-1688 creation that was essentially an income tax on agricultural earnings. For most of the period of warfare between 1688 and 1715, Parliament set the Land Tax rate at 4 shillings on the pound (20 percent). As can be seen in Table 4.1, the Land Tax was a particularly important source of revenue during the War of the Spanish Succession. Given that wealthy landowners made up of the vast majority of Members of Parliament (MPs) during the eighteenth century (and the vast majority of voters), parliamentary support for the Land Tax raises interesting questions about why the landed classes accepted this new measure. In Chapter 5 I argue that the tax was actually

---

[10] It should be noted, however, that the bank did not serve as a monopoly lender to government.

a subject of significant partisan strife between Whigs and Tories. After 1715, while Parliament kept revenues at sufficient levels to service the public debt, it reduced the rate for the Land Tax.[11] As a consequence, the share of revenues derived from taxes on land was considerably lower. The tax burden instead shifted increasingly to excise taxation. The political motivations for this change in tax policy that took place under Robert Walpole are also considered in Chapter 5.

In addition to raising new types of revenue, the British monarchy borrowed heavily to fund the wars between 1688 and 1715, and the share of expenditures met by borrowing was particularly high during the War of the League of Augsburg between 1689 and 1697. As a result of sizable long-term borrowing, by 1713 U.K. public debt had reached six times annual revenues. In this same year the U.K. government devoted half of its revenues to debt servicing. Though the government borrowed less during the period of peace after 1714, overall public debt continued to rise, reaching eight times annual revenues by 1742.[12]

Yields on U.K. Government Debt

Given the absence of secondary market data for long-term government debt during this period, a first cut at measuring credibility can be attempted by observing initial yields on British government issues, as reported by Dickson (1967) and Homer and Sylla (1991). These can be compared with rates reported for borrowing by the Estates of Holland.[13] Figure 4.1 shows a clear long-term decline in British yields between 1688 and 1742, but it also raises several important questions about existing descriptions of politics and government finance in Great Britain. For one, there was very significant variability in yields in the years after 1688, and for a brief period between 1710 and 1713 the British government actually

---

[11] The Land Tax was reduced to 15 percent in 1717 and 10 percent in 1722; it remained at 10 percent for most of the period until 1740. See Holmes (1993: 368).

[12] One event I do not consider here was the South Sea Bubble of 1720, which was a financial crisis involving a plan to convert government debt into equity in a private trading company. While it was a major event, the South Sea Bubble did not result in a major change in default premia on government debt, which explains why I have not given it greater consideration in this study. See Garber (2000) for a recent review of the crisis.

[13] Unfortunately, no continuous series exists for Dutch interest rates during this period. The rates reported here are collected from t'Hart (1999), Homer and Sylla (1991), and Veenendaal (1994). While these data are incomplete, there seems to be unanimous agreement that the rates at which the Dutch government was able to borrow were low and quite stable during this period.

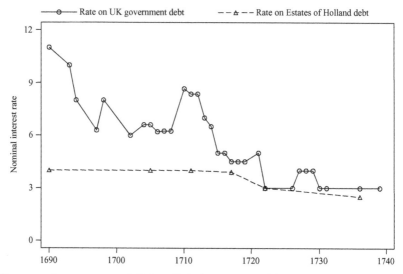

Figure 4.1. Interest rates on British and Dutch government debt, 1689–1742.
Source: Dickson (1967), t' Hart (1993), Homer and Sylla (1991), and Veenendaal (1994).

found itself paying interest rates that were higher than those that had prevailed before the Glorious Revolution.[14] Moreover, the spread between yields on British government debt and Dutch government debt remained sizable until the early 1720s, more than thirty years after the Glorious Revolution.

Before assuming a political explanation, there are several potential economic explanations for the variation observed in post-1688 British government yields. Given a limited supply of capital, increased government demand for funds during wartime would place upward pressure on interest rates independent of any change in investor perceptions of default risk. Likewise, variation in expected levels of inflation would influence yields since investors knew that their real rates of return would depend on movements in goods prices.[15] Additional privileges granted to lenders could provide another explanation for variations in yields. About a third of the loans issued by the British government during this period

[14] Homer and Sylla (1991) list three separate interest rates for government borrowing before the Glorious Revolution: 8 percent in 1640, and 1665, and 6 percent in 1680. Each of these rates is equivalent to or lower than the rates reported by Dickson (1967) and Homer and Sylla (1991) for the period 1710–13.

[15] Of course, inflation might also be deliberately generated by a government in order to reduce the real value of outstanding debt, but I am referring here to changes in inflation that are exogenous to government policy.

provided investors with an additional benefit of this sort, usually in the form of participation in a lottery. Likewise, the two loans associated with the establishment of the Bank of England (1694) and the New East India Company (1698) gave investors monopoly privileges to issue currency and to trade with certain regions. One would expect to observe lower interest rates on these loans relative to loans that did not entail any special privileges.

To examine in a systematic fashion whether the economic factors listed above are a sufficient explanation for post-1688 variation in British yields, I have estimated several simple time-series regressions. The annual quantity of government borrowing is included to control for the effect of increased demand for funds on interest rates.[16] As a proxy for expected future inflation, I have included the current rate of inflation, based on changes in producer prices and after applying a Hodrick-Prescott filter to the price series in order to provide a better measure of trend inflation.[17] I have also added a linear time trend to control for the effect of long-run changes that might have led to a decline in interest rates. One possibility here is that interest rates fell on government debt as the overall capital stock in Great Britain grew. A growing capital stock would imply a reduction in the rate of return on capital in the economy. The linear time trend also captures the argument that it took time for people to realize that the institutional changes begun in 1688 would not be reversed.[18] I also considered including a dummy variable *lottery* that takes a value of 1 for each loan where lenders received lottery or other privileges in additional to regular interest payments. The coefficient on this variable was never statistically significant, and so I have excluded it from the final estimates (other results were unchanged when it was included).

As an alternative to explanations emphasizing economic factors, I also explore to what extent yields on British government debt were correlated with trends in partisan control of government. This involves asking whether the changing electoral fortunes of the Whig and Tory parties were associated with changes in government yields. This is an initial test of one observable implication of my argument about party government, and it is explored in much greater depth in Chapter 5. The variable *Whig control* is

---

[16] Taken from Mitchell (1988).

[17] The source for the price index is Schumpeter (1938). Using a consumer goods index that includes goods other than cereals does not significantly alter the results.

[18] North and Weingast (1989) suggest that the changes initiated during the Glorious Revolution were not secure as long as Louis XIV failed to recognize the new British monarch.

Table 4.2. *Explaining Yields on U.K. Government Debt*

	(1)	(2)
Net government	.093	.105
borrowing	(.064)	(.072)
Trend inflation	.565	1.87***
	(.532)	(0.60)
Time trend	−.121***	−.042**
	(.013)	(.017)
Whig control	−1.00***	
	(0.20)	
Whig majority		−.008***
		(.002)
Number of observations	31	31
F test	$p \leq .001$	$p \leq .001$
R^2	0.86	0.85

Note: Heteroskedastic-consistent standard errors in parentheses. *, **, and *** indicate significance at the 10%, 5%, and 1% levels, respectively.

scaled from 0 to 2, taking a value of 2 if there is a Whig majority in both the House of Commons and the House of Lords, a value of 1 if there is a Whig majority in either house, and a value of 0 otherwise.[19] While the Whig party arguably enjoyed a majority in the Lords for most of the period considered here (with the important exception of the years 1712–14), the pattern of majority control in the Commons was much more volatile during the period before 1715.[20] As an alternative measure, I included a second partisan variable *Whig majority*, which measures the size of the Whig majority in the House of Commons in number of seats. For years in which the Tories had majority control in the Commons, this variable takes a negative value.

Table 4.2 reports the result of two different specifications, each using a different partisanship variable. Even after controlling for economic determinants and a time trend, a shift in partisan control of government from Tory to Whig is estimated to result in a significant drop in interest rates. Based on regression 1 a shift from Tory control of both Houses to Whig control of both Houses is estimated to result in a drop in the interest rate

[19] Data from the House of Commons are compiled from Hayton (2002) and Holmes (1993), while data for the House of Lords are drawn from Speck (1970).
[20] As discussed in Chapter 5, the Whigs had a Commons majority in 1688–89, from 1694 to 1700, and briefly in 1708 and 1709. The Whigs established lasting supremacy in the Commons after 1715.

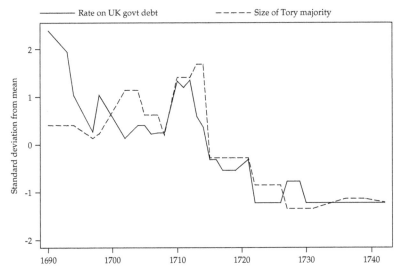

Figure 4.2. Interest rates on debt and partisan control of the House of Commons. Variables transformed to mean = 0, standard deviation = 1.

on government debt by 2 percent. Using regression 2, a 200-seat electoral swing in favor of the Whig party within the Commons is estimated to result in a 1.6 percent drop in interest rates on government debt. To give a visual sense of the relationship between partisan control and interest rates on government debt, Figure 4.2 plots interest rates on U.K. government debt against the size of the Tory majority in the Commons between 1689 and 1742. Both variables have been transformed to have a mean 0 and standard deviation of 1. The fit between the two series is remarkably close, as Tory majorities were associated with a higher cost of borrowing.

One potential problem with my regression specification is that net government borrowing and the interest rate on government debt may be jointly endogenous. When governments borrow more, this places upward pressure on interest rates, but when interest rates are high, governments may also have incentives to borrow less in equilibrium. To deal with this issue I repeated the regressions reported in Table 4.2 while replacing the net government borrowing variable with a dummy variable for war years. After inclusion of this variable the coefficients on both partisan variables remained negative and statistically significant.

Another potential concern with the results in Table 4.2 is that one or more variables may be nonstationary. While unit root tests suggested that this was not the case for inflation or government borrowing, the interest rate on government debt may be nonstationary.[21] This is of course not a surprising finding given the significance of the time trend coefficient in regression 1. As a robustness check I repeated regressions 1 and 2 using data that has been detrended by regressing each variable on a time trend and then saving the residuals. In these regressions the coefficients on the two variables *Whig control* and *Whig majority* remained virtually unchanged and highly significant.[22] Finally, the coefficients for the two partisanship variables also remained significant after exclusion of several outlying observations.[23]

In sum, these econometric tests suggest that there was substantial variation in interest rates on U.K. government debt after 1688 that cannot be explained by economic factors such as increased demand for funds, nor by a simple time trend. This result is consistent with an observable implication of my first argument concerning constitutional checks and balances. Even with the institutional changes of the Glorious Revolution, credibility of government debt was by no means guaranteed after 1688, as there appear to have been periods of relatively high interest rates. In addition, the fact that interest rates were highly correlated with trends in the partisan control is a result that is consistent with my second argument about party government. Yields on government debt were lower during periods of Whig control, and the historical discussion in Chapter 5 considers this issue in greater detail.

Bank of England Share Prices

From its creation in 1694, the British government relied increasingly on the Bank of England as a source of short- and long-term loans, and during the course of the eighteenth century it also relied increasingly on the bank to manage government debt. Rather than automatically assume a scenario of ever increasing power and influence for the institution, however, it is important to consider the extent to which eighteenth-century observers thought it possible that Crown or Parliament might take actions such

---

[21] Based on both an Augmented Dickey Fuller test and a Philips-Perron test. A related potential concern is autocorrelation, but the estimates were virtually unchanged when using Newey-West standard errors instead of those reported here.

[22] Ideally, the relationship between yields on debt and the other variables might also be reestimated using an error-correction model, but the numerous gaps in the sample combined with the limited number of observations made this technique impractical.

[23] Outliers were excluded that had a DFBETA statistic for which the absolute value was greater than the absolute value of $2/\sqrt{N}$.

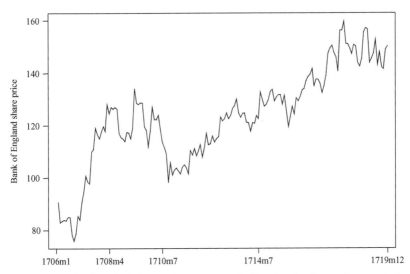

Figure 4.3. Bank of England share prices, 1706–1718. "1708m4" refers to the arrival of a Whig government in April 1708; "1710m7" refers to the arrival of a Tory ministry in July 1710; "1714m7" refers to July 1714 when the Whigs returned to power.

as defaulting on debts owed to the bank or undermining privileges enjoyed by its shareholders. Reports by observers at the time suggest that there were several periods when the Bank of England's future was placed in doubt. The two best documented of these episodes involve the creation of the rival Land Bank in 1696, which was promoted by a group of politicians who would subsequently become Tory leaders, and the fears for the bank's future at the time of the Tory electoral landslide of October 1710.[24] A systematic assessment of this issue can be performed by analyzing trends in Bank of England share prices, for which high frequency data is available beginning in 1709. During periods where the perceived probability that the government might interfere with the bank's operations increased, one would expect the share price to fall.

Figure 4.3 plots monthly Bank of England share prices between January 1706 and December 1718.[25] As can be seen, there is a clear upward trend in the share price, but several other features are also apparent. While the period leading up to the Whig government between April 1708 and

---

[24] These episodes are considered in more detail in Chapter 5. On the Land Bank episode, see Andréades (1909). Morgan (1922) discussed the electoral campaign of 1710 and its impact on the bank. See also Carruthers (1996).

[25] Data compiled by Neal (1990) from Castaing (1698–1711).

July 1710 was associated with a significant increase in bank share prices, the arrival of a Tory government during the summer of 1710 was associated with an equally dramatic drop in the Bank of England's share price. The share price subsequently recovered, but it took until the middle of 1714 to return to the peak it had reached under the previous Whig government. Econometric support for this partisan interpretation has recently been provided by Wells and Wills (2000), who have estimated a vector autoregression to identify significant breaks in the prices of individual stocks on the London stock market between 1698 and 1730. Using this methodology, they identify a significant negative break in Bank of England share prices associated with the Tory election victory of October 1710.

What these findings suggest is that the Bank of England after 1694 was far from immune to trends in partisan control of government, and in particular there was a significant perceived risk that the bank would fare poorly under a Tory government. This finding is consistent with my third argument, which suggests that bureaucratic delegation can be an effective means of commitment only when government creditors have the political power to resist attempts to override bureaucratic decisions. Chapter 5 considers this link between partisanship and the Bank of England in greater detail using historical evidence.

Links between Public Debt and Other Markets

While this study focuses on the politics of public debt, one of the broader political economy debates about Britain during this period is whether the Glorious Revolution resulted in increased security of property rights not just for government creditors, but for the economy more generally. North and Weingast (1989) make this causal link quite explicitly, suggesting that commitment to repay public debt helped lead to the growth of private financial markets in general. To support this claim, they cite evidence collected by Dickson (1967) on the growth of the English stock market. Given that many of the companies traded on the stock market in its early days depended on a government-granted monopoly, the link between government credibility and stock market development would seem very clear.

Clark (1996) has challenged North and Weingast's conclusion, using data on land rents in England from the sixteenth century through the early nineteenth century. If an institutional change results in government commitment not to expropriate property, then he argues one should logically observe a drop in the rate of return on farmland. In fact, Clark's data show quite convincingly that neither the Glorious Revolution nor any of the events immediately following it were associated with a significant drop in land rents. While Clark takes this as an indication that political changes in England post-1688 had no effect on the overall security of property rights, his data may actually support a more nuanced conclusion. For reasons that have yet to be identified, relative security of property rights for landowners may have been established well before the Glorious Revolution, but the market for government debt was clearly different, as it took considerably longer to reduce the risk of default on sovereign debt.

4. French Government Borrowing, 1689–1742

In 1689 institutions governing public borrowing in France continued to be characterized by the three features described in Chapter 3: weakness of national representative institutions, heavy use of borrowing through intermediaries, and the sale of offices to generate war finance. This section reviews French public finance during the period of warfare at the end of Louis XIV's reign (1689–1715) and during the subsequent period of the Regency (1715–23).

Financial and Political Institutions under Louis XIV

In terms of its prerogatives to borrow, spend, and tax, the French monarchy under Louis XIV was not constrained by any representative institution at the national level. As argued in Chapter 3, the Estates General had enjoyed little influence over policy since the mid-fifteenth century, and the last Estates General before the revolution was called in 1614. Louis XIV had power to create new laws, which were announced as Edicts or Arrêts du Conseil. Regional *parlements*, of which the Paris *parlement* was the most important, were charged with determining whether royal decisions conflicted with existing law, and as a result they technically had veto power, but any decision by a *parlement* to protest a royal decision could be overridden by the king through a procedure known as a *lit de justice*. As a consequence, then, the *parlements* could at best make it slightly costly for the king to pass a law.[26] In addition to the *parlements*, several French provinces in the eighteenth century retained representative assemblies known as Estates. This was true of the provinces known as the *pays d'état*, which had been integrated into the French royal domain later than other areas.

[26] For the best concise review of ancien regime French political institutions, see Richet (1973).

A partial exception to this full royal discretion was in the area of taxation, due to the way revenues were collected. While many royal decisions, such as the option to suspend interest payments on certain loans, could be easily implemented from Paris, implementation of other policy changes was more difficult. New taxes actually needed to be administered by the *parlements*, and even if a new tax had been imposed as part of a *lit de justice*, a *parlement* might in practice delay implementation. With this said, Hoffman (1994) argues that this problem was reduced under Louis XIV's long reign, thanks to the creation of a core of royal officials (the *intendants*) who could administer taxes directly, and thanks to improved possibilities for sanctioning recalcitrant *parlements*. In the *pays d'état*, taxes remained administered throughout the eighteenth century by the provincial Estates. An annual contribution made by each of the *pays d'état* to the royal finances, the oddly named *don gratuit* (free gift), was negotiated directly between the Estates and the monarchy.

A second continuing characteristic of French financial institutions was the resort to venality to raise revenue. Louis XIV had actually begun his reign determined to restrict the sale of offices to raise revenue, and on several occasions he even abolished a large number of existing offices. With the resumption of war after 1688, however, Louis XIV made heavy use of this type of finance (Doyle 1996).

A final key aspect of French government finance under Louis XIV was that the monarchy continued to rely heavily on indirect borrowing from venal officeholders and other bodies. Indirect borrowing can be seen as a form of bureaucratic delegation to the extent that it involved the monarch delegating certain powers (control over future revenues) to officials. As had been the case in previous periods, the Crown would generally grant the right to some future revenue stream to a group of officials in exchange for an immediate cash advance. In the case of venal officeholders the Crown could also agree to increase the level of future payments to officeholders, known as *gages*. Generally the officeholders obtained money to advance to the Crown by borrowing on private financial markets. The collateral for the loans taken out by the officeholders could include the market value of their offices, the value of future *gages* payments, or the value of future tax revenues. In addition to borrowing from venal officeholders, the Crown also borrowed indirectly via regional assemblies such as the Estates of the *pays d'état*.[27]

---

[27] See Potter (1997, 2000), Potter and Rosenthal (1997), and Rebillon (1932).

Root (1989, 1994) and Bien (1989) argue that individual royal officials who had purchased offices realized that they could profit by banding together with other creditors in corporate bodies. A crucial feature of corporate groups such as the *secrétaires du roi* and the *fermiers généraux* was the fact that they functioned under a principal of limited liability. In the event that the corporation was pushed into bankruptcy by actions such as a royal refusal to make interest payments on loans granted by the corporation, individual members would be liable only up to the value of their offices.[28]

Public Finances under Louis XIV

Like Great Britain, the French monarchy after 1688 found it necessary to borrow heavily to finance the War of the League of Augsburg (1689–97) and the subsequent War of the Spanish Succession (1702–13). Because royal borrowing at this time relied on ad hoc loans that often involved a degree of coercion, it is difficult to produce quantifiable indicators of default risk of the sort that I have developed for Great Britain. Nonetheless, using available evidence one can still establish several basic conclusions. The fact that the French government after 1688 did not produce unified financial accounts also makes it difficult to track the total quantity of royal borrowing. Forbonnais (1758) made a retrospective effort to compile information on royal finances during the period of warfare between 1689 and 1715. During the War of the League of Augsburg (1689–97), according to his estimates 61 percent of royal expenditures were raised by taxation and 39 percent by the creation of new venal offices.[29] For the War of the Spanish Succession (1702–13), the figures appear to show that the French monarchy relied much more heavily on both sale of offices and on borrowing.

With regard to the composition of taxation, Mathias and O'Brien (1976) have shown that for the period after 1715 the share of revenues from direct taxes was significantly higher in France than in Great Britain.[30]

---

[28] Another feature of corporate bodies was that creditors as a group might carry more bargaining weight in negotiations with the monarchy than would individual lenders. So, for example, if the monarchy defaulted on debt owed to a single officeholder, it might well expect to continue borrowing elsewhere. The same strategy might not be feasible with debt owed to a corporation, to the extent that a corporation consisted of a sizable fraction of total creditors.

[29] Forbonnais data reported by Bonney (1999).

[30] For 1715, Mathias and O'Brien calculate that 61 percent of total French revenues were derived from direct taxes, whereas 34 percent were derived from indirect taxes.

As Mathias and O'Brien take pains to note, however, the extremely frag-
mented nature of the French tax system implied that there were actually many individuals, and in particular the nobility, who benefited from
exemptions from certain direct taxes, such as the *taille*. Moreover, when
the monarchy introduced a new direct tax in 1710, the *dixième*, for which
even the nobility would not be exempt, this move raised a storm of political protest, and the measure was repealed.[31]

Estimates for the total stock of French public debt at the end of the
War of the Spanish Succession vary. Félix (1994) has produced a figure of
1777 million livres tournois, which would include both loans contracted
during the wars of 1689–1713 and previous debts. This is equivalent to
more than nine times French annual royal revenues, implying that the ratio of debts to revenues in France was roughly double that of the United
Kingdom during the same time period.[32] This figure for the stock of public
debt would be much higher if one added the value of venal offices that, like
other forms of debt, needed to be serviced with annual payments. Doyle
(1996) estimates that the French monarchy raised roughly 700 million
livres tournois from creation of offices between 1689 and 1713. Finally,
while there is some uncertainty about the scale of annual French debt
servicing costs at the end of the War of the Spanish Succession, it is interesting to note that there is little indication that the ratio of debt servicing
costs to annual revenues was much higher in France than in Britain at the
same time.[33]

The fact that both the French and British monarchies were able to run
unprecedented debts during the years before 1715 points to the potential weakness of using quantity borrowed as a measure of credibility. In
contrast, a look at the terms on which the French government borrowed
shows clearly that when wealth holders lent to it freely, they often did so
at interest rates that incorporated a substantial default premium. Between
the beginning of the War of the Spanish Succession in 1702 and the arrival
of a Tory government in 1710, the British Crown was able to borrow at

---

[31] No doubt as a result of the *dixième*'s repeal, the share of French revenues derived
from direct taxation dropped from 61 percent in 1715 to 48 percent in 1725 (Mathias
and O'Brien 1976).

[32] If one instead took the ratio of debt to gross domestic product, then the U.K. figure
would be significantly higher.

[33] Based on the 85 million livres tournois of debt servicing for 1715 reported by Marion
(1919), and the 166 million in gross revenues reported by Forbonnais (1758) the
ratio would have been 51 percent. The ratio would have been much higher, however,
with net revenues (excluding revenues from creation of offices). Weir (1989: 101–2)
presents a number of different estimates.

rates that never exceeded 6.6 percent. The French monarchy, in contrast, was on occasion forced to pay interest rates as high as 8.3 percent on new issues of *rentes* (Saugrain 1896). Louis XIV's ministers were sometimes able to sell *rentes* at lower rates of interest, but in many of these instances, the sale involved a significant degree of coercion. Potter (2000) suggests that coerced loans were frequent during the War of the Spanish Succession.

Finally, regardless of whether lenders to the French monarchy anticipated the risk of a default, the most obvious evidence that the French monarchy was not fully committed to repaying its debts is that the Crown reneged on debt contracts. In 1710 the French government took the initial step of reducing interest payments on all existing *rentes* to 5 percent. Subsequently, payments on some *rentes* were further reduced to 4 percent.

Evidence on Indirect Borrowing

Given their difficulty obtaining access to credit, French monarchs throughout the eighteenth century sought to borrow indirectly through intermediaries and to establish new bureaucratic institutions that might allow them access to credit at lower rates of interest. As previously discussed, a number of researchers have focused their attention on this method of royal borrowing in recent years, including Bien (1989) and Root (1989, 1994). I suggest here that there is insufficient evidence to show that indirect borrowing offered the French Crown an effective means of credible commitment. The exception to this conclusion involves borrowing through the Estates of the *pays d'état*, a subject that has been considered by Potter (1997, 2000) and Potter and Rosenthal (1997).

Bien (1989) and Root (1989, 1994) have based their arguments about indirect borrowing on the fact that groups of officeholders could borrow freely at between 5 and 5.5 percent interest when the Crown was borrowing at significantly higher rates. They take this as implying that the Crown was more committed to repaying money borrowed indirectly than it was to repaying money borrowed directly. Potter (1997, 2000) has criticized this interpretation. He argues that rather than decreasing the risk of default, the primary effect of indirect borrowing may have been simply to transfer the risk of default from private wealth holders to the officeholders. While the officeholders were legally obliged to repay any debts contracted with private creditors (otherwise they might have their offices seized), the officeholders themselves had little recourse if the Crown took actions such as suspending *gages* payments or redirecting revenues that had been allocated to a group of officeholders. Potter (2000) notes that in 1709 during the War of the Spanish Succession the Crown did precisely this in response to a fiscal crisis. The comprehensive study on venality by Doyle (1996) demonstrates that when fiscal pressures grew especially severe, French monarchs regularly chose to postpone or reduce payment of *gages* to officeholders. There were also more subtle means for the monarchy to revise unilaterally contracts it had established with officeholders. A threat to create new offices within a particular *corps* would generally prompt existing officeholders to offer a cash payment in exchange for not pushing the proposal forward.[34] The multiple pressures that the French Crown could exert on officeholders helps explain why these groups were willing to borrow and then advance the borrowed funds to the Crown despite the risk entailed.

In addition to borrowing from groups of venal officeholders, the French monarchy also borrowed indirectly through the provincial Estates of the *pays d'état*. In cases where the monarchy borrowed indirectly through the provincial estates, the estates issued debt for purchase by private creditors, and this debt would be repaid with future revenues that the Crown agreed to cede to the Estates. So, for example, the Estates of Burgundy were given the right to collect tolls from people transporting goods on the Saône River (Potter 1997). The Estates of Brittany had a similar arrangement with the Crown (Rebillon 1932).

The major difference between borrowing through venal officeholders and borrowing through the provincial Estates was that in the latter case the Crown showed more reluctance to alter contracts unilaterally. Potter (1997) conducts a thorough study of royal borrowing through the Estates of Burgundy, and he reports that despite periodic attempts by the Crown to reallocate revenues generated by the tolls on the Saône, the Estates of Burgundy were almost always successful in opposing such efforts. Likewise, Rebillon (1932) mentions no examples of the monarchy redirecting revenues raised by the Estates of Brittany. Rebillon (1932) and Potter (1997) note that the Estates of Brittany and of Burgundy were able to raise money at 5 percent interest even in cases where the monarchy was paying significantly higher rates for loans that it contracted directly. As argued above, this is not necessarily evidence of the effectiveness of this form of borrowing as a commitment mechanism, because groups of

---

[34] The motivation here would be that creation of new offices would reduce the market value of existing offices (given the existence of a secondary market for offices).

venal officeholders were also often able to raise funds at 5 percent interest. Nonetheless, it does leave open the question of why the Estates were able to resist attempts by the Crown to alter contracts unilaterally. Despite this success, the provincial Estates remained a secondary source of funds for the monarchy.[35]

Public Finance under the Regency, 1715–1723

As had been the case with previous royal transitions, the death of Louis XIV in 1715 was followed by a series of measures to default on royal loans. The Regent who ruled France in place of the young Louis XV convened a *chambre de justice*, a special tribunal designed to investigate whether creditors had taken "illicit" action such as breaking usury laws. This could result in severe fines, imprisonment, or both. While the *chambre de justice* of 1715 had disastrous consequences for some individual creditors, Hoffman, Postel-Vinay, and Rosenthal (2000) suggest that it actually netted less than 100 million livres in fines, a tiny proportion of the overall royal debt.[36] The monarchy also used currency devaluation at this time to reduce the real value of debts.

The dire fiscal situation left by Louis XIV prompted a number of proposals to reform French political and financial institutions. The first of these was a suggestion by several senior ministers that the Regent should call the Estates General, which had not met since 1614. According to the memoirs of one adviser, the duc de Saint-Simon, calling the Estates would allow the Regent to make public the dire financial situation in which Louis XIV had left the kingdom, and it would allow the Estates to choose among various alternative solutions.[37] As discussed in detail in Chapter 6, Saint-Simon's suggestion echoed the ideas of three aristocrats, the abbé de Fénélon, the duc de Beauvilliers, and the duc de Chevreuse, who in 1711 had written a text calling for royal power to be limited by an Estates General that would have veto power over legislation and that would meet regularly every three years (and not at the discretion of the king, as had been the case with previous Estates General).[38] In the end, the

---

[35] Potter (2000) suggests that it represented less than 3 percent of total royal borrowing in the period before 1715. Potter and Rosenthal (1997) suggest that by 1789 the combined debts of the *pays d'état* amounted to one-sixth of total royal debt.

[36] Dutot (1738) seems to give a somewhat larger figure of a reduction in the debt by 600 million livres thanks to the various devices used after Louis XIV's death.

[37] Saint Simon (1985: vol. 5, p. 338).

[38] Fénelon (1711: 97–125). See also the discussion in Richet (1973).

Estates General was not called, and in the opinion of Sargent and Velde (1995), this decision represented a major missed opportunity for France to adopt the sort of political institutions that had improved public credit in England. While it is impossible to say with certainty what would have transpired if the Estates General had been called, Chapter 6 argues that the intended effect of convening the Estates was actually to trigger a default.

A second reform proposal following the death of Louis XIV was to establish a national bank in France. The Scottish financier John Law proposed a project that was inspired to a significant extent by the experience of the Bank of England. Law's bank would act as banker to government, and he sought to give it greater freedom than the Bank of England enjoyed to issue paper currency. Credibility for this paper currency would be ensured via a royal guarantee. Law also planned to convert existing royal debts into equity held in a joint-stock company. Like its British counterparts, the East India Company and the South Sea Company, this company would have monopoly privileges on trade with a geographic area.[39] Law's plan amounted to a form of bureaucratic delegation to the extent that the monarchy would have granted certain powers to the bank, and in return this would help improve the monarchy's access to credit.

In 1716 the Regent gave Law permission to create a scaled-down version of his bank, the Banque Générale. The following year, Law was given permission to organize the Compagnie des Indes, a privately owned joint stock company in which shares could be purchased by redemption of government debt. In 1719, Law's bank was converted into a full-fledged national bank, renamed the Banque Royale. The transformed institution now served as banker to the government, and its note issue was guaranteed by the crown. The Banque Royale engaged in a massive expansion of its note issue during 1719, an action that was prompted by an attempt to support the price of Compagnie des Indes shares. This was intended to speed up the process of converting royal debt into equity held in the company. During 1720 Law's system fell apart as the price of shares in the Compagnie des Indes dropped as dramatically as it had risen, and as public confidence in the notes issued by the Banque Royale was badly shaken. By mid-1720 Law's bank was liquidated, and he was forced to flee the country. One major legacy of Law's experiment was that significant price inflation during 1719 and 1720 dramatically reduced the real value of outstanding royal debt. As a result, his policies led indirectly to default.

---

[39] The most recent survey of Law's policies is Murphy (1997). See also Faure (1977), Garber (2000), and Lüthy (1959–61).

While in the popular imagination John Law's system has acquired a reputation as a dangerous gamble that was bound to go wrong, recent work has highlighted the fact that the basic economic assumptions underlying his project were not unsound (Bonney 1999; Garber 2000; Murphy 1997). Instead of being fundamentally flawed, his plan was wrecked by the decisions of 1719 to increase dramatically the issue of bank notes. In Chapter 6, I consider the political pressures that might have pushed Law into taking this action.

In sum, the history of royal finance during the Regency period raises several important questions that Chapter 6 investigates by considering partisan politics in France at the time. First, would calling the Estates General have improved credibility of government? I argue to the contrary. Second, what were the underlying reasons for the failure of Law's Bank? I argue that the failure of Law's experiment illustrates how attempts to improve credibility through bureaucratic delegation will prove fruitless in an absolute monarchy.

5. Sovereign Borrowing in Great Britain and France, 1742–1793

Both because of improved availability of data and due to changes in borrowing practices, I have considered borrowing by the French and U.K. governments during the later eighteenth century in a separate section within this chapter. As the eighteenth century progressed, U.K. government borrowing became routinized with the creation of a single type of government bond, the consol, for which there was a well-developed secondary market. In France the monarchy did not simplify its borrowing practices through the creation of a single type of bond, but it did implement changes by opting increasingly for the anonymous sale of securities, rather than relying primarily on coaxing officeholders into purchasing debt. As in the United Kingdom, these bonds were traded on secondary markets. These changes in France occurred as part of a broader transformation in French financial markets, which has been emphasized by Hoffman et al. (2000). While agreeing with their observation that French financial markets evolved significantly during this period, I show that there remained very significant default risk on French royal debt.[40]

---

[40] One might draw a comparison here between France in the late eighteenth century and a number of emerging market governments today that have obtained increased access to private capital thanks to the development of new markets, but without a significant reduction in default risk on public debt.

Table 4.3. *British Public Finance during the Seven Years' War, 1756–1763 (in annual terms, million £)*

Annual spending	Land taxes	Customs and excise	Net borrowing
15.8	2.1	6.0	7.1
	13%	38%	45%

Note: Figures do not sum to 100% because of additional stamp taxes and post office taxes.
Source: Mitchell (1988).

Trends in Public Finance

The series of Franco-British conflicts of the later eighteenth century, beginning with the Seven Years' War (1756–63), necessitated heavy recourse to government borrowing. During the course of the Seven Years' War the British government borrowed the funds for approximately 45 percent of its total expenditures, with the rest being raised by revenue, as shown in Table 4.3. It is also noteworthy that the proportion of British revenues raised by taxes on land during the Seven Years' War was only half the proportion raised by the Land Tax in the wars at the beginning of the eighteenth century.[41] By the end of the conflict total outstanding British public debt was equivalent to 13.5 times annual revenues, a much higher figure than at the end of the previous period of conflict.

Public finance data for France during the Seven Years' War have been collected by Riley (1986, 1987). Based on data covering the years 1756–59 and 1761, the French monarchy funded roughly 40 percent of its total expenditures through borrowing, a figure quite close to that for Britain.[42] One difference between France and Britain was that the ratio of French public debt to annual revenues at the end of the war was considerably lower than in Britain. Outstanding French debt was equal to 7.3 times annual revenues in 1763 (a figure that does not include the outstanding capital of venal offices).[43] Finally, as had been the case fifty years earlier, the French government in 1763 appears to have found itself devoting a lower proportion of annual revenues to servicing than did the

---

[41] Although the land tax between 1756 and 1763 was set at the same rate of 4 shillings on the pound that had prevailed between 1689 and 1715.

[42] This figure for borrowing includes both issue of long-term loans and creation of new venal offices.

[43] Based on data from Riley (1987).

British government. Following calculations by Weir (1989), debt servicing represented 39 percent of French revenues in 1764. Based on data in Mitchell (1988), for Great Britain the debt servicing ratio was actually higher (48 percent).[44]

A key difference between French and U.K. government borrowing during this period was that the French government defaulted, while the British government never did so. The French monarchy no longer resorted to techniques such as calling a *chambre de justice*, but it instead used other means to alter debt contracts unilaterally. In 1759 the monarchy suspended interest payments on two short-term debt instruments. This partial default was prompted by fiscal pressures generated by the Seven Years' War (Riley 1986). A much more significant default occurred in 1770 when the Finance Minister again suspended interest payments on short-term debts, and on this occasion payments were never resumed. Short-term loans were instead consolidated into long-term loans at lower rates of interest. In addition, the French monarchy converted a number of tontine loans into annuities that paid lower rates of interest (Velde and Weir 1992).

While the ancien régime made repeated use of default during the eighteenth century, it is interesting to note that public finance did not become more stable after the beginning of the French Revolution in 1789. By mid-1789 the Constituent National Assembly had become the key political decision-making body in France. On November 14, 1789, the king's finance minister, Jacques Necker, made a proposal to turn an existing private bank, the Caisse d'Escompte, into a full-fledged national bank with an increased capital and the monopoly right to issue bank notes.[45] The proposal subsequently became the subject of considerable debate. In the end the deputies of the Constituent National Assembly decided in favor of issuing a new currency, the *assignats*, backed by proceeds from the sale of church lands, but they decided against transforming the Caisse d'Escompte into a national bank. Monetary policy would instead be set directly by the legislative authorities. Sargent and Velde (1995) have seen this as another missed opportunity for the French government to establish credibility through institutional reform. Chapter 6 considers the politics behind this decision.

---

[44] This suggests that subsequent French defaults may have been due to problems meeting interest payments on short-term debt, not general insolvency. Weir (1989) shows that even in 1788 the French debt servicing ratio was not significantly higher than the British debt servicing ratio.

[45] *Archives Parlémentaires*, vol. 10, pp. 56–65.

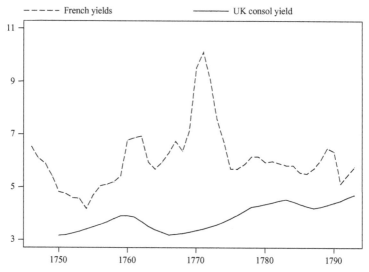

Figure 4.4. French and British government bond yields, 1746–1793.
Source: Neal (1990) and Velde and Weir (1992).

Yields on Government Debt

Velde and Weir (1992) have made a painstaking effort to produce a time series of yields on French government debt during this period, which can be compared with yields from British government bonds (known as consols). While yields on British consols remained within a band between 3 and 5 percent, fluctuating little from year to year, yields on French government debt were higher on average and much more variable. The average difference between U.K. yields and French yields was 2.2 percent (see Fig. 4.4). Since credibility cannot be measured directly, to judge whether this difference reflected a default premium paid by the French government, the best way to proceed is to consider alternative explanations. As discussed previously, in addition to any default premium, yields on government loans will also be influenced by expected levels of inflation and changes in demand for capital.

To investigate determinants of French and U.K. yields, I performed two time-series regressions for each country, estimating the bond yield as a function of net government borrowing and trend inflation (Table 4.4). The first regression for each country uses variables in levels, while the second uses variables that have been first-differenced to make them

Table 4.4. *Explaining Yields on Government Debt, 1746–1793*

	(1) U.K. levels	(2) U.K. differenced	(3) France levels	(4) France differenced
Net borrowing	0.03***	0.12***	−0.002	−.001
	(0.01)	(0.03)	(0.002)	(0.01)
Trend inflation	0.12	0.15***	0.31	2.17***
	(0.09)	(0.04)	(0.22)	(0.76)
Constant	3.65***	0.03**	5.95***	−0.11
	(0.12)	(0.01)	(0.23)	(0.10)
N	44	43	32	31
R^2	0.27	0.53	0.07	0.32

Note: Heteroskedastic-consistent standard errors in parentheses. *, **, and *** indicate significance at the 10%, 5%, and 1% levels, respectively.

Source: Mitchell (1988), Neal (1990), Riley (1986, 1987), Velde and Weir (1992), White (1989). Several missing values for French net borrowing were imputed using spending data.

stationary.[46] For the United Kingdom, both trend inflation and net government borrowing are positively correlated with the bond yield, as theory would predict. This result for net borrowing in particular fits well with the basic observation that U.K. yields peaked during three periods of increased military spending: (1) the Seven Years' War, (2) the American War of Independence, and (3) the French Revolution. In the regression for France, trend inflation has a positive coefficient that is significant in the regression using first-differenced data, but the coefficient on net borrowing is not significant in either regression. The biggest difference between the two sets of regressions, however, involves the overall goodness of fit. The *r*-squared statistics are much higher in the U.K. regressions. This may suggest that while the market for U.K. government debt became increasingly predictable in the late eighteenth century, this was not the case in France, as periodic partial defaults had a major influence on market expectations.

Given that trends in net borrowing and inflation cannot account for the gap in yields between France and Great Britain in the latter eighteenth

---

[46] Unlike the previous series of regressions, interest rates on government debt during this period appear to have been difference-stationary rather than trend-stationary. As in the previous regressions, trend inflation was estimated by taking the change in Hodrick-Prescott filtered prices.

century, it seems logical to suggest that the French government paid a sizable default premium on its debt issues. The other obvious indication here is that the two most significant increases in French yields occurred following the partial government defaults that took place in 1759 and again in 1770.

6. Summary

The material presented in this chapter supports the widely held view that the British government after 1688 gained credibility as a borrower, while the French monarchy failed to do so. Beyond this basic comparison, however, the evidence also raises a number of additional questions about the politics of government finance in France and Great Britain. First, were higher default premia in France attributable to the lack of a representative assembly and the absence of a national bank? Second, what can account for significant variations in British interest rates before 1715, as well as periodic runs on Bank of England shares? I have offered a preliminary answer to this question here by showing that Whig governments faced lower costs of borrowing than did Tory governments. Finally, why did French reform experiments such as John Law's bank inevitably fail? The next two chapters seek to provide detailed answers to these questions using historical evidence on partisan politics and government finance.

5

Partisan Politics and Public Debt in Great Britain,
1689–1742

1. Introduction

While the Glorious Revolution of 1688 signaled a major change in the relationship between Crown and Parliament, the same period also witnessed the emergence of another political phenomenon: the formation of two cohesive political parties. During this period, English society was divided over ideological issues such as religious toleration, as well as over an economic dimension of conflict. This involved the cleavage between those who derived their income from agricultural revenues, "the landed interest," and those whose income derived from finance, "the monied interest." I argue in this chapter that the conflict over noneconomic issues such as religious toleration had a major impact on the choice of economic policies, in particular with regard to debt. Credible commitment was facilitated by the fact that owners of government debt were part of a larger Whig coalition that took a common stance on multiple issues. In other words, a "bourgeois revolution" was possible in England only because of an alliance between the monied interest and other groups in British society. This helps explain how default risk might be lowered even in the case of a legislature where owners of debt (or their representatives) are in the minority. An alternative interpretation, that government creditors were more an independent lobby, is undermined by the fact that members of the "monied interest" consistently sought election in Parliament and that their fortunes were clearly tied to the Whig party.

As historians of this period have emphasized, the cohesiveness of political coalitions was reinforced by the development of political party organizations. An understanding of partisan politics is critical for explaining trends in public borrowing in Great Britain after 1688. My argument emphasizing party formation can also help explain variations in default premia on British public debt over time. Trends in default premia were clearly linked to shifts in the electoral fortunes of the Whig and Tory parties, and contemporary observers realized this fact. Finally, the chapter suggests that after 1722, as divisions over issues such as religious toleration and foreign policy became less salient, the use of political patronage also played an increasingly important role in holding the Whig coalition together.

In terms of method, the chapter considers whether the observable implications of the three main arguments presented in the Chapter 1 conform to historical evidence. In asking these questions I rely primarily on the extensive secondary literature that has developed on British politics during the period, supplementing this with use of primary sources in several specific areas.[1]

My first argument concerns the necessity and the sufficiency of constitutional checks and balances for achieving credible commitment. Great Britain had the same set of formal political institutions during the period on which I focus (1688–1742).[2] As a result, I am unable to examine here whether changes in institutions were correlated with changes in credibility. As an alternative, I suggest that the existence of episodes after 1688 where government commitment to repay debt was placed in doubt raises questions about the sufficiency of checks and balances for reducing default risk. Chapter 4 has already established that on several occasions after 1688 the British government was forced to borrow at higher interest rates than had prevailed before the Glorious Revolution. The current chapter considers these episodes in greater detail, reviewing historical evidence that demonstrates that scares with regard to public debt were linked to the arrival of Tory governments. The same was true for Bank of England share prices.

My second argument, which concerns party formation, has several observable implications. First, as mentioned in Chapter 4, historical evidence that trends in partisan control were closely linked to trends in government credibility is consistent with the argument. Second, if the party government hypothesis is accurate, then one should expect to see that government creditors were members of the party that tended to be associated with low default premia when it was in power. The historical evidence

---

[1] I have chosen to end the inquiry in 1742 both for reasons of space and because the years between 1688 and 1742 were the period where interest rates on U.K. government debt first declined significantly. It seems most useful for comparative purposes to focus on how credibility was first established.

[2] One significant change that did occur was the Anglo-Scottish union, but this arguably had little effect on debt politics.

here shows clearly that U.K. government creditors were associated with the Whig party but not with the Tories. Furthermore, one would expect to see evidence of voting cohesion within the Whig party, and in particular that even those members of the party who did not represent government creditors voted to support debt repayment. Finally, if the party government hypothesis is accurate, then within the Whig party we should expect to see evidence of specific mechanisms to reinforce voting cohesion.

My third argument suggests that attempts to improve credibility through bureaucratic delegation can be successful only when government creditors have significant power within a representative assembly. The key observable implication of this proposition involves a comparison between the British experience with the Bank of England and the multiple French attempts to establish a national bank. As such, the evaluation is divided between this chapter and the next. This argument also implies that the extent to which a national bank increases credibility will depend on trends in the partisan control of different veto points. Chapter 4 has already presented evidence that suggests that Bank of England share prices fell dramatically following the Tory election victory of October 1710. This chapter considers whether the historical record provides further support for this interpretation.

The remainder of this chapter begins with a presentation of the most salient issues in British politics after 1688. This is followed by a discussion of the political organization of the Whig and Tory parties. I then consider whether the observable implications of my arguments are met for three historical periods: the reign of King William III (1688–1702), which coincided with the War of the League of Augsburg (1689–97); the reign of Queen Anne (1702–14), which coincided with the War of the Spanish Succession; and a third period (1714–42), much of which was dominated by the Whig leader Robert Walpole. This was a period of relative peace. Table 5.1 presents a list of key political events during these three periods.

2. Political Divisions over Issues

While a majority of its citizens may have drawn satisfaction from the fall of James II, England after 1688 remained very much a "divided society," to use the term applied by two historians of the period.[3] The electorate

---

[3] Holmes and Speck (1967). For more detailed reviews of divisions over political issues, see Hayton (2002) and Holmes (1967). This same terminology has been used by other historians writing about the period, including Kenyon (1977), Plumb (1967), and Stone (1980).

Table 5.1. *Key Events in British Politics,*
1688–1742

1688	Glorious Revolution
	William and Mary rule jointly
1689	Land Tax
	Act of Toleration
	Beginning War of League of Augsburg
1694	Triennial Act
	Bank of England created
1702	Beginning reign of Queen Anne
	War of the Spanish Succession
1707	Union with Scotland
1713	War of the Spanish Succession ends
1714	George I becomes king
1722	Walpole becomes Prime Minister
1742	Resignation of Walpole

remained divided over five key issues: religious toleration, divine right and
the hereditary monarchy, foreign policy, constitutional restraints on the
executive, and questions of taxation and government finance. Preferences
with regard to each of the first three issues were highly correlated, as individuals who supported religious toleration tended to oppose traditional
theories of the monarchy, and they also advocated an activist foreign
policy involving war against Catholic France. Most importantly for the
subject of this book, however, preferences over taxation and finance did
not coincide with preferences on the ideological issues. Landowners in
particular were split over ideological issues, with some favoring religious
toleration and some opposed. A final phenomenon to mention is that
if the political debate on each of these four issues was particularly intense during the reigns of King William III (1688–1702) and Queen Anne
(1702–14), in the period after 1715 passions with regard to issues such as
religion and the succession gradually began to calm. As discussed below,
it is unclear, however, to what extent this was due to a convergence in
underlying preferences on the part of different groups or, alternatively,
to a new style of compromise management pursued by Robert Walpole
during his tenure in office.

Religious Toleration

One of the most fundamental issues in British politics after 1688 was that
of religious toleration. While Great Britain by 1688 was overwhelmingly

Protestant, there remained an important divide between those who ad-
hered to the Church of England and those who worshipped in churches
of other denominations including Baptists, English Presbyterians, Inde-
pendents, and Quakers. Church of England supporters often referred to
members of these other churches as "nonconformists" or as "Dissenters."
A Whig majority in Parliament voted an Act of Toleration in 1689, which
permitted the Dissenters to establish their own places of worship.[4] While
no significant group of parliamentarians subsequently supported repeal of
the Act of Toleration, there was an intense debate after 1689 over the rights
of Dissenters to hold places in Parliament or other public office. Nominally, any holder of public office was required to be a Church of England
member, but this rule was not always strictly enforced, and officeholding Dissenters frequently evaded the restriction through the practice of
"occasional conformity." In substance this involved doing the minimum
necessary in terms of Church of England membership while continuing
membership in a Dissenting congregation.

Debate over the practice of occasional conformity and over the status
of the Church of England more generally was a constant of British political
life after 1689, and it was a dispute that grew in ferocity after 1700.[5] The
members of the Tory party consistently supported the established Church
of England. Cries of "the Church in danger" were a staple of Tory electoral
rhetoric from the late 1690s, and Tory members of Parliament repeatedly
attempted to pass legislation restricting the practice of occasional conformity. This goal was accomplished by two statutes signed in 1711 and
1713.[6] Tory preferences here were consistent with those expressed before the Glorious Revolution. The Whig party, in contrast, was generally
more favorable to toleration of Dissenters, and Whig parliamentarians
most often opposed Tory efforts to establish an Occasional Conformity
Act. However, this support for toleration did not extend to Catholics,
as Whig pamphleteers often criticized the Tories for being in league with
Catholic forces on the European continent. Legislation of 1711 and 1714
that restricted the rights of Dissenters was overturned by a Whig majority
in 1719. Subsequently, the Whig government led by Robert Walpole took
more of a compromise stance on the issue, supporting religious toleration

---

[4] The act specifically excluded Catholics from benefiting from this provision.
[5] See Kenyon (1977: 63–82). He reports that the controversy over occasional conformity was heightened when a leading London official attended both a Church
of England service and a service from a dissenting congregation on the same
day.
[6] On the "Church in danger," see Holmes and Speck (1967: 116–17).

but declining to pass further legislation to expand the formal rights of the Dissenters.[7]

While toleration of dissent remained a bitterly divisive question throughout the reign of Queen Anne, reaching its peak during the trial of Henry Sacheverell in 1710, a number of authors have observed that in the years after 1715 the issue gradually became less salient, and this was particularly true after the repeal in 1719 of legislation restricting the rights of Dissenters. One reason for this may have been Robert Walpole's compromise policy. Alternatively, there may have been an exogenous decline in the salience of this issue in British politics. Speck (1977) and Holmes and Szechi (1993) attribute this fact in part to the recognition by Church of England supporters that the Dissenters posed less of a challenge to the established order than had been originally imagined. What's more, the number of new Dissenting congregations licensed under the Toleration Act declined significantly.[8] Stone (1980) suggests that a gradual decline in enthusiasm for religion led to the issue's becoming less prominent in political debates. Holmes (1993: 350–51) concurs, suggesting that if in 1709 it was possible for a particularly politically charged sermon to sell 100,000 copies, by the 1720s religious literature was read by a devoted but more narrow public. Religious fervor would increase again in the 1730s with the development of new evangelical churches, but it would not enter national politics in the same way.

Divine Right and the Hereditary Monarchy

Civil conflict in England throughout the seventeenth century had been heavily influenced by the debate over the status of the monarchy and the question of whether kings ruled by divine right or whether their sovereignty was instead limited by the need for consent from Parliament and people. In the aftermath of the Glorious Revolution the debate over divine right was closely linked to the question of succession to the throne. The ambiguous legal basis for James II's replacement with William III and Mary II in 1688–89 left a degree of uncertainty over the succession. This uncertainty inevitably had religious overtones, because James II was

---

[7] The principal exception to this Whig support for toleration involved the tactical move by several Whig leaders to support the restrictive legislation of 1711.

[8] Speck (1977) observes that 1,260 dissenting congregations were licensed between 1701 and 1710. This was the period where toleration was most frequently debated in Parliament. In contrast, between 1731 and 1740, roughly the last decade of Robert Walpole's tenure as prime minister, only 448 new congregations opened.

a Catholic and his son, born in 1688, was also baptized as a Catholic. While it was generally acknowledged that after the death of both William and Mary, the Crown would pass to Mary's younger sister Anne, who was a Protestant, the provisions for the succession after Anne's death were very unclear, because Anne herself was childless.[9] One possibility was that Anne might be succeeded by the son of James II, commonly referred to as the Pretender, but this would mean placing a Catholic upon the throne. Alternatively, a proposal was developed to transfer the succession to Sophia of Hanover, which would keep the throne in Protestant hands. This policy was strongly supported by the Whigs. It was approved by Parliament in 1701 as the Act of Settlement, which barred any Catholic from acceding to the throne of England and which officially transferred the succession to the House of Hanover.

While the majority of English citizens after 1688 would have clearly preferred not to have a Catholic monarch, the Act of Settlement was to prove controversial because it appeared to some on the Tory side of politics to violate the fundamental principle of a hereditary monarchy. As has been noted by many authors, the Tories placed a much higher premium on royal sovereignty, even if the claim of a purely hereditary succession had been something of a fiction in previous periods of British history as well.[10] This placed the Tory party in a difficult position, however, because opposition to the Act of Settlement laid them open to criticisms of Jacobitism.[11]

As had been the case with the issue of religious toleration, the division over the succession to the throne began to gradually diminish in importance as a political issue after 1715, and in particular after the failure of the Atterbury Plot of 1722. This transformation can be attributed in part to the fact that it would have been increasingly difficult to reestablish a purely hereditary monarchy without allowing a Catholic to ascend to the throne. This fact was made abundantly clear by the Jacobite Rebellion of 1715, in which the Pretender attempted to invade Britain with a small force. The rebellion helped split the Tory Party between those opposed to the action and those who favored it.[12] One should not take this diminished

---

[9] Following the death of her sole remaining heir, the Duke of Gloucester.

[10] Dunham and Wood (1976) argue that as a result of precedents created by several monarchs being deposed, Parliament by the late 1480s had a strong say in whether a particular individual acceded to the throne.

[11] Jacobites sought to restore James II (and subsequently his son) to the throne.

[12] In a more long-term sense, a number of authors have suggested that there was a gradual shift in opinion in Great Britain away from ideas emphasizing the Divine Right

salience of the succession issue to mean that it was absent from parliamentarians' minds during the Walpole era, though. Efforts by Whigs to paint the Tories as Jacobites would continue throughout Walpole's period of Commons leadership.

Foreign Policy

Great Britain after 1688 also faced major foreign policy decisions, in particular over the extent to which it should become embroiled in wars on the European continent. One of William III's main objectives in claiming the throne was to gain access to greater resources in the protracted military struggle between France and the Netherlands. As a consequence, while James II had been nominally allied with Louis XIV, William sought almost immediately to plunge England into a war with France. What followed was a period where two wars were fought in the space of twenty-five years (1689–97 and 1702–13). While many saw these conflicts as being necessary to prevent Louis XIV from establishing hegemony on the European continent, a number of Tories in particular saw them as an excessive commitment and instead favored a less costly strategy based on the use of Britain's naval forces.

As the War of the Spanish Succession dragged on, it became an extremely divisive issue, and one that was inevitably linked to debates about religion, since Protestant Great Britain was waging war against Catholic France.[13] In general election campaigns Tory party pamphleteers took every opportunity to tag the war effort as a costly enterprise that was being waged for the benefit of foreigners (European Protestants) and financial interests (those profiting from lending to the government).[14] Whigs, in contrast, emphasized the need to pursue the struggle against an absolutist and "papist" French monarchy. The Treaty of Utrecht, which ended war with France, was initially a controversial measure, negotiated by a Tory administration in 1713. Subsequently, however, the death of Louis XIV in 1715 reduced fears of French hegemony in Europe.

---

of Kings in favor of a more contractarian view of the monarchy where sovereignty was held by the will of Parliament. See Hazard (1961), Kenyon (1977), and Stone (1980).

[13] Given the close correlation between preferences with regard to religious toleration and preferences with regard to war with France, Schofield's argument that conflict over foreign policy had an impact on conflicts over economic issues is similar to my own line of argument (Schofield 2001a, b).

[14] The best example of this rhetoric can be found in Swift (1711a).

Restraints on the Executive

In addition to the specific debate about the status of the monarchy, there was a broader debate in seventeenth- and eighteenth-century England about the necessity of limitations on the executive. After 1688 this debate referred increasingly to restraints on both monarch and Ministry.[15] It was a key feature of what has become known as the debate between "Court" and "Country," reflecting two political groupings that had preceded the Whigs and Tories. While people who subscribed to a Court ideology favored a strong executive, the Country ideology emphasized restrictions on the powers of the executive, whether the executive was a monarch or minister. Key questions regarding executive prerogative after 1688 included whether a standing army should be permitted, how frequently elections should be called, and whether it was legitimate for royal officeholders to serve in the House of Commons. Unlike the issues of religion, divine right, and foreign policy, members of the Whig and Tory parties did not fall consistently on one side of this debate. The majority of Whigs in the years immediately after 1688 were on the Country side of this debate. So, for example, they supported the Triennial Act of 1694, which mandated elections to the House of Commons every three years. Progressively, however, and in particular during periods where they controlled the Commons, a large number of Whigs abandoned their earlier qualms about executive authority. This was made most clear after 1716 with the passage of the Septennial Act, which was designed to preserve a Whig majority in the Commons. There remained, however, a minority of Whigs who sided with their party on religion, foreign policy, and finance, but who increasingly fought a rear-guard action in support of certain Country principles.

Finance and Taxation

While individual preferences with regard to religious toleration, the succession, and foreign policy were highly correlated in England after 1688, questions of finance and taxation constituted an additional dimension of conflict that cross-cut the ideological dimensions. England's military engagements after 1688 needed to be financed by some mix of new taxes and new debts. Financing expenditures through debt was less costly to the extent that lenders to government anticipated that debts would actually

---

[15] The "Ministry" was the term used in the early eighteenth century for the ministers of the Crown. It can be seen as an early version of what would later become known as the Cabinet.

be repaid. Given that the principle source of taxable income in England at this time was revenue from agricultural production, government borrowing created an ex post facto distributional conflict between taxing land in order to repay debt on one hand or, alternatively, taxing government bond holders by defaulting. It was to prove of crucial importance, however, that preferences with regard to this issue did not coincide with those on other issues, as Great Britain's landowning majority was deeply split over the issues of religious toleration, foreign policy, and the hereditary monarchy.

The conflict between what would become known as the "monied interest" and the "landed interest" gained initial prominence due to three developments: (1) Parliament's creation of a long-term national debt, (2) the establishment of the Bank of England (1694), and (3) the tax on land income, set initially at a rate of 20 percent. The stance on each of these measures was clearly partisan, in particular with regard to the Bank of England. Whig leaders in Parliament consistently supported the proposals above, while the Tories sought to find alternative mechanisms of raising funds (Horwitz 1977: 129–31). It was during the War of the Spanish Succession (1702–13), however, that partisan conflict over finance and taxation reached its peak. In election campaigns the Tory party made much of the idea that heavy taxation was impoverishing landowners while owners of government bonds profited handsomely. Though it did not default or declare a moratorium on debt payments, a Tory majority in the Commons did reduce the land tax rate to 10 percent in 1713.

While partisan disputes over religious toleration, the succession, and foreign policy gradually diminished in intensity after 1715, finance and taxation remained very present in political debates. The chief reason for this was that while the British government was no longer borrowing heavily to finance military expenditures, servicing the debt that had accumulated during the wars up to 1713 required maintaining the land tax. The land tax was raised under a Whig administration in 1716, only to be returned to 10 percent when the Whig Robert Walpole assumed the leadership in the Commons in 1722. As discussed below, Walpole preferred to pursue a compromise policy with regard to land taxation in order to avoid opposition from Britain's landed majority.

3. Party Organization: Whig versus Tory

Both the Whig and Tory parties during the late seventeenth and early eighteenth centuries employed effective means of organization that were designed to improve their chances of electoral success and to help maintain a common voting stance in the House of Commons as well as the House of Lords. Because this subject has been fiercely debated among historians, it is worth first reviewing trends in the historiography before presenting detailed evidence on party organization. During the early twentieth century the standard interpretation of early eighteenth-century politics given by historians such as Macaulay (1861) and Trevelyan (1933) was that the struggle between the Whig and Tory parties was the most salient feature of political debate. The interpretation was seen as holding for the period up to 1714, and perhaps later into the eighteenth century. The party interpretation was seconded by American historians such as William Thomas Morgan (1920), but it came under sharp criticism in the 1950s, most notably by Robert Walcott (1956). Walcott claimed that patterns of voting in the House of Commons undermined any argument emphasizing the unity of party groups.[16]

Since the mid-1960s Walcott's thesis has been fiercely criticized, initially by Holmes (1967), Plumb (1967), and Speck (1970), and more recently by historians who have produced abundant, detailed evidence about the extent to which the Tory and Whig parties after 1688 operated as cohesive units that resembled modern political parties.[17] The current historical consensus also suggests that the Whig and Tory parties continued to play a major role in shaping political debate during Robert Walpole's tenure as leader of the Commons (1722–42), although the methods of party organization evolved considerably during this time.[18] In what follows I present evidence on membership, voting behavior, methods of communication within parties, and devices used to sanction those who defected from the party line.

Party Membership

If the majority of both Whig and Tory politicians in the eighteenth century were landowners, there were still very significant differences in the composition of each group. Among landowners, it has been commonly

---

[16] Walcott's argument was heavily inspired by the work of Lewis Namier, who had emphasized the importance of family connections when considering the politics of late-eighteenth-century Britain.

[17] Hayton (2002) provides a thorough review of this literature.

[18] The same can also be said for contemporary observers. In his essay, "Of the Parties of Great Britain" (1742), David Hume suggested that, at the time of his writing, the division between Whig and Tory continued to be the principal feature of national politics.

suggested that Whig support tended to be drawn from the aristocracy and large landowners in general, while Tory support tended to be drawn from the gentry and smaller landowners. Authors have also suggested that Tory support was drawn from more peripheral regions of the country, while Whig support was more likely to be drawn from the home counties.[19] In addition, the Whig party had a membership that was much more heterogeneous than the Tory party, as it included groups other than large landowners and aristocrats. The Whig party was the party most closely associated with the financial interests who lent to government after 1688, and it also included a number of individuals who were strongly motivated by their dissenting religious beliefs. It is particularly interesting to note that the heterogeneous composition of the Whig party was frequently criticized by Tory writers such as Jonathan Swift, as illustrated by the following quote:

> For I do not take the Heads, Advocates, and Followers of the *Whigs*, to make up, strictly speaking, a *National Party*; being patched up of heterogeneous, inconsistent Parts, whom nothing served to unite but the Common Interest of sharing in the Spoil and Plunder of the People.[20]

With regard to dissenters and the Whig party, the biographies compiled for the *House of Commons 1690–1715*, which has recently been published by the History of Parliament Trust, show that among the 39 known Dissenters who served in the House of Commons during this period, 31 voted consistently with the Whigs, and none voted consistently Tory (see Hayton 2002 for details). When the sample is increased to include probable and possible Dissenters, 138 of 166 MPs voted consistently Whig, only three voted consistently Tory, and a further 25 were either impossible to classify or changed affiliation during the period. In terms of numbers, there were on average 54 certain, probable, or possible Dissenters in each of the eight Parliaments between 1690 and 1708, after which their numbers decreased drastically due to the Tory electoral landslide of 1710. This would mean that this group made up roughly a quarter of the Whigs in each Parliament at this time.

The Whig party also included a number of government creditors in its ranks. Tory political rhetoric during the early eighteenth century railed frequently against a "monied interest" composed of government creditors, primarily based in London and who were closely allied with the

---

[19] These conclusions rely on scattered evidence, though. Holmes and Speck (1967) cited evidence from Kent where large landowners were predominantly Whig.

[20] *The Examiner*, no. 35, April 5, 1711.

Whig party. Data from multiple sources strongly support the assertion that government creditors were predominantly associated with the Whigs, although one should not generalize this to assume that all owners of financial capital were Whigs.[21] Though he acknowledges this may be an underestimate, Hayton (2002) calculates that in each Parliament between 1690 and 1710, there were between twenty-seven and thirty-five Whig "monied men" in the House of Commons. Given that these individuals were almost invariably based in London, they would also have been among the MPs who were most regularly in attendance for parliamentary sessions. As a consequence, the "monied interest" constituted a small but significant block of Whig MPs. (If all members attended – which was rarely the case – 257 votes was the minimum necessary for a majority in the Commons.)

Among directors of the Bank of England during the period 1694–1715, De Krey (1985) has demonstrated that thirty were clearly identifiable as Whigs, while only three were clearly identifiable as Tories.[22] A pamphlet written by an opponent of the Bank of England at the time complained specifically about the fact that Whig MPs were allowed to also serve as bank directors.[23] Likewise, among Bank of England Shareholders, Whigs outnumbered Tories by two to one.[24] Patterns of ownership in other joint stock companies established after 1688 were similar. The majority of New East India Company directors and shareholders had Whig sympathies.[25]

Sedgwick (1970: 71) shows that in Parliaments after 1715, "with few exceptions" the numerous Bank of England and East India Company directors who served after 1715 were supporters of the Whig government. While records do not exist to identify firmly the partisan orientation of owners of other types of government debt, there is no obvious reason to suspect that the pattern should be different from that of the

---

[21] The evidence reviewed in Hayton (2002) for the period before 1715 shows that if one considers financial interests more generally, MPs were evenly split between the Whigs and Tories. As emphasized by De Krey (1985), the key difference was that Tory financial interests were far less likely to be the individuals who benefited directly from the post-1688 revolution in government finance.

[22] Carruthers (1996) provides similar figures.

[23] The same pamphlet also clearly indicates that the bank was associated with the Whig party. Broughton (1705).

[24] Data compiled by De Krey (1985).

[25] The exception here was the directorship of the South Sea Company, established under a Tory government in 1711. This is not surprising, though, given that the directors of the South Sea Company were appointed by the government rather than being elected by shareholders.

Bank and the New East India Company. In addition, Dickson (1967) presented substantial evidence showing that through the middle of the eighteenth century, government creditors tended overwhelmingly to be based in London. London merchants and financiers tended to be Whigs (De Krey 1987). Sedgwick (1970) also shows that the broader mercantile community in Parliament after 1715 was overwhelmingly Whig.[26]

Voting Behavior

Evidence on the importance of party can also be gleaned from voting records of members of the House of Commons and the House of Lords. The key question here is whether individuals tended to vote consistently with either the Tories or the Whigs. As Krehbiel (1993) has persuasively argued, the fact that members of a party tend to vote together does not in and of itself demonstrate that party structures have an independent effect on outcomes. Voting cohesion may instead be simply due to similarities in underlying preferences. Nonetheless, even for those who take Krehbiel's argument seriously, demonstrating voting cohesion remains an important first step toward investigating the importance of party. To address Krehbiel's critique I subsequently show that Whig landowners in particular tended to vote against their own individual preferences with regard to tax policy.

While neither the House of Commons nor the House of Lords kept records of individual votes on bills before 1742, available evidence still suggests a high degree of voting cohesion. This conclusion is based both on comments from firsthand observers of debates as well as on records of individual Commons votes, known as division lists. Individual parliamentarians often drew up prospective or retrospective lists of MP stances on specific votes, and a number of these have survived to this day.[27]

---

[26] According to his calculations, MPs from the "monied" interest made up roughly 13 percent of Whig MPs at this time.

[27] The fact that only a small portion of votes was actually recorded raises the question of whether those that did survive can be regarded as a random sample. On one hand, it would seem quite reasonable to regard the process through which some lists have been lost over the years due to fire, and so on, as being a random one. It should also be acknowledged, however, that the process through which parliamentary managers decided to record some votes and not others was undoubtedly not a random one. In all likelihood, lists were compiled either prospectively or retrospectively only for particular votes. It does not seem to have been the case, however, that MPs drew up division lists primarily for close votes, nor was it the case that the division lists primarily recorded lopsided votes. There is no clear reason to believe that the surviving division lists reflect votes where party solidarity was atypically high.

Horwitz (1977) was among the first to provide detailed evidence on parliamentary voting during the reign of King William III (1688–1702). Based on a sample of eight division lists, he identified 421 MPs whose name was present on two or more lists. Within this group, 86 percent always voted with their party. Among those who crossed party lines on at least one occasion, only a handful were identifiable as Whigs. This suggests a slightly higher degree of cohesion among Whig members of the Commons. Figures for the House of Lords are similar.[28]

Data on voting during the reign of Queen Anne (1702–14) point to a similarly high degree of voting cohesion. Speck (1981) records that 88 percent of Whig MPs never wavered in their allegiance, and a similarly high proportion of Tories always voted with their own party. The situation in the Lords was again similar to that in the Commons. Based on seven division lists recorded in Holmes (1967), 71 percent of Lords voted consistently with either the Tories or the Whigs. Among those who crossed party lines there was a roughly even split between Whigs and Tories.

For the period between 1715 and 1742, Sedgwick (1970) compiled data from thirteen separate division lists. During these years the Tories showed remarkable consistency in voting against the Whig ministries that controlled the Commons during this period, with virtually no defections recorded.[29] The average percentage of Whigs who voted with their party's position was also quite high. On average, 79 percent of Whig party members voted in favor of proposals made by the Whig Ministry.[30] Nonetheless, over time a faction known as the "Old Whigs" developed, which frequently voted against the Walpole Ministry. This can be seen in part by comparing voting behavior of government officeholders with behavior of nonofficeholders.[31] The frequency with which Whig officeholders voted with the Ministry was much higher than the same figure for those Whigs

---

[28] Based on a sample of four division lists, only 24 percent of Lords ever wavered from a consistent Tory or Whig position.

[29] Only three out of 145 Tories voted for the Septennial Act in 1716, and only three out of 131 voted for a bill on the peerage in 1719. In the other 11 votes the entire Tory group voted against the Ministry.

[30] Unfortunately, Sedgwick did not report voting records of individual MPs. Rather than providing a figure for the percentage of MPs who voted consistently with their party, for each vote he records the number of Whig party members who voted for or against the proposal.

[31] Government offices during this period included a wide variety of positions, ranging from the purely honorific to offices where the holder was actually expected to perform a task. All offices carried a salary.

who did not hold office (90 percent vs. 71 percent).[32] Officeholders were even more likely to vote with the Whig Ministry during Robert Walpole's tenure (1721–42) than they were in the period immediately before his arrival.[33] As described below, this undoubtedly reflects the fact that Walpole made it a firm practice to sanction officeholders who voted against him. With this said, it should be remembered that despite the usefulness of patronage, in order to maintain his majority Robert Walpole still required the consistent support of a significant number of Whigs who did not hold a royal office.

Communication

The most basic form of party organization in Great Britain at this time involved members coordinating their actions in advance of parliamentary debates. Members of the Whig party were meeting regularly as early as 1674 at the Green Ribbon Club.[34] After the Glorious Revolution, party organization became more developed, in particular for the Whig Party. Beginning in 1693–94 a group of four Whig parliamentarians known as the Junto established both a coherent means of negotiating strategy and a high degree of control over the party rank and file. Their dominance within the party would continue for the remainder of the reigns of William and of Anne, and it is well reflected in the observation of a Tory backbencher that the Whig election victory of 1708 would render Parliament superfluous, "for all matters which used to be its business are now arranged in private meeting."[35] There were regular dinners of Whig party leaders during this period, including members of both the Commons and the Lords, which served the purpose of plotting parliamentary strategy. In addition, there appears to have been a hierarchy of meetings, as summit conferences of Whig leaders were followed by meetings where the party line was disseminated to the rank and file.[36] In contrast with this apparently close

---

[32] A t-test massively rejected the null that the means for the officeholding and nonofficeholding sample were equal.

[33] On three Commons votes between 1717 and 1719, the percentage of Whig officeholders to vote against the Ministry was 22 percent, 13 percent, and 22 percent. On the nine Commons votes for which we have data during Walpole's tenure as prime minister, the average rate of defection by officeholders was only 8 percent.

[34] Jones (1961) suggests that these gatherings generally occurred in advance of parliamentary debates and allowed Whig MPs to plan strategy.

[35] Cited in Holmes (1967: 288).

[36] See the evidence collected by Jones (1991, 1997). His conclusion about a hierarchy of meetings remains somewhat speculative, but there does appear to be solid evidence

coordination between leaders of the Whig party, Holmes (1967: ch. 9) suggests that leaders of the Tory party were often hampered by a lack of communication at the top.

In addition to private communications, regular meetings of the parliamentary Whig party in London taverns continued to be an important element of party organization after 1688. From 1694 to 1700 the Rose Tavern was a regular venue for Whig MPs to meet in advance of House of Commons sessions to be briefed by party leaders.[37] During this period the Tories met regularly at the Vine Tavern. After 1700, Whig party organization became even more sophisticated, with the creation of the Kit-Kat Club. This was a more exclusive club whose members met frequently to plot strategy. Importantly, it also contained members of both the Lords and the Commons. The Kit-Kat Club remained crucial to Whig party organization until 1712 when, during the Whig's period in opposition, it was replaced with a new organization, the Hanover Club (Hayton 2002).

The Tories also convened meetings of parliamentary meetings, in particular at the beginning of parliamentary sessions. Holmes (1967: 294) reports that these sessions were often attended by up to 150 members. In some cases, though, instead of serving as a means for party leaders to plot strategy and disseminate information to the rank and file, Tory political clubs were created by backbenchers who sought to steer policies in a more extreme direction. The best example of this phenomenon was the October Club, which gained prominence after the Tory election victory of 1710. Members of the October Club repeatedly pressured Commons leader Robert Harley to adopt policies more favorable to the Church of England, while the club also fiercely opposed the financial policies that were benefiting the "monied interest." The October Club's vociferousness prompted the Tory writer Jonathan Swift to write a letter to the October Club members suggesting that their strategy was so extreme as to be counterproductive.[38]

---

of regular meetings among senior officials. Jones's evidence here extends earlier evidence identified by Holmes (1967).

[37] Sir Richard Cocks reported meeting at the Rose Club with 125 other Whigs in February 1701 to coordinate strategy for the election of the next Speaker of the House of Commons (1698–1702: 61–62). Hayton (2002) reports that these meetings were sufficiently institutionalized for chairmen to be appointed.

[38] Swift (1711b). The October Club also called for Harley to remove all government officeholders who had Whig sympathies. A second organization, the March Club, played a similar role as a backbench pressure group.

Beyond the London-based political clubs, the Tory party also made use of a system of regional whips designed to ensure that MPs actually attended regular sessions of the House of Commons. Given early eighteenth-century traveling conditions, ensuring that party members actually showed up was no small consideration. In the House of Lords, problems of attendance were lessened by the existence of a proxy system. Holmes (1967) reports that the four Junto Lords were particularly effective in exploiting this system.

Sanctions

If a "significant" party is defined as one where members commit to pursuing certain policies that occasionally diverge from their most preferred outcomes, then members will inevitably face incentives to deviate on certain votes. Given these incentives, one would expect successful parties to develop centralized mechanisms to sanction those who defect from the party line. For Calvert and Fox (2000), the centralized nature of sanctions is the principal distinction between a significant party and a coalition that is simply held together by the threat that defection will be met with defection. Leaders of both the Tory and the Whig parties had a number of different mechanisms at their disposal to ensure cohesion among members. These mechanisms seem to have been most prominent in the case of the Whigs.

One of the crucial aspects of the political clubs that developed during the reign of Queen Anne was that membership in them was highly prized. On one level membership could be seen as valuable because it allowed individual Whigs a greater chance to influence their party's policy. Additionally, one can see membership as having been valuable because of the social function it provided for members. Whigs who failed to vote the party line could expect to be expelled from the Kit-Kat Club.[39]

In addition to being excluded from political clubs, MPs who voted against their own party also faced the risk of not being selected as candidates in future elections. This was all the more credible as a threat before 1714 in that elections to the House of Commons occurred on average once every two years. In contrast, after 1715 and the passage of the Septennial Act, elections occurred only every seven years. Elections to the House of Commons during the early eighteenth century were divided between two types of constituencies: counties and boroughs (the latter generally being

---

[39] Holmes (1967: 297–98) cites the example of the Duke of Somerset's expulsion.

much smaller). There appear to have been no formal rules other than a property requirement restricting candidacies for Parliament. In practice, though, for the county constituencies it was impossible for individuals to present themselves as candidates without the support of a local magnate (usually a large landowner). Speck (1970) reports that candidacies in the counties were inevitably decided on by a "selectorate" of the gentry. In cases where the gentry could not agree on a list of candidates, they met separately to form rival Whig and Tory lists. Local patrons also seem to have been critical for the success of candidacies in the smaller borough constituencies.[40]

National leaders of the Whig party in particular seem to have relied heavily on local political organizations to enforce the party line. Whig leaders at the national level could attempt to persuade local magnates to withdraw support from a particular individual who had proven untrustworthy.[41] Holmes (1967: 311–12) reports examples of a number of Whig MPs during the reign of Queen Anne who, following a defection on one or more parliamentary votes, were subsequently excluded from presenting themselves as candidates for the House of Commons. As further evidence of the power of the Whig leadership, Holmes (1967) shows that after the Whig electoral defeat of 1710, party leaders succeeded in finding safe seats in by-elections for prominent candidates who had recently been defeated.

In addition to sanctions made possible by party institutions, leaders of a parliamentary majority in eighteenth-century Great Britain were also able to use state patronage as a lever to ensure voting cohesion. The practice of granting MPs paid royal offices, known as "places," began under Charles II in the 1670s and was managed by one of his ministers, who was humorously referred to as the "Bribe Master General" (Holmes 1993: 112). The places were generally little more than sinecures that provided a regular income. The Crown also found reasons to grant some MPs pensions when no offices were available. Estimates for the number of placeholders during the reign of Queen Anne vary, with most authors identifying between 100 and 120 placeholders (Hayton 2002; Speck 1977). This was far from sufficient to ensure a Commons majority in support of the Ministry, but it was still a significant aid. Unfortunately, we lack accurate data for this period on the frequency with which placeholding MPs, when compared with nonplaceholding MPs, voted consistently with their party.

---

[40] See the review by Hayton (2002), as well as Speck (1970).
[41] Assuming of course that the local magnate had continued to support party policy. Tory party organization appears to have been more loosely based at the local level.

During Robert Walpole's tenure as Prime Minister, patronage became much more significant as a means of maintaining majority support in the Commons. Estimates of the exact number of officeholding MPs vary, but all sources point toward a dramatic increase in numbers compared with the pre-1714 period. Sedgwick (1970) reports an average of 183 officeholders for the period 1729–42. This represented 65 percent of the vote necessary to form a Commons majority. Speck (1977) suggests that the number of officeholders expanded to 160 soon after Queen Anne's death in 1714 and reached 220 by 1760. As previously argued, however, even with this increase in the number of officeholders, during the post-1714 period leaders such as Robert Walpole still found it necessary to maintain support from a number of Whig MPs who did not hold offices. As a consequence, it would be inaccurate to suggest that the stability of Walpole's coalition was due exclusively to patronage.

In addition to increasing the number of MPs who profited from offices and pensions, Robert Walpole also established a more direct link than had previously existed between voting and the rewards of officeholding. Before 1714 there was a clear expectation that officeholders should support the Ministry on important votes concerning finance in particular. However, Holmes and Szechi (1993) report that minor officeholders were not expected to support the Ministry on every vote. Walpole made things much more explicit by requiring that officeholders vote with the Ministry on all bills. Otherwise they could expect to be dismissed.

4. Partisan Politics and Public Debt

Given the evidence on partisan divisions and party organization, the next logical step is to take a closer look at individual episodes in policy making over time. This section addresses four specific observable implications of my argument about party formation and credible commitment. First, it provides clear evidence to show that government creditors were closely associated with the Whig party, while they were not associated with the Tory party after 1688. Second, it demonstrates that even landowning members of the Whig party voted consistently in favor of maintaining the land tax that was necessary to service government debt. Third, it shows that there were clear examples where negotiations over financial policy were explicitly linked to negotiations over other types of policy, which is also consistent with the party formation argument. Finally, the section shows that crises of confidence in public finance were often generated by partisan political events.

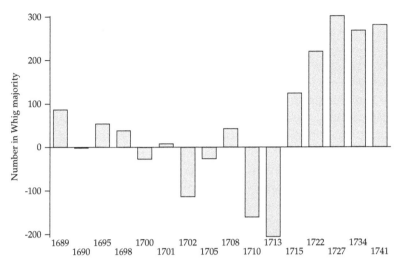

Figure 5.1. Majorities in the Commons, 1688–1742.
Source: Hayton (2002), Holmes (1993), and Holmes and Szechi (1993).

Before considering events in more detail, it is useful to first review the evolving pattern of partisan control of government in Great Britain after 1688. Figure 5.1 shows the differential between Whig and Tory strength in the Commons after each election between 1689 and 1741. Apart from the Convention Parliament of 1689, the reign of King William III (1689–1702) was one where the parties were fairly evenly matched in the Commons. During the reign of Queen Anne partisan swings grew larger, culminating in the Tory elections landslides of 1710 and 1713. After the death of Queen Anne the pattern of partisan politics changed again, as the Whig Party maintained a continuous majority in the Commons through the fall of Walpole in 1742 (in fact, Whig dominance continued until the 1760s).

The pattern of control in the House of Lords was similar to that in the House of Commons. The Whig party held a small majority in the Lords after 1688, which it seems to have held until 1712, when Queen Anne created twelve new Tory peers. There was then a Tory majority in the Lords for the next few years, but after 1715 the Whigs once again gained control of the upper chamber.

Politics under King William III, 1689–1702

As mentioned previously, the outbreak of the War of the League of Augsburg (1689–97) prompted William III's government to seek new opportunities for raising finance. On the revenue side a series of reforms initiated before 1688 had resulted in more stable and predictable collections for the Crown. In addition, under William III new revenue was generated by the Land Tax, which from 1693 was set at a rate of 20 percent. The other major change in terms of finance during this period involved the first long-term loans contracted by the English Crown and the creation of the Bank of England. Both the creation of the Land Tax and the increase in government borrowing (implying future taxes on land) generated significant opposition in Parliament. I suggest here that the new policies were made possible by the support of a Whig coalition, managed by the Whig leaders known as the Junto, and composed of both the "monied interest" and a group of landowners.

During the first years of his reign, William III had attempted to rule with a mixed administration including both Whig and Tory ministers. As this strategy proved increasingly unworkable, beginning in 1693 he opted for a Ministry that was dominated by Whigs. Horwitz (1977) has provided the most detailed synthesis of British politics during this period, and his evidence suggests, interestingly, that the creation of the Bank of England was made possible thanks to a logroll with the Triennial Act of 1694. During the years immediately following the Glorious Revolution, the majority of Whigs still favored strong restraints on the executive, and one means to achieve this goal was to have frequent elections to Parliament. In early 1693 William vetoed an initial triennial bill passed by the Commons that would have required him to call new elections every three years. By early 1694 the Whigs sought to propose a new Triennial bill, and on this occasion a prominent Whig whom William sought to grant a ministerial position announced that he would not accept the offer unless William gave his assent to the Triennial bill. At roughly the same time, the Scottish entrepreneur William Paterson gained the support of several prominent Whig merchants for his proposal to create a national bank in England. Toward the end of 1694 both the Triennial bill and the bill creating the Bank of England were passed in the Commons with the support of the Whigs. Contemporaries who witnessed the votes saw the two as being explicitly linked, and their statements refer directly to a deal between different interests within the Whig party.[42]

---

[42] Horwitz (1977: 138) reports a remark: "[O]ur affairs go on merrily with relation to the land forces, for which the gentlemen will have the triennial bill." Affairs "with relation to the land forces" in this statement refers to the financing of William's army in Europe with money raised from the loan provided by Bank of England shareholders.

Following the Junto's rise to power in 1693–94, Whig party control over the Commons grew increasingly sophisticated, and this resulted in consistent policies in favor of taxing land income to fund the war effort, supplemented by borrowing. If MPs in 1692 had observed that Commons votes were highly unpredictable, by 1696 Whig parliamentarians were preparing sessions on a nightly basis at the Rose Club, provoking complaints from some Tories that "questions were brought ready prepared" to the Commons.[43] On one occasion in 1697 the Whigs conferred at the Rose Club to coordinate support for a bill extending the Bank of England's charter and privileges (Horwitz 1977: 187). This followed an unsuccessful attempt by opponents of the Whigs to create a "Land Bank" that would have been a rival to the Bank of England and that would have issued notes backed by land holdings.[44] This is powerful evidence that the bank's success depended on political support in Parliament from the Whig party. In addition, Horwitz (1977: 213) concludes that there were explicit links made in many cases between maintaining land taxes and passing other legislation: "[T]he commitment of Whigs in office and on the backbenches to the continuation of the war was reinforced both by the bestowal of places for the ambitious and by concessions on reform questions for the principled."

After the end of the war in 1697 there was less need for borrowing, but the British government needed to maintain taxes at a sufficiently high level in order to meet debt servicing payments. During the 1698 election campaign the Whig majority in the Commons came under criticism for "heavy taxes" as well as for its reliance on officeholders (Horwitz 1977). The Tories also pressured after the war's end for the government to renege on certain debts, and in particular those contracted with the New East India Company. This was prompted both by a desire to avoid further taxes necessary to repay the loans and by the fact that the Tories were closely linked with a rival corporation, the Old East India Company.[45] Finally,

---

[43] MP cited in Horwitz (1977: 208).
[44] Clapham (1958: 34) observes that positions with regard to the Land Bank depended heavily on party affiliation, with the Whigs opposing and the Tories supporting. Support for the Land Bank was also consistent with support for the interests of landowners, since they would have been advantaged by the creation of this sort of Bank.
[45] See Carruthers (1996) and De Krey (1985) for data showing that a high percentage of New East India Company directors were Whigs, while the reverse was true for the Old East India Company. This reflects the more general pattern whereby Whigs were closely associated with financial institutions created after 1688, while the few stock companies created before the Glorious Revolution were more likely to be associated with the Tories.

the end of the war also coincided with fractures in the Whig coalition in Parliament, as a group of "Country Whigs" opposed the Junto over issues such as whether a standing army should be maintained.

Despite some tensions within the Whig coalition, evidence shows that after 1697, most Whigs maintained a united front on other issues including religious toleration, the succession, and maintaining the land tax in order to repay debts. The parliamentary diary of Sir Richard Cocks, a Whig with strong Country sentiments, is particularly interesting in this regard. Despite being a landowner from a landowning constituency, and despite his explicit dislike of the Land Tax, Cocks repeatedly made Commons speeches in favor of land taxation to support the war effort (pre-1697) and to repay debts (after 1697).[46] In March 1699 Cocks actively opposed Tory attempts to renege on debts owed to the New East India Company.[47] The evidence from the Cocks diary seems to reflect a broader trend within the Whig party where landowning MPs from landowning constituencies voted to support continued land taxation, against their immediate economic interest but consistent with their party platform.

Politics under Queen Anne, 1702–1714

The reign of Queen Anne, which began in 1702, coincided with renewed war between France and Great Britain. The War of the Spanish Succession would last until 1713 when a Tory government negotiated the Treaty of Utrecht. Partisan control of government during these years can be divided into three separate periods: divided government between 1702 and 1708, unified Whig government between 1708 and 1710, and unified Tory government from 1710 to 1714. It is evident for these two latter periods in particular that government credibility was linked to the shifting fortunes of the Whig and Tory parties and that debt repayment continued to depend on the support of a Whig coalition composed of both government creditors and landowners.[48]

From 1702 to 1708 there was a Tory majority in the Commons, while the Whigs retained control of the House of Lords. Queen Anne opted

---

[46] During the 1701 session he made a speech indicating that he did not favor the land tax, but recognized it as necessary to counter the threat of foreign (French) aggression. Cocks (1698–1702: 103).

[47] Cocks (1698–1702: 19–20). In 1701 he made a second speech urging the Commons to honor outstanding debts to the New East India Company shareholders (p. 133).

[48] Hayton (2002) and Holmes (1967) provide the best overviews of parliamentary politics during this period.

for a Ministry that included representatives of both parties. Though her own sympathies appear to have been closer to the Tory party, it has been suggested that Anne, like William III, initially chose a mixed Ministry in order to avoid becoming dependent on a single party. This was a period of mixed government where the Earl of Godolphin and the Duke of Marlborough, two political figures who were less explicitly aligned with either party, gained prominence. As Lord Treasurer, Godolphin managed consistently to produce the parliamentary majorities necessary to pursue the government's financial policies.

The electoral success of the Whigs during the 1708 election created pressures on Anne to bring more Whigs into the Ministry, and the end result was a brief period of unified Whig government, where the Whigs controlled both Houses of Parliament as well as the Ministry. Consistent with a partisan interpretation of the politics of public debt, the brief period of Whig control saw several legislative initiatives that were very favorable to government creditors. Most importantly, the Bank of England's charter was renewed in 1709, and its monopoly privileges were significantly extended despite vociferous opposition from the Tory members of the Commons (Clapham 1958: 65). Writing of this period, Daniel Defoe remarked that "the [Whig] Junto had wrought up so great a majority into Engagements to stand by them on all Occasions, by Voting unanimously in every thing that concerned the Ministry."[49]

After a brief period of unified Whig government, political events in 1710 led to a dramatic reorientation as the Whigs were expelled from the Ministry and they suffered a crushing electoral defeat. The Whigs briefly retained control over the House of Lords, but the Tory leader, Robert Harley, was soon able to put together a majority in that assembly as well. In addition to the effect of popular dissatisfaction with the war effort, the principal event precipitating this political change was the decision by Whig ministers in late 1709 to put on trial a well-known clergyman with Tory sympathies who had made a highly publicized sermon attacking the Whig interpretation of the Revolution of 1688, the Dissenters, and the financial interests (most notably, the Bank of England). It is interesting to note in this regard that Tory criticisms of the Whigs often focused simultaneously on the question of dissent and on opposition to the "monied interest," which was symbolized by the Bank of England.

As previously described in Chapter 4, the Tory electoral landslide of 1710 was accompanied by higher rates of government borrowing and by

---

[49] Defoe (1710c).

a drop in Bank of England share prices. Contemporary observers drew a direct link between heightened fears of a default and the Tory victory. During the summer of 1710, as Queen Anne was removing Whig ministers, a delegation of directors from the Bank of England visited the Queen to warn her that further dismissals would do irreparable harm to public credit (De Krey 1985). Subsequently, many observers noted that the drop in Bank of England shares at this time was precipitated by the Tory electoral landslide.[50]

During the next four years (1710–14) with a Tory majority in the Commons, Tory political rhetoric attempted to capitalize on the idea of a conflict between the landed interest and the monied interest.[51] The Tory leader, Robert Harley, employed both Daniel Defoe and Jonathan Swift as political pamphleteers. At Harley's prompting, Defoe wrote several pamphlets claiming that the deterioration in public confidence in government debt after 1710 was based on the mistaken assumption that credibility depended on which party was in power.[52] Defoe wrote a follow-up essay in 1711 that made similar arguments.[53] The fact that Harley found it so necessary to use Defoe to deny the link between partisanship and access to public credit suggests that there was a very close link in the public mind between party and public credit.

Jonathan Swift made more of an effort in his writings to castigate the Whig party as a selfish faction that pursued a land war with France in order to serve the interests of foreign powers and of government creditors who were reaping handsome profits. Swift's best-known pamphlet from this period was *The Conduct of the Allies* (1711), where he suggested the true motive for the war was "the mutual Indulgence between our General and Allies, wherein they both so well found their Accounts; to the Fears of the *Mony-changers*, lest their *Tables should be overthrown....*"[54] In the same

---

[50] See the evidence presented in William Thomas Morgan (1922), as well as the anonymous monograph, *An Impartial View of the Two Late Parliaments*. In his *Essay on Publick Credit*, Daniel Defoe also referred to the events of 1710.

[51] In addition to the well-known writings of Jonathan Swift, the comments by Pittis (1711) on the proposal that only landowners should be eligible to serve as MPs illustrates this rhetoric quite well: "The Qualification Bill incapacitating all men to serve in Parliament, who have not some Estate in Land, either in Possession or certain Reversion, is perhaps the greatest security that ever was contrived for preserving the Constitution, which otherwise might in all too little time, lye wholly at the Mercy of the money'd Interest."

[52] Defoe (1710b).

[53] Defoe (1710a).

[54] His emphasis. Davis (1951) argues that Swift conferred closely with several Tory government ministers before writing this pamphlet, and that it was

pamphlet Swift actually referred to the threat of default by suggesting, "Since the Monied Men are so fond of War, I should be glad, they would furnish out one Campaign at their own Charge."

Not surprisingly given its composition, Robert Harley's Ministry from 1710 found it much more difficult than previous administrations to gain access to long-term credit. Harley himself sought to steer a moderate policy course, but others in his party were less eager to do so. While the Whig government in 1708 had been able to borrow long-term at 6.25 percent, in 1710 and 1711 the Harley administration was forced to pay over 8 percent per year, and as a further inducement to investors, it was forced to add certain lottery privileges to each of these loans. Like its predecessors, the Harley Ministry also relied on granting monopoly privileges to joint stock companies in order to raise funds, in particular with the creation of the South Sea Company. The South Sea Company was different, though, from the two other companies in one fundamental way. While subscriptions to the Bank of England and the New East India Company were purely voluntary, the South Sea Company was created by an involuntary conversion into equity of short-term navy debts that the government was having great difficulty servicing.[55]

Robert Harley after 1710 attempted to gain support of financiers, in particular with the idea that the South Sea Company might serve as a rival to the Whig-controlled Bank of England and East India Company.[56] In courting the monied interest, however, he was continuously undermined by the fact backbench Tory groups, and the October Club in particular, were vociferously opposed to any policies that they saw as benefiting the monied interest. The October Club pressed, among other things, for revoking the Bank of England's charter.

Politics during the Walpole Era, 1715–1742

The death of Queen Anne in 1714 marked a major watershed in British politics. While most of the period between the Glorious Revolution and

---

intended to serve as a statement of government policy at the outset of the new Parliament.

[55] The parliamentary act creating the South Sea Company did not oblige investors to accept this conversion, but it stipulated no other provision for repayment of the short-term debts. In reference to this forced conversion, Dickson (1967) states, "The establishment of the South Sea Company got rid of the floating debt, with the grudging acquiescence of the financial community in the City."

[56] This included a failed attempt by the Tories to gain a majority of seats on the Bank of England's court of directors in 1711 (Clapham 1958: 65).

the death of Anne had been one of war, England from 1715 to 1742 entered into a lengthy period of peace. In electoral terms, 1715 also marked the beginning of a long period where the Whigs held a sizable majority in the House of Commons. Finally, the terms of the political debate began to change (albeit slowly) after 1715. As debates over existing issues such as religious toleration and the royal succession became less prominent, by the end of the Walpole era the political conflict in England centered increasingly around the claim that the Whig government under Robert Walpole represented an oligarchy of financial interests, and that to support its policies the government was resorting to corrupt and tyrannical measures. These included expansion of the number of placemen in Parliament, the repeal of the Triennial Act, and restrictions on civil liberties. During this period the Whigs who supported Walpole largely abandoned their onetime emphasis on individual liberty with respect to Crown and executive. Restrictions on the executive were instead supported by a group of opposition Whigs, frequently referred to as the "Old Whigs."[57]

The immediate years after 1715 were a period of transition within the Whig party as new leaders supplanted the aging members of the Junto. MPs including Stanhope, Sunderland, Townshend, and Walpole disputed control of the party, and for a brief period after 1717, Walpole actually led a Whig faction in the Commons that regularly voted with the Tory minority against the Ministry led by Stanhope. Robert Walpole established undisputed leadership over the parliamentary Whig party in 1721, following the disaster of the South Sea Bubble and after the deaths of Stanhope and Sunderland. Walpole was appointed First Lord of the Treasury and Chancellor of the Exchequer and has frequently been seen as England's first Prime Minister.

Robert Walpole's success in maintaining majority support for debt repayment was attributable in part to the same factors that had held the Whig coalition together between 1688 and 1715. For one, government creditors remained a key element of the Whig coalition, and they appear to have increased their representation in Parliament during this period.[58] In addition, because ideological issues remained relevant for a time, a number of landowners also supported the Whig party line even if this

---

[57] For reviews of politics during the Walpole era, see Holmes and Szechi (1993), Plumb (1956, 1967), and Speck (1977).

[58] Sedgwick (1970) lists twenty-seven Bank of England directors who served as MPs between 1715 and 1754, which is certainly an increase from the previous period.

also implied continuing the Land Tax. With regard to the succession, while the coronation of George I of Hanover was increasingly seen as a fait accompli after 1715, there were a number of uprisings by Jacobites after 1715 who supported the restoration of the Stuarts to the throne. As a consequence, the need to defend the Hanoverian succession remained a motivating force for a number of Whigs after 1715, and Speck (1977) suggests that Robert Walpole never hesitated to play on fears of Jacobitism in order to reinforce his coalition. Likewise, the question of religious toleration retained importance after 1715, though as previously emphasized, the issue became less salient over time.

Walpole also relied on other devices to hold his majority together. While patronage had been used by ministers to procure majorities in the Commons at least since the reign of King Charles II, as noted above, Walpole significantly expanded the number of placemen in Parliament. This increased use of patronage, and the stipulation that officeholders were required to vote with the Ministry on all bills, may have helped compensate for the fact that issues such as religious toleration gradually became less salient in political debates after 1715. This heavy use of patronage also had its costs. A number of Whigs became disillusioned with what they saw as Walpole's corrupt policies. By the 1730s the splinter group calling itself the "Old Whigs" became increasingly active in opposing Walpole on certain votes.

Another new element in Walpole's strategy involved political compromise, as his Ministry took steps to shift some of the burden for government taxation from taxes on land toward indirect taxation, especially in the form of excise taxes.[59] Walpole was himself a landowner from a predominantly landowning constituency, and historians of the period agree that he made consistent attempts to lower the rate of the land tax whenever practical, keeping it at a rate of 10 percent for most of his period of rule (Holmes and Szechi 1993). That Walpole kept land taxes low helps explain one reason why potential opposition from landowners within his own party was mollified. It would be inaccurate to say, however, that tensions between the landed interest and the monied interest were also diminished by diversification of landholders into government debt.[60] In addition, political rhetoric generated by the Tory opposition during the

---

[59] This part of Walpole's strategy has also been emphasized by Schofield (2001a, b).

[60] Dickson (1967) shows convincingly that government creditors were overwhelmingly based in London at least through the 1760s. This remained true despite the fact that ownership of government stocks expanded considerably, reaching a total of about 60,000 owners at this time.

Walpole era continued to emphasize the division between a "monied interest" that was enjoying excessive profits and a landed sector of the economy that was being forced to bear the brunt of taxation.[61]

One possible interpretation of the increased resort to excise taxes by Walpole is that they were borne primarily by the popular classes who were politically disenfranchised and by those commercial groups that were not part of the Whig coalition. As O'Brien (1988) cautions, however, it is difficult to make firm judgments about the relative burden of excise taxes on different households with existing data. In any case, opportunities for increasing excise taxes were not unlimited, as a proposed increase in 1733 that would have also allowed abolition of the land tax provoked one of the greatest crises of Walpole's period of rule (Plumb 1956; Speck 1977). Walpole's proposals of 1733 to improve enforcement of customs and excise collections generated a storm of popular protest, and as a result he was forced to abandon them.[62] Even without these changes, during Walpole's period of leadership, excise taxes increased very significantly as a share of government revenue.

One final significant aspect of Whig party rule after 1715 is that continued support for debt repayment was not matched by continued support by the Whigs for individual liberties and restraints on the executive. Whig majorities after 1715 passed a Septennial Act (1716), which more than doubled the period between parliamentary elections; they passed the Riot Act, which greatly restricted right of free assembly; and they approved numerous other restrictions on individual liberties, such as the suspension of habeas corpus. By most accounts, the principal objective of these measures was to reduce the danger of popular protest.[63] In sum, then, this suggests that the Whig majority under Walpole relied increasingly on both patronage and restrictions on democratic participation in order to assure political stability and the perennial nature of its power. It was precisely these restrictions, on civil liberties and the prevalence of patronage that the American revolutionaries of the late eighteenth century reacted against when they criticized the English government during and after the Walpole era (Stone 1980). The issue of how political stability was maintained is considered at greater length in Chapter 7.

---

[61] See Speck (1977) as well as Kramnick (1968), who provides a detailed analysis of the rhetoric of Bolingbroke, one of the most outspoken Tories.

[62] Opposition appears to have been in part generated by fears about handing arbitrary power to tax inspectors.

[63] See Kenyon (1977), in particular.

5. Summary

Parliamentary representation of government creditors was critical in allowing the British monarchy after 1688 to borrow at unprecedented low interest rates. However, I have argued that the fact that creditors had influence over parliamentary decisions was itself dependent on the emergence of cohesive political parties in Britain. Government creditors gained power as part of a Whig coalition that was composed of heterogeneous interests and held together by political compromise. During the turbulent period between 1688 and 1715, trends in interest rates on government loans closely tracked the shifting electoral fortunes of the Whig and Tory parties, providing further support for the party hypothesis. It was only after the final triumph of the Whigs over the Tories in 1715 that interest rates on U.K. government borrowing finally converged with prevalent rates for government debt in the Netherlands.

6

Partisan Politics and Public Debt in France, 1689–1789

1. Introduction

It has become received wisdom in recent years that the weakness of representative institutions in eighteenth-century France undermined the monarchy's credibility as a borrower. A logical implication of this argument is that if the Crown had revived the Estates General, it would have been able to borrow at lower rates of interest. While recognizing that this is a counterfactual question that cannot be answered with certainty, in this chapter I argue that default risk on sovereign debt in France had as much to do with the balance of partisan forces in French society as with the weakness of representative institutions. In fact, the observed absence of credibility in France is consistent with an alternative argument that credibility for sovereign debt would have been absent even if English-style institutions had been adopted. What was missing in France was the possibility for a coalition such as the English Whigs to form, based on a compromise between financial interests who had invested in government debt and other social groups. This finding supports my argument that constitutional checks and balances may not suffice to ensure commitment, while it is also consistent with my second main argument about the effect of party formation in a plural society. In considering eighteenth-century French politics I also hope to shed light on another recent debate concerning the extent to which it was possible, in the absence of national representative institutions, for the French Crown to gain credibility by bureaucratic innovations such as indirect borrowing or establishing a national bank. I conclude that the French experience provides an excellent illustration of the inefficacy of bureaucratic delegation as a commitment device under autocracy.

Though some of the arguments considered in this chapter are counterfactual, it is still possible to evaluate them rigorously by identifying different observable implications of each explanation and then investigating whether these implications are consistent with historical evidence. To do this I consider three separate episodes of attempted or proposed institutional reform.

The first instance involves the proposal made after the death of Louis XIV in 1715 to call the Estates General. If the argument that this was a missed opportunity to credibly commit is accurate, then we might expect to observe that those who recommended calling the Estates foresaw that it would reduce the risk of a royal default. Sargent and Velde (1995) cite several late-eighteenth-century thinkers who saw a direct link between representative institutions and improved public credit, but they do not consider this earlier episode in detail. Based on the experience of past Estates General, we can investigate whether those elected to the Estates would have had a clear interest in seeing that royal debts were repaid. I suggest that historical evidence points in the opposite direction of Sargent and Velde's argument. Those who recommended calling the Estates in 1715 actually hoped that the assembly would choose default over new taxes, and given the structure of public debt holdings in France at this time, it seems likely that creditors would have been poorly represented within the Estates. Finally, possibilities for a Whig-style coalition to form between government creditors and liberal aristocrats would also have been limited, due to the existence of conflicts between these two groups over other issues.

The second episode of failed reform involves John Law's Banque Royale, which briefly served as France's national bank (1719–20), and his project to convert royal debt into equity in a trading company, the Compagnie des Indes. As argued in Chapter 4, while Law's project has acquired a reputation for being impractical, recent observers have argued that the economic principals on which it was based were not fundamentally unsound. The plan offered an opportunity to convert royal debt into equity, and if it had succeeded, the Banque Royale would have been able to offer advantages similar to the Bank of England in terms of public credit. Ultimately, Law's project was undone by an excess issue of bank notes in 1719, followed by hesitation in adopting deflationary policies. In Section 3 of this chapter I argue that the failure of Law's plan illustrates the inefficacy of bureaucratic delegation as a commitment device in an absolute monarchy. I support this claim with two types of evidence. First, there are clear indications that the Regent who ruled France at the time pushed Law into the excess issue of bank notes and subsequently into delaying deflationary adjustment. Second, contemporary observers directly attributed the failure of the project to unbridled royal prerogative.

The final episode of failed reform involved a series of financial decisions made by the French Constituent Assembly in 1789 and 1790. Rather than opt for a national bank modeled on the Bank of England, as had been proposed by the King's minister, Jacques Necker, the deputies of the Constituent Assembly voted to create a new currency, the *assignat*, which would be backed by the proceeds of sale of church lands. Subsequent decisions to significantly increase the supply of *assignats* led to high inflation and indirect default as the real value of royal debts was reduced. I suggest in Section 4 of this chapter that this outcome was attributable above all to the balance of partisan forces within the Constituent Assembly. I consider observable implications of this argument involving the weak representation of government creditors and the absence of possibilities for creditors to form a cross-issue coalition of the sort represented by the Whig party in Great Britain.

2. The Proposal to Call the Estates General (1715)

Following the death of Louis XIV in 1715, some of the new Regent's counselors suggested that it might be an opportune time to call the Estates General, France's national representative body, which had not met for over a hundred years. The Estates had been a representative organ that met whenever the King proposed it, and up to 1614 it was not uncommon to summon the Estates at the beginning of a new reign. One motivation for summoning the Estates involved the financial crisis that Louis XIV had left as part of his legacy. By 1715 the government was unable with current taxes to service the debts that had been contracted during the period of warfare between 1689 and 1713. The Regent might also have called the Estates in order to help solidify his power. After a long reign, France was now governed by a Regent acting for the child Louis XV, and from the beginning there were questions about the Regent's legitimacy. One key reason for this lack of legitimacy was that in 1715 the Regent had taken actions akin to a coup d'état in order to alter several provisions in Louis XIV's will.

Saint-Simon's Proposal to Call the Estates General

One of the Regent's close advisors, the duc de Saint-Simon, suggested that calling the Estates General would allow the Regent to make public the dire financial situation, and it would force the Estates to choose between two alternative solutions: default or new taxes. Saint Simon's suggestion was in fact only the most recent in a series of proposals made by French aristocrats between 1700 and 1715 who favored reinvigorating French national representative institutions. Sargent and Velde (1995) have seen the Regent's subsequent refusal to call the Estates as a missed opportunity for France to adopt the same sort of institutional mechanism for commitment that had been so successful in Great Britain.

While we cannot know with certainty what would have transpired if the Estates had been called, one way to approach this issue is to consider the motivations of those who made the proposal. Fortunately, the duc de Saint-Simon left an extremely detailed memoir that has become a classic reference for historians of the period. Contrary to the interpretation that calling the Estates would have reduced default risk, Saint-Simon actually makes quite clear that he believed calling the Estates General would provide a convenient way to declare a state bankruptcy. It would also avoid the Regent having to assume personal responsibility for a default. Saint-Simon based his analysis on the assumption that given the composition of the Estates, one would expect most members to prefer default to the alternative of increasing taxes so as to allow debt to be serviced:

An obvious reflection shows that the Estates General will be almost entirely composed of people from the provinces, especially for the First and the Third Estates. In contrast, almost all the individuals or corporate bodies which bear the immense burden of the King's debts are financiers based in Paris. The provincial nobility, while obliged by financial ruin to marry beneath itself, has few debts outside of the provinces and none contracted with the King's creditors, who are all financiers living in Paris and officers such as *secrétaires du Roi*, *trésoriers de France*, and all sorts of *fermiers généraux*; people who are unlikely to be deputies for the Third Estate. As a consequence, the great majority of deputies from the three orders will have a personal interest and an interest for their constituents in preferring bankruptcy to the possibility of increased taxes, and they will pay little heed to the ruin and the cries which bankruptcy will cause.[1]

Saint-Simon continued in his memoirs by arguing that the Regent should explain the financial situation of the government to the Estates and then declare that any decision taken by the Estates would be binding, so absolving himself of responsibility for the decision. He also noted that it might be best to avoid default on one type of debt, the *rentes sur*

---

[1] *Mémoires* (1715: 342), author's translation. For similar statements in a piece attributed to Saint-Simon, see "Projets de Gouvernement Résolus par Monsieur le duc de Bourgogne, Dauphin," Bibliothèque de l'Arsenal, Paris.

l'Hôtel de Ville, because of the political power held by owners of this debt. Assuming the Estates met with equal representation for the Clergy (First Estate), the Nobility (Second Estate), and the bourgeois (Third Estate), then Saint-Simon assumed that the Paris-based creditors of the government would have little or no representation in the First and Third Estates, and they would be outnumbered in the Second Estate by the provincial nobility.[2] In the case of the Estates General held in 1614 it is true that Parisian nobles made up only 10 percent of the Second Estate deputies, so Saint-Simon's assertion seems accurate on this account.[3]

Evidence from Government Debt Holdings

The basic logic underlying Saint-Simon's argument is also supported by data on holdings of French government debt. Up to 1715 when it sold debt, it is well known that the French Crown relied heavily on financing from lenders grouped under the general term *financiers*. As the detailed work by Dessert (1984) has shown, the *financiers* were overwhelmingly royal officeholders, just as Saint-Simon claimed.[4] Among the *financiers*, 79 percent also claimed to be nobles, although the vast majority of those in this category had recently acceded to this status (holding certain royal offices allowed a family to be "ennobled"). Only 13 percent of the *financiers* came from families that had been among the nobility for three generations, and as a result, few of the people who directly purchased royal debt were from the upper nobility, defined as those families that had a more ancient claim to nobility.[5]

A sample of Parisian notarial records compiled by Hoffman, Postel-Vinay, and Rosenthal (1995, 2000) shows that for the period before 1715, nobles and royal officers were the most important lenders to government (see Table 6.1). The one exception here is the sample from 1711, near the end of the War of the Spanish Succession, where merchants played an increasingly important role as creditors. The well-known study by Lüthy

[2] No standard voting rule existed for the Estates General.
[3] Data presented in Hayden (1974).
[4] Some 85 percent of Dessert's sample of 534 *financiers* were officeholders (pp. 86–87).
[5] One caveat here is that even if the upper nobility did not directly purchase royal debt, Dessert (1984) argues that *financiers* who lent to the crown often acted as intermediaries for other individuals, including the upper nobility. His study presents a number of such cases but does not provide firm quantitative evidence to support this argument. Even if some members of the upper nobility did lend to the crown, it seems unlikely that payments on these loans would have constituted their principal source of income.

Table 6.1. *Loans to the State by Social Category in France (%)*

Category	1682–1700	1730–88
Nobles and officers	60	54
Merchants and bourgeois	17	27
Clergy	7	9
Crafts	3	3
Institutions	11	–

Source: Hoffman, Postel-Vinay, and Rosenthal (1992, 1995, 2000)

Table 6.2. *Loans to the State by Region in France (%)*

	1690–1710	1730–49	1750–69	1770–89
Paris	84	75	60	63
Provinces	14	13	39	19
Foreign	4	12	1	18

Source: Hoffman, Postel-Vinay, and Rosenthal (2000: 169)

(1959–61) argues that during these years, the resources of traditional government creditors had been exhausted, and as a result, the monarchy was forced to turn to Geneva-based bankers for funds. In terms of the total stock of government debt, however, one would expect that nobles and officers remained the most important creditors.

The data compiled by Hoffman et al. (2000) also support Saint-Simon's assertion that most government creditors were based in Paris. This was the case for 84 percent of creditors in the period before 1715. While their sample is drawn exclusively from Parisian notarial records, we can draw this conclusion because government loans were almost always marketed with the help of Paris-based notaries. As a result, even loans made to the government by provincials would appear in their sample. As Table 6.2 shows, it was not until the late eighteenth century that the French government's geographic base of creditors became somewhat more diversified.

Proposals to Call the Estates as Part of an "Aristocratic Reaction"

If government creditors would have been a small minority within any Estates General held in 1715, and deputies bargained only over the issue of finance and taxation, then Saint-Simon's expected outcome of default seems plausible. One can also suggest that the broader configuration of preferences in French society made it improbable that government creditors could form a majority coalition by joining with liberal aristocrats, as had taken place with the Whig party in Great Britain. Unlike in Great Britain, where government creditors and liberal aristocrats had similar preferences on issues such as religious toleration, in France the upper nobility, who were more likely to have interests in land, and the newer nobility, who were more likely to lend to the state, found themselves in opposition with each other. This was true both with regard to finance and taxation and with regard to other political issues. In other words, French politics lacked a cross-cutting cleavage that might have opened up possibilities for political compromise.

The divisions between upper nobility and government creditors in France can be illustrated by considering their opinions on the constitutional issues that were a major subject of discussion in France in the latter years of Louis XIV's reign. These debates touched in particular on the issue of restraints on royal power. As had been the case in Great Britain in 1688, there were many groups in France in 1715 who supported restrictions on the monarchy. This was in part prompted by the extreme personalization of rule under Louis XIV. However, the solutions to this problem advocated by the upper nobility and by those who had gained a noble title more recently were quite different. Since at least the early seventeenth century, members of the upper nobility had, on repeated occasions, sought to propose reforms that would have reinforced their own position within French society while simultaneously weakening the position of the crown, the *financiers* (government creditors), and the more recently arrived nobility in general. Saint-Simon's proposal to summon the Estates General was in fact seen by French eighteenth- and nineteenth-century observers as part of a broader project in France at this time to restore the position of the upper nobility at the expense of newer arrivals.[6] Marmontel (1819) suggests that Saint-Simon's main goal was to reverse the system, first put into place by Cardinal Mazarin under Louis XIII, that had sought to emancipate the king from dependence on the upper nobility.

Modern authors have shown how Saint-Simon's proposal was merely the latest of a series of similar proposals made by the upper nobility in the last years of Louis XIV's reign. Richet (1973) notes that beginning in 1711, three key figures at the Court – the abbé de Fénelon, the duc de Beauvilliers, and the duc de Chevreuse – began collaborating to make

---

[6] It should be noted here that the distinction between nobles who were well established and the more recent arrivals always carried a large element of hypocrisy. Saint-Simon's own family had not been members of the nobility for more than a few generations.

proposals for new forms of governance after the death of Louis XIV. Saint-Simon was also associated with this group. In his proposal for an Estates General, Fénelon suggested that membership of the Second Estate should be restricted to the "ancient and high nobility," which would marginalize the *financiers*, and he also called for a selective default on debts.[7] Fénelon recommended calling triennial meetings of the Estates in order to check the power of the king.

While the movement led by Fénelon and others was an aristocratic reaction in the sense that it sought to return France to the situation that had prevailed in the early fifteenth century when the Estates General had greater power, it is important to recognize that these authors were still liberals for their time.[8] Nor was the spirit of this movement very different from the desire expressed by the early Whigs in England to return to the constitutional precepts first established by the Magna Carta in the thirteenth century. The difference was that in England there was not a sharp conflict between an upper nobility represented by individuals such as Saint-Simon and newer arrivals who lent to government, but who also sought to be accepted as nobles.

A final important aspect of the aristocratic reaction in France was that its leaders were not only concerned about restricting royal authority and undercutting the *financiers*; they were also highly critical of taxes that infringed upon traditional exemptions held by the nobility and large landowners in particular. Toward the end of the War of the Spanish Succession, a desperate Louis XIV had introduced a new tax, the *dixième*, which fell on all revenues regardless of social class. Marmontel (1819) suggests that Saint-Simon "compared the *dixième* to these numerous impositions which had always made the Creator indignant," and sarcastically suggests that Louis XIV was "tormented with religious fright" when he was asked to approve the new tax. The *dixième* was finally abolished in 1717 during the Regency government and under pressure from the upper nobility. Similarly, Saint-Simon's proposal to the Estates General

[7] As a justification for this, he suggested, "The King has had the misfortune to take money from the hands of all the good families of the realm, and from the people, in order to pass it to *financiers* and usurers. We would have him transfer it from the *financiers* and usurers, into the hands of the people and the good families" (pp. 389–92).

[8] Richet (1973) suggests that "at this stage of historical development, liberalism necessarily had commonalities with the aristocratic ideal." The upper aristocrats also actually shared many opinions with merchants regarding the need to abolish the restrictions on trade and commerce present in France.

may also have been motivated by the fact that he was himself a large landowner.[9]

The above evidence strongly suggests that had the Estates General been called by the Regent in 1715, this would not have led suddenly to a commitment to repay debts. Unlike the English case, French government creditors would have been few in number within the Estates General. In addition, the pattern of political divisions in France at the time would have made it difficult for government creditors to form a coalition with other groups as had happened in Great Britain with the Whig party.

3. The Experience of John Law's Bank (1715–1720)

As previously discussed in Chapter 4, the failure of the *chambre de justice* significantly to reduce royal debts left the French monarchy in 1715 in need of alternative solutions for its financial problems. It was at this point that the Regent became intrigued with the proposal by the Scottish financier John Law to create a bank issuing paper currency and to convert existing government debt into equity in a joint stock company. In 1716 Law was given permission to create the Banque Générale, which could issue bank notes that could be used for payment of taxes, and in the following year the Regent allowed him to organize the Compagnie des Indes, the shares of which could be purchased with cash or by voluntary redemption of government debt. In 1719 the Banque Générale was converted into a national bank and became the Banque Royale. I argue here that the subsequent history of Law's bank illustrates the ineffectiveness of bureaucratic delegation as a commitment device in an autocratic system.

Expansion and Collapse of Law's System

Law massively expanded the scale of his scheme when in September 1719 he proposed to have the Compagnie des Indes rapidly acquire all outstanding government debt in exchange for shares. This was a critical turn in policy. Lüthy (1959–61) claims that when he first proposed his plan in 1715, Law had estimated that it would take up to twenty-five years to pay off all royal debts. Abandoning this earlier timetable in order to retire the royal debt quickly, Law engaged in three massive share issues

---

[9] See, e.g., Marmontel (1819: 340): "Saint-Simon, who owned land, and who owned little royal debt, saw the territorial tax and especially the *dixième*, as a gross iniquity, and royal bankruptcy as just."

in September and October of 1719, and each of these issues was accompanied by a substantial issue of Banque Royale notes in order to help support the price of shares.

The first several months of 1720 saw two important flip-flops in policy by Law that raise questions about the political pressures he faced. By early 1720 Law realized that he had overexpanded by issuing too much paper currency in order to maintain an artificially inflated share price. On February 22 a decree was published in Paris introducing measures that effectively ended the policy of printing Banque Royale notes to support artificially the price of shares in the Compagnie des Indes. The price of company shares would now be strictly determined by the market. This action seemed to be a clear indication that Law had recognized that he had erred in overexpanding the supply of Banque Royale notes. On March 5, however, a decree was published that reversed the decision of February 22. The new policy instead provided a guaranteed price of 9,000 livres for Compagnie des Indes shares in notes of the Banque Royale. This policy was itself reversed by a decree of May 21, 1720, imposing a significant reduction in the gold price of both Banque Royale notes and Compagnie des Indes shares. Finally, the decree of May 21 was reversed a week later, but at this point the market price of Compagnie des Indes shares fell precipitously. Law quickly fell out of favor, and he was forced to flee France.

Explaining Law's Failure

While there is considerable debate about Law's thinking during the first months of 1720, most authors agree that his project was undone by excess note issues, followed by the subsequent hesitations in adopting a deflationary policy.[10] For a political economy account, then, the key question is, what considerations might have pushed Law into a hasty expansion and subsequently made him reluctant to pursue deflation?

Faure (1977) argues that Law had a need to continually please the Regent so that the complete plans for his bank could be carried out.[11] The implicit threat was that the Regent could unilaterally decide to liquidate Law's bank and his other financial ventures. Given that the Regent himself was in a somewhat precarious political position, Law may well have

---

[10] See Faure (1977), Garber (2000), and Murphy (1997).
[11] Faure (1977) also places heavy weight on what he sees as Law's risk-taking personality.

faced a strong incentive to overissue bank notes. Increasing the issue of bank notes allowed the monarchy to reduce its indebtedness, as well as to distribute money to political favorites.

As an astute observer of events at court, Saint-Simon also refers to the fact that Law was subject to the Regent's desires to secure his rule:[12]

That which hastened the demise of the Bank and of Law's System was the incomprehensible prodigality of the duc d'Orléans [the Regent], who, without limit and, if that is possible, without choice, could not resist the temptation, even with those whom he knew, no doubt, to be hostile to him. He distributed notes to each and everyone and frequently let himself be defrauded by people who ridiculed him and who respected only their own arrogance.[13]

A slightly different account of Law's demise is presented by Dutot (1738), a contemporary observer who was a principal administrator of the Banque Royale. Dutot claims that Law was undone by a "cabal" of those who were most threatened by his plans. He attributes the collapse in confidence in Law's system to the efforts of Law's political enemies to convince the public that the project was doomed. Among Law's enemies, Dutot singles out the venal officeholders who had served as the principal lenders to the monarchy and whose position would obviously be jeopardized if Law succeeded in establishing a new mechanism for royal finance (p. 200). That Law's system undermined the position of existing *financiers* has also been argued by Dessert (1984), Lüthy (1959–61), and Murphy (1997).

While it is difficult to establish whether the fall in share prices in the spring of 1720 was driven by a "cabal" of Law's enemies, a better indication of the fact that Law was under political pressure can be seen from the reversal of policy of March 5 in particular. Dutot (1738) argues that Law was forced into this decision by the Regent, who did not truly wish to see the deflationary measures of February 22 implemented. The Regent had in fact previously made a statement to the General Assembly of the Compagnie des Indes in January 1720 that the share price should remain at 10,000 livres. One obvious explanation for this preference is that if the Compagnie des Indes share price were not artificially supported, this would retard attempts to retire the stock of royal debt.[14] The extensive work by Murphy (1997) shows that Law attached great importance to the objective of retiring the royal debt, and this might help explain the

---

[12] Erlanger (1938: 259) expresses a similar opinion.

[13] Saint-Simon, *Mémoires* (1720: 605–6). Saint-Simon also noted that Law "had the ability to issue bank notes at will in order to garner support" (vol. 7, p. 577). Other evidence for this can be found in vol. 7, pp. 428–29, 503–5.

[14] Faure (1977) places much less faith in this argument.

March 5 decision (though not the inconsistency between the decisions of February 22 and March 5).

Whether the Regent published the March 5 decree in order to satisfy Law's enemies or for other reasons, the more fundamental point seems to be that John Law's system was undermined by its dependence on unconstrained royal power. While the Bank of England when threatened was defended by a Whig coalition in Parliament, Law's bank lacked similar political defenses. After the failure of Law's system in 1720 and the continuing success of the Bank of England, a number of contemporary observers actually drew the conclusion that a national bank was not feasible in an absolute monarchy, because a sovereign would always retain the power to expand the supply of bank notes excessively or to take actions that would similarly undermine a national bank. In a fascinating article, Kaiser (1991) shows that it was commonplace in the early eighteenth century to argue that lenders to absolutist regimes suffered from special risks and that Law's system failed for precisely this reason. Kaiser's frequently cited article has popularized a quotation from Saint-Simon that suggested that creation of a national bank in France was bound to be a futile exercise:

As good as this establishment could be in itself, it could not exist except in a republic or in a monarchy like England, whose finances are governed only by those who provide them and who provide them only as much as it pleases them. (cited in Kaiser 1991)

Opinions such as these would continue to be expressed throughout the eighteenth century and would even be mentioned in the debates on public finance in the French Constituent Assembly of 1789–91.

Interestingly, when first proposing his experiment, Law took the point of view that an absolute monarch would have an *easier* time establishing his credit. Law claimed that "an absolute prince who knows how to govern can extend his credit further and find needed funds at a lower interest rate than a prince who is limited in his authority" (John Law cited in Kaiser 1991: 6). Even after the failure of the system, Law's deputy, Dutot (1738), continued to suggest that failure had more to do with a "cabal" of Law's enemies rather than with the nature of royal power in France. Part of his argument here is based on the fact that England in 1720 suffered a similar episode with the South Sea Bubble (even if he fails to recognize the obvious differences between the two episodes). More generally, he firmly rejects the notion of a link between form of government and credibility:

One will tell me no doubt that with a government such as ours, it is impossible to prevent the King from printing paper money at his whim.... I cannot be persuaded that outrages involving credit are the natural outcome of our form of government. The same thing happened in England, and I would add here to argue against this opinion, that the cabal formed by envy, jealousy, and treason, had a much greater role in the destruction of the System than did despotism. (p. 280)

Placing Law's Experience in a Broader Context

John Law's system was only the most ambitious of a number of efforts by the French monarchy before 1789 to obtain better access to credit through contractual arrangements with royal officials and with provincial assemblies. As discussed in Chapters 3 and 4, the monarchy had for several centuries borrowed indirectly from venal officeholders. It would continue to do so after 1720, though this financing option became less important for royal finances over the course of the eighteenth century. In addition, the monarchy borrowed indirectly from provincial Estates in *pays d'états* such as Burgundy and Brittany. In Chapter 4, I suggested that with the exception of borrowing from the provincial Estates, there is not clear evidence that efforts to borrow through intermediaries were an effective commitment mechanism. As argued by Potter (1997, 2000) when the monarchy borrowed from venal officeholders, this seems to have resulted in a transfer of default risk to the venal officeholders, without necessarily reducing the probability the monarchy would default.

The main factor that plagued indirect borrowing through venal office-holders is the same one that undermined Law's system. Given the concentration of power in the hands of the monarch in ancien régime France, any contract written with a group of venal officeholders could ultimately be unilaterally modified to suit the monarch's needs. Had venal officehold-ers gained power within a representative assembly, they might have been able to resist these attempts. While it was more of an appeals court, the *parlement* of Paris throughout the eighteenth century did frequently serve as the defender of officeholder interests against the Crown, but ultimately the Crown retained the ability to override the *parlement*.

While the monarchy may have found it advantageous to unilaterally modify contracts with venal officeholders, its financial relationship with the provincial assemblies of the *pays d'état* was very different. Potter (1997, 2000) describes how the monarchy granted the Estates of Burgundy the right to collect certain taxes, the *octrois sur la Saône*, and how it was then able to borrow from the Estates, who in turn issued securities backed by the future revenues from the *octrois*. In theory, the monarchy retained the right to revise this contract unilaterally by suspending the right of the Estates to collect the *octrois*, much as it revised contracts with venal officeholders. In practice, this did not occur during the eighteenth century, even if the monarchy did use other devices to pressure the Estates of Burgundy into providing funds.[15] This raises the question of why the monarchy found it costly to reallocate the *octrois sur la Saône*. This trend is all the more surprising in that, by 1789, debts owed to representative assemblies of the *pays d'états* amounted to 16 percent of the monarchy's total debt (Potter and Rosenthal 1997).

Though Potter (1997) contrasts the relationship between the Crown and the Estates of Burgundy with the relationship between the Crown and other corporate bodies in eighteenth-century France, ultimately it remains uncertain why the case of the Estates of Burgundy was different. Potter and Rosenthal (1997) review a number of potential explanations for the non-interference of the monarchy in tax collections of the Estates of Burgundy. One possibility is that there were personal relationships between French monarchs and the holders of Burgundian bonds, but they acknowledge this argument fails because the expansion of royal borrowing from the Estates occurred after the decline in influence of the Condé, the most powerful Burgundian family at the royal court. Future research should continue to explore the reasons why the Estates of Burgundy were able to resist attempts by the French monarchy to unilaterally alter contracts.

4. Public Finance in the French Constituent Assembly (1789–1791)

The Constituent National Assembly (1789–91) and its successor assemblies during the French Revolution represent a clear case where establishing representative institutions failed to improve credibility of debt repayment.[16] Beyond this conclusion, however, there remains the question of why the Constituent Assembly failed in this regard. One potential explanation emphasizes the assembly's refusal to create a national bank similar to the Bank of England.[17] In this section I propose an alternative argument: The lack of credibility in France after 1789 was due above all to a balance of partisan interests that gave the individuals who would have been the proposed national bank's shareholders little influence over policy.

---

[15] See Ligou (1965).

[16] This point has also been emphasized by Hoffman, Postel-Vinay, and Rosenthal (2000).

[17] Sargent and Velde (1995). One could add to this interpretation by arguing that the reluctance of the Constituent Assembly to create constitutional checks and balances (involving a royal veto over legislation and a bicameral legislature) further diminished the likelihood that French representative institutions would allow credible commitment.

Evidence on the distribution of interests and the pattern of coalition formation within the Constituent Assembly strongly suggests that even if a national bank had been created, it might have fared no better than did the Caisse d'Escompte, an earlier bank created by the monarchy in 1776 that was pushed into insolvency by incessant royal demands for credit.[18] Unlike the situation in Great Britain where the Bank of England's shareholders were part of a legislative majority, those in the Constituent Assembly who favored having a national bank were not a part of any durable coalition in France. In making this argument, I show how it is related to broader historical discussions on the French Revolution, which have emphasized the failure of centrist and center-left deputies in the Constituent Assembly to form a liberal majority coalition (Furet and Richet 1963).

My argument in this section proceeds in four steps. After reviewing the debate on public finance, I first show that the private bankers who supported the plan to create a national bank were a very small minority within the Constituent Assembly. Second, I argue that the pattern of preferences over political issues in France at this time limited possibilities for financial interests to form a cross-issue coalition such as had occurred in England between the "monied interest" and liberal aristocrats. This derived from the fact that preferences over all major issues in France were distilled into a single dimension of political conflict between "left" and "right," so there was no cross-cutting cleavage as existed in Great Britain. The marginalization of financial interests also derived from the hostility to Parisian interests on the part of provincial deputies. Third, I argue that the pattern of party organization in the Constituent Assembly further undermined the position of the private bankers. Financial interests were most closely associated with a centrist group, the Society of 1789, but this political club failed to generate as effective an organization as did parliamentary groups on both the right and the left. Finally, the possibility for the private bankers to form part of a majority coalition was also undermined by the resort to political unrest by deputies of both the left and the right in the Constituent Assembly. This is a subject that is considered in greater detail in Chapter 7.

The Debate over Public Finance, 1789–1791

By mid-1789 the Constituent National Assembly had become the primary political decision-making body in France, and it moved quickly

---

[18] See Says (1865) on this point.

in June and July of 1789 to affirm that it would honor all debts contracted by the monarchy.[19] At the same time, the assembly failed to
agree on tax increases that could have provided an alternative solution
to the monarchy's fiscal problems.[20] Facing a situation of near default on
royal debts, on November 14, 1789, the king's finance minister, Jacques
Necker, made a proposal to turn an existing private bank, the Caisse
d'Escompte, into a full-fledged national bank with an increased capital
and the monopoly right to issue bank notes.[21] The short-term motivation for creating this bank was that the Caisse d'Escompte's shareholders
would be advancing a significant sum of money to the monarchy. The more
long-term motivation was clearly to emulate the success of the Bank of
England.

Necker also made another proposal for solving the monarchy's short-
term fiscal problems. A number of deputies had suggested as early as
September 1789 that lands owned by the Catholic Church in France could
be sold and the proceeds used to service existing debts. Opponents of
the measure castigated this as an unjust expropriation of property. Pro-
ponents suggested that since the Church had merely been holding the
lands as a trustee for the French nation, reclaiming the lands was fully
justified.[22]

In the end, the deputies of the Constituent National Assembly decided
against creating a national bank but in favor of the sale of church lands.
They also voted to create a new unit of exchange, the *assignat*, which at
this stage was essentially a security offered by the government to repay
debts. The *assignats* were to be backed by the proceeds from the sale of the
church lands, and decisions about the quantity of *assignats* to be issued
would be made directly by the Constituent Assembly. One plausible reason
that many have offered for this decision is that the failed experience
of John Law's bank left many in France with the impression that any

---

[19] *Archives Parlémentaires*, vol. 8, p. 230. The question of why Louis XVI called the
Estates General (which evolved into the Constituent Assembly) rather than simply
defaulting on his debts has been a major subject of interest among historians. For
reasons of space I do not consider this issue in detail here.

[20] See White (1995) for a more detailed discussion of this debate. White argues that
subsequent evolution of public finances during the Revolution resembled a "war
of attrition" between creditors who demanded full repayment and taxpayers who
refused increased taxes. Hoffman et al. (2000) argue that parliamentary groups held
off solving the monarchy's fiscal problem so as to extract favorable constitutional
concessions from Louis XVI.

[21] *Archives Parlémentaires*, vol. 10, pp. 56–65.

[22] For the different justifications offered, see Vovelle (1972).

scheme involving paper money was foolhardy. If this were the principal motivation, however, one would also expect the assembly to have opposed turning the *assignats* into a paper currency, but this is precisely the course of policy that the Constituent Assembly subsequently embarked upon. There was an initial decision in December 1789 for an issue of *assignats* earning 5 percent interest and worth 400 millions livres tournois.[23] In September 1790, after a lively debate, the Constituent Assembly essentially converted the *assignat* into a new form of paper money by giving it a legal rate, having it earn o percent interest, and by authorizing the printing of a further 800 millions livres in value. Subsequently, a loss of public confidence in the notes combined with further issues to generate hyperinflation in France.[24]

Membership of the Constituent Assembly, 1789–1791

The Constituent Assembly was formed as a result of the disintegration of the Estates General, which had been called by Louis XVI to solve France's financial crisis. In the spring of 1789 the Third Estate deputies voted to declare that they alone were the legitimate representative assembly of France, leaving the deputies from the First and Second Estates (clergy and nobility, respectively) the option of either joining the new assembly or returning home. The vast majority of First and Second Estate deputies accepted this invitation and as a result, in June of 1789 the new Constituent Assembly had 604 deputies who were formerly from the Third Estate, 295 from the clergy, and 278 from the nobility (Tackett 1996: 20).

A generation of historians beginning with Alfred Cobban's well-known work (1964) have argued that contrary to earlier Marxist interpretations of the French Revolution, the deputies of the Third Estate in the Constituent Assembly did not in their majority reflect the rising commercial bourgeoisie suggested by Marxist theory. The Third Estate representation was instead dominated by lawyers and royal officeholders. If it did represent a bourgeoisie, then, the Third Estate was largely a noncommercial bourgeoisie, as bankers and merchants made up only

---

[23] As noted by Brugière (1992), this sale resembled past occasions where the French Crown had forced its creditors into accepting a rescheduling of its debt.

[24] See Sargent and Velde (1995), Velde and Sargent (1990), and White (1995) for a further discussion.

a small fraction of the deputies.[25] In this context, the shareholders of a national bank would have been poorly represented within the assembly.

While accepting that the Third Estate was not composed of a commercial bourgeoisie of the type envisaged by Marx, several recent books have presented evidence that political positions adopted by deputies in the Constituent Assembly depended heavily on social origin. Applewhite (1993) collected detailed information on parliamentary behavior, finding that among the deputies who served in the Constituent Assembly between 1789 and 1791, members of the clergy and the nobility voted overwhelmingly on the right, while representatives of the Third Estate voted overwhelmingly on the left and center. The studies by Timothy Tackett (1989, 1996) have also shown that nobles tended to vote on the right while members of the Third Estate were much more likely to be aligned on the left. When the Constituent Assembly split into a distinct "left" and "right," more than 80 percent of the deputies from the former group were from the Third Estate, while more than 90 percent of "right" deputies were from the nobility and the clergy.

Divisions over Issues

Observers of the Constituent Assembly in 1789 quickly adopted the terms "left" and "right" to describe deputies' political positions, because of the tendency for deputies with common interests to sit together in the same part of the hall. That deputies could be placed into the categories of "left", "right," or "center" was made all the easier by the fact that opinions over the great issues of the day tended to be distilled into a single dimension of political conflict. So deputies who had a "left" opinion with regard to taxation and finance also tended to have a "left" opinion on other issues such as religion and the monarchy. The financial interests who supported the national bank plan of November 1789 were most closely associated

---

[25] For a review of this historical debate, see Doyle (1980) and, more recently, Tackett (1996). Cobban calculated that 85 deputies (13 percent of the Third Estate) from the Estates General of 1789 were either merchants or manufacturers, but only one of these was a banker. Tackett's evidence also supports the idea that there were few bankers in the Estates General. Doyle (1996) calculates that 45 percent of Third Estate deputies in 1789 were venal officeholders. A significant number of Second Estate representatives were also venal officeholders, generally army officers.

with the centrists in the assembly and the centrist group, the Society of 1789. One implication of this tendency for politics to collapse into a single dimension of conflict was that there were fewer possibilities for the formation of a cross-issue coalition as had taken place in Great Britain after 1688. This subsection presents evidence on deputy opinion over four major issues: aristocratic privilege, the future of the monarchy, religious toleration, and public finance.

Public Finance. One significant issue encountered by the deputies of the Constituent Assembly was state finance. More specifically, this involved a debate over the means that could be used to address the French monarchy's budgetary problems. As discussed above, the deputies in 1789 faced a variety of options. These included a default on debt, new taxes, sale of church lands to repay debt, money creation, or attempting to raise finance by establishing a national bank. Though this was quite a wide menu of options, it is possible to describe most of the variation in deputy opinion over state finance in terms of a single dimension that corresponds closely to the underlying "left" versus "right" split in the Constituent Assembly. Far left deputies such as the future Jacobin leader Marat favored solving the fiscal crisis through outright repudiation of debt (Albertone 1990). More moderate elements on the left opposed default and instead favored the solution of selling church lands, combined with issuing the new currency, the *assignats*. Center-left deputies tended to support the initial issue of *assignats*, voted in December 1789, but they opposed subsequent issues of the new currency (Albertone 1990; Tackett 1996). Finally, deputies on the right of the assembly vigorously opposed both the sale of church lands and the creation of the *assignats*. They also opposed default and as a result do not seem to have offered a clear solution to the fiscal crisis.

Deputies also had varying attitudes with regard to the possibility of creating a national bank. The most fervent supporters of this proposal appear to have been Jacques Necker, who was himself a banker, as well as several members of the Constituent Assembly who were shareholders of the Caisse d'Escompte. The shareholders of the Caisse d'Escompte were originally primarily Swiss bankers, but over time the pattern of shareholding became somewhat more diversified (White 1990). Within the Constituent Assembly the shareholders of the Caisse d'Escompte were most closely connected with the center-left group, the Society of 1789, which had a number of private bankers in its ranks. In parliamentary debates, members of the Society of 1789 generally favored the idea of creating a national bank.[26] They also took a firm line opposing excess issues of *assignats*.[27]

Opponents of the proposal to create a national bank had a variety of motivations. For some, there was clearly a tactical incentive to delay approving any project that might solve the monarchy's fiscal problem and thus reduce its future dependence on the Constituent Assembly.[28] For many others, opposition stemmed precisely from the fact that the bank proposal would grant special privileges to a consortium of bankers. These deputies often argued that a national bank would be useful above all to the "bankers and capitalists of Paris."[29] Albertone (1990) suggests that for many of the provincial members of the left, the bank was also to be opposed because it would be a predominantly Parisian institution.[30] It is noteworthy in this regard that the Marquis de Condorcet, who was a member of the Society of 1789, felt it necessary to write a tract arguing that no fundamental economic conflict existed between Paris and the provinces.[31] Finally, in addition to the above criticisms, one Society of 1789 member, the duc de La Rochefoucauld, lodged a different sort of dissenting opinion. He opposed the bank proposal based on the claim that the Bank of England under Walpole had facilitated corruption, patronage, and excess influence for ministers. Fear of repeating the Walpole experience would also be cited by opponents of creating a national bank in the newly independent United States.

[26] See, in particular, the speeches by Dupont de Nemours (*Archives Parlementaires,* vol. 10 pp. 137–45) and Lecouteulx de Canteleu (vol. 10, pp. 392–94). Antoine Lavoisier, a shareholder of the Caisse d'Escompte (and also a royal officer) was another noteworthy parliamentarian associated with the Society of 1789 who supported creating a national bank. See Lavoisier (1789). Other Society of 1789 members who spoke in favor of a bank included Adrien Duquesnoy, who wrote a pamphlet supporting Necker's plan; Monneron, who also produced a pamphlet; and Dufresnoy, another shareholder of the Caisse d'Escompte. See Say (1865). Tackett (1996: 286) suggests that the Society of 1789 was composed to a great extent of aristocrats, bankers, and merchants.
[27] See the contributions in the *Mémoires de la Société de 1789* from September 1790.
[28] As emphasized by Hoffman, Postel-Vinay, and Rosenthal (2000).
[29] Deputy Bouchotte cited in *Archives Parlementaires,* vol. 10, p. 270. See also the speeches by Lavenue (*Archives Parlementaires,* vol. 10, pp. 135–36), the Comte de Custine (vol. 10, p. 145), and the Baron de Cernon (vol. 10, p. 281). See also Say (1865: 10) and Custine (1789).
[30] This opinion is supported by Mirabeau's speech opposing the bank proposal *Archives Parlementaires* (vol. 10, p. 130), and by the journal of one of the Constituent Assembly members, Adrien Duquesnoy.
[31] See his article in the *Journal de la Société de 1789,* July 10, 1790.

Aristocratic Privilege. A second major issue considered by the Constituent Assembly involved aristocratic privilege. On August 4, 1789, by majority vote, the Constituent Assembly annulled all privileges enjoyed by members of the nobility, including tax exemptions, special legal exemptions, and the provision that only those who could demonstrate several generations of noble lineage could hold certain offices of state. As described by both Furet and Richet (1963) and Vovelle (1972), the second half of the eighteenth century had seen a significant movement by the upper nobility to push the Crown into restricting the access of venal officeholders to certain privileges. Subsequent to the August 4 vote, observers of politics in the Constituent Assembly would divide the assembly between those who sat on the "right," known initially as the *aristocrates*, who had opposed the abolition of privileges, and those who sat on the "left." As previously noted, Tackett (1996) shows that on votes such as this, the majority of aristocratic members of the assembly voted against the proposal, as did the clergy. The centrist deputies who would become associated with the Society of 1789 voted with the left to abolish aristocratic privileges. This pattern of preferences made it more difficult to construct a coalition including both members of the Society of 1789 and the *aristocrates*, given that the two groups were not natural allies on the issue of privilege.

The Monarchy. Left and right in the Constituent Assembly were also distinguished by their attitudes toward the future of the French monarchy and toward the future design of any French representative institutions. Initially in 1789 those on the right favored maintaining royal prerogatives, and as a consequence this group was also often referred to as the *monarchiens* or in some cases the *anglomanes* because of their preference for English-style institutions. The *monarchiens* sought to preserve a royal veto, and they also sought to establish a two-chamber Parliament with an upper chamber that would be reserved for the nobility (Harris 1986). If achieved, this program would have satisfied the program laid out by nobles such as Saint-Simon earlier in the eighteenth century, involving limitation of royal power and the reinforcement of the position of the upper nobility. Opposition to the *monarchiens* came both from centrist deputies of the Society of 1789, such as Sieyès, who favored a unicameral Parliament with more limited royal powers, as well as from deputies who were further to the left. As with the question of aristocratic privilege, the distribution of preferences concerning the future of the monarchy also made it less likely that centrist deputies of the Society of 1789 could form a coalition with the aristocrats, who tended to vote on the right on this issue. It also made it more difficult for the centrist deputies to form a coalition with those deputies on the far left who supported abolition of the monarchy.

Religion. A fourth issue that divided the deputies of the Constituent Assembly was religion. The key distinction between France and Great Britain on this issue is that in France by 1789 the nobility was entirely of one religious persuasion (Catholic) and largely in favor of having Catholicism as the state religion. While France in the sixteenth and seventeenth centuries had been torn by violent religious conflict, by the eighteenth century this conflict had been decided in favor of a Catholic France. This was a result of the military campaigns waged by Louis XIII and Louis XIV, culminating in the revocation of the Edict of Nantes in 1685.[32]

The issue of religion resurfaced in French politics in 1789 as a result of the Declaration of the Rights of Man. This text, which was voted by the Assembly, opened the door to the reestablishment of religious toleration, and as a consequence a number of the nobles who sat in the Constituent Assembly offered a counterproposal to make Catholicism the state religion. This proposal did not obtain a majority in the Assembly, and Applewhite (1993) and Tackett (1996) both show that opinions on this issue were highly correlated with the stance that deputies took with regard to royal prerogative. This then provides a further reason why it would have been difficult to form a Whig-style coalition in France. The centrist and center-left deputies who were the main supporters of the national bank proposal also supported religious toleration, but there were relatively few aristocrats who took a liberal view on this issue.

Party Organization

Even if divisions over issues made it difficult for the centrist deputies of the Society of 1789 to form a cross-issue coalition with other groups, one might still expect the centrists to have enjoyed significant influence over legislation, precisely because of their pivotal position within

---

[32] Lüthy (1959–61: 19–20) suggests that in the early seventeenth century, as much as one-third to one-half of the nobility were Protestants. This figure subsequently shrunk dramatically, and the period of repression known as the Dragonnades (1680–85) led to the conversion of the remaining Protestant nobility. A large number of Protestants fled to England and other European countries at this time.

the Constituent Assembly. In practice, the Society of 1789 was influential in the assembly during the early months of 1790. The society failed to construct a durable majority, however, and over time the most prominent feature of legislative organization in the Constituent Assembly was to become the polarization of the assembly into two distinct camps.

Recognizable factions began to form soon after the Constituent Assembly took shape during the summer of 1789. Political organization appears to have occurred initially on the right. Tackett (1989, 1996) studies the way in which deputies who had opposed the measures voted by the Assembly during August 1789 (abolition of aristocratic privileges, Declaration of the Rights of Man) responded by organizing. Early organization among these deputies was facilitated in some cases by the fact that they either knew each other personally or had served together in provincial assemblies.[33] In addition, as has been noted by several authors, among the nobles who sat in the Constituent Assembly, a much higher percentage came from the upper nobility than had been the case in the Estates General of 1614 (Vovelle 1972).

There is some evidence that the conservative nobles and clergy in the Constituent Assembly acted as a cohesive unit. So, for example, the two groups met regularly to plan parliamentary sessions, and their decision to enter into the Constituent Assembly in the first place was apparently taken in concert. Tackett (1989) cites evidence from firsthand accounts of several left-wing deputies who by August 1789 began complaining of an opposing faction of clergy and nobles that was voting as a bloc. With the formation of the group of *monarchiens* during 1789, factional organization was taken to a new level as a central committee was formed that sent out instructions regarding votes to a series of subcommittees (Tackett 1989). The *monarchiens* would continue to be a potent political force in the Constituent Assembly through 1791.

Legislative organization on the French right was followed by counter-organization on the left.[34] During the fall of 1789 a large group of center and left deputies formed the Société des amis de la Constitution, which became better known as the Jacobin Club, from the name of the convent

---

[33] For the clergy, political organization was facilitated by the institutions of the church, and as Applewhite has shown, the clergy was predominantly situated on the right. Tackett (1989) observes that over 40 percent of the nobility who sat in the Constituent Assembly were Paris residents who would have known each other personally from both social and professional occasions.

[34] See the discussion in Maintenant (1984) and Tackett (1989).

where its members regularly held their meetings.[35] Views about the degree of centralization and cohesion within the Jacobin Club differ significantly among historians of the period. Tackett (1989) suggests that the Jacobins actually exceeded the right-wing *monarchiens* in the sophistication of their organization, which involved a central committee that served as guide for the large number of affiliated clubs in the provinces. Gueniffey and Halévi (1992) and Kennedy (1979, 1982, 1984) argue that there was a much lower degree of central control. Gueniffey and Halévi argue, for example, that local Jacobin clubs continued to regularly correspond with non-Jacobin Paris-based groups, such as the Society of 1789. Speaking of a somewhat later period (October 1791 to June 1793), Kennedy (1984: 663) observes:

The Paris society, rather than being a controlling force, at times provided almost no leadership. The provincial clubs which numbered more than 1500 were often in conflict with Paris or with each other. Moreover, the network was in a perpetual state of flux, as clubs went into and out of operation.

Despite the early formation of the Jacobin Club, one prominent feature of the French left during the Constituent Assembly was its lack of cohesion. The Jacobin Club had begun as a broad organization designed to mobilize all those who felt that the gains of the Revolution were jeopardized by the right, but during 1790 and 1791 various splinter groups were formed by individuals who felt that far left deputies were gaining too much influence within the organization. The first of these was the Society of 1789, founded by a group of moderate deputies in early 1790 who sought to consolidate the early gains of the Revolution. Initially, the deputies who joined the group also remained part of the Jacobin Club. The Society of 1789 began life as a dining club, and one that had a heavy representation of wealthy individuals from Paris, including aristocrats, merchants, and bankers. The rest of the Jacobin party, in contrast, had a much higher percentage of provincial representatives, especially small-town lawyers and officeholders.[36]

The Society of 1789 quickly became a rival of the Jacobin Club, and Tackett (1996) suggests that during the early part of 1790 the society succeeded in engineering a legislative majority in favor of a compromise on foreign policy-making powers. It also obtained a moderate outcome

---

[35] For histories of the Jacobin Club, see Kennedy (1979, 1982, 1984), Maintenant (1984), and Tackett (1996).

[36] See the evidence presented in Tackett (1996).

regarding the royal veto. After these initial successes, however, the Society of 1789 quickly lost influence within the Constituent Assembly. Different explanations have been offered for this outcome. Gueniffey and Halévi (1992) suggest that the group suffered from a lack of cohesive organization, as it was essentially an overgrown Parisian dining club.[37] It is one of the ironies of this period that precisely because of the centrist nature of their opinions, one might have expected the deputies of the Society of 1789 to remain a powerful force within the Constituent Assembly, but this centrist position failed to translate into lasting influence. The end result was that the group of deputies most closely linked to those who would have been shareholders of a national bank found itself in the minority.

5. Summary

Though it is true that the French government paid more for its loans than did the British government during the eighteenth century, we should not automatically assume that credibility was absent because France lacked the "English-style" institutions of a strong national parliament and a national bank. In this chapter I have instead argued that high default risk for sovereign debt in France derived ultimately from the balance of partisan forces in French society. As a consequence, had the Estates General been called in 1715, this might have triggered a default rather than a commitment to repay debt. This was the view of several contemporary observers. Likewise, when a national assembly was finally reintroduced in 1789, those who had the most direct interest in seeing that a national bank succeed failed to construct a durable majority coalition within the Constituent Assembly. Finally, I have also suggested that eighteenth-century French history provides an excellent illustration of the futility of absolute monarchs attempting to make commitments through bureaucratic delegation. Apart from the interesting exception of indirect borrowing through the assemblies of the *pays d'état*, French monarchs continued to unilaterally revise contracts that they had entered into with royal officeholders. John Law's attempt to establish a national bank foundered for a similar reason; the monarchy retained the authority to change provisions of policies of Law's bank without heed for its long-term solvency.

[37] See the discussion in Tackett (1996), as well.

7

The Stability of Representative Institutions
in France and Great Britain

1. Introduction

In Chapter 2's theoretical discussion I assumed that political actors respect the basic rules of representative institutions. This has been a useful simplifying assumption to aid development of my arguments. Ultimately, however, the question needs to be asked: What happens if the losers from legislative bargaining are not obliged to respect the rules of the political game? Will the arguments developed in Chapter 2 hold up if one drops the assumption that those in the minority must accept a majority decision no matter how distasteful they find it? Another question involves the role of monarchs in their dealings with representative assemblies. What prevents a ruler from pitting different factions in an assembly against one another and subsequently subverting the legislature's prerogatives? From an empirical point of view there are also important questions to answer. Why did the vast majority of Tories in England after 1715 accept the policies chosen by a Whig majority, rather than resorting to extraconstitutional tactics? Likewise, it would be useful to understand why British monarchs after 1688 did not profit more directly from the conflict between Whigs and Tories to pursue a strategy of divide and rule. Finally, in the case of France one would need to explain why factions within the French Constituent Assembly (1789–91) and the Legislative Assembly (1791–92) repeatedly resorted to extraconstitutional tactics.

This chapter explores the determinants of democratic stability by relaxing the assumption that politicians must accept the policies chosen by a majority. I extend the model from Chapter 2 by allowing the minority player an "outside option" of resorting to extraconstitutional measures to try and overturn majority decisions. Two main conclusions appear from this extension to the model. First, when a society is characterized by multiple political cleavages, party formation can have a moderating effect on policy and lead to credible commitment even when there is a threat of unrest. As a result, the theoretical arguments from Chapter 2 are not dependent on the assumption that the rules of the democratic game are fully respected. Second, I conclude that the mere risk of the minority exercising an outside option will not always be sufficient to prompt the majority to moderate its policies. I then argue that even if the threat of an outside option being used does not prompt the majority to compromise, when there are multiple political cleavages in society, the process of forming a durable legislative majority may nonetheless lead simultaneously to moderate policy choices and to a reduced likelihood of extraconstitutional action. Finally, I also consider alternative explanations of democratic stability offered by Olson (1993, 2000) and by Weingast (1997a). Weingast introduces a new dimension to the issue by considering how a legislature divided into different factions might succumb to a monarch who pursues a strategy of divide and rule.

The empirical sections of this chapter consider to what extent the observable implications of my model, as well as the alternative hypotheses offered by Weingast (1997a) and Olson (1993) are supported by historical evidence from representative assemblies in Great Britain after 1688 and in France after 1789.

For Great Britain the key question is why a country that had suffered from a lengthy period of political instability before 1688 suddenly underwent a transition to stable representative government with a limited monarchy. One key reason involved the fact that in Great Britain, preferences on noneconomic issues cross-cut the economic division between the landed interest and the "monied interest." Historical evidence suggests that the cross-cutting character of political cleavages provided the room for politicians such as Robert Walpole to propose moderate policies that had the simultaneous effect of cementing the Whig coalition and of minimizing incentives for radical Tories to revolt. I also argue that the development of cohesive political parties may explain why British monarchs after 1688 found it difficult to pursue a strategy of divide and rule with respect to parliamentary groups.

For France the key empirical question considered in this chapter is why a stable form of representative government did not emerge in 1789. While there are many potential explanations here, I argue that instability of representative institutions may have been linked to the relatively zero-sum nature of political conflict within the Constituent Assembly, combined with a polarization of preferences between "left" and "right." French society after 1789 faced a number of political issues similar to those faced in the United Kingdom, but the divisions over these issues did not tend to cross-cut each other. Furthermore, political preferences across this single dimension were also quite polarized between those who supported and those who opposed revolutionary change. Within this context there was less likelihood that the process of political bargaining would result in policies sufficiently moderate that all legislative groups would respect majority decisions.

2. Modeling the Sources of Democratic Stability

Existing formal models of democratic stability frequently focus on the idea that the shadow of the future gives groups an incentive to refrain from extraconstitutional action. A current minority may respect democratic decisions if it has a reasonable expectation of becoming the majority party at some point in the future. Likewise, a current majority may have an incentive to moderate its policies if it faces a risk of becoming the minority party after the next election.[1] While these arguments are convincing, it also makes sense to ask what factors may increase respect for democratic outcomes independent of the shadow of the future. This is relevant because in many democratic contexts, a single party holds power for a considerable length of time. This was certainly true of the Whigs in Great Britain after 1715.

Political Bargaining under Threat of Unrest

One way to incorporate the possibility of extraconstitutional action within a legislative bargaining game is to allow the minority to exercise

---

[1] Przeworski (1991) presents a basic model where the decision to rebel is in part a function of expected future electoral gains. Dixit, Grossman, and Gul (2000) develop a model where, in a two-party system, the repeated character of elections can lead to an equilibrium where electoral winners implement compromise policies. In a slightly different setup, Weingast (1997a) considers how the shadow of the future can help heterogeneous social interests to cooperate in order to resist encroachments on their basic rights by a sovereign. Finally, Miller (1984) also relies on future expected electoral gains in order to explain democratic stability. He argues that in contexts where policies are likely to be unstable (given standard social choice assumptions), then those unsatisfied with policy today will know that the current policy is unlikely to remain in place for long.

an "outside option" if it is particularly dissatisfied with the set of policies approved by the majority. Powell (1996, 1999) has used this idea in a two-player alternating-offers bargaining game to consider how the threat of a solution imposed by force is likely to alter bargaining outcomes in international relations.[2] In a domestic political setting, Ellman and Wantchekon (2000) have considered how the threat of unrest may influence electoral outcomes. In a legislative bargaining context, an outside option for the minority might represent a number of different actions, such as the threat of inciting popular violence to intimidate legislators or, in extreme cases, the threat of full-scale rebellion.

In the modified legislative bargaining game presented in this chapter, subsequent to any majority decision, the player who is not part of the majority may be able to exercise an outside option. This outside option represents a set of policies $(\theta_q, \tau_q, \rho_q)$ for the tax rate on land, the tax rate on capital, and the level of religious toleration. The minority player and the other players each derive utility from this set of policies according to the utility functions presented in Chapter 2. This set of policies could be interpreted as a certain outcome or, more realistically, as the expected result of an outside option for which the result was subject to uncertainty. All players also pay a cost c if the outside option is exercised. This cost can be seen as representing the use of resources for extraconstitutional action (as well as to oppose it). I assume that information about the availability of an outside option is revealed only subsequent to a majority decision being taken. This simplifies the analytics of the game by ruling out the possibility that a player might attempt to convey information about the value of his or her outside option by posturing and making more extreme proposals during the bargaining stage. The game proceeds in the following sequence.

1. Players receive their exogenous endowments e and z, and they choose whether to consume their capital endowment or to save it.
2. One of the three players is chosen at random to propose a set of policies for taxation and religious toleration, which is then voted on, without possibility for amendment, under simple majority rule. If two players

---

[2] Esteban (2001) has proposed a generalization of this approach. Humphreys (2001) has also considered political conflict in environments where actors may have options other than accepting a majority decision.

vote in favor of the proposal, the policy is implemented. If there is no agreement, a new player is randomly selected to propose and the stage is repeated.

3. Nature determines whether the minority player has an outside option. With probability p the minority player has an outside option $(\theta_q - \tau_{q'}, \rho_q)$. With probability $1 - p$ the minority does not have access to an outside option.

4. The minority chooses whether to exercise its outside option (if it has one), and the game ends.

In this game the majority does not observe in stage 2 whether the minority has an outside option, but I assume that it does observe p, which represents the likelihood that the minority will have an outside option. For simplicity I also assume that the majority knows the expected outcome from a potential outside option $(\theta_q - \tau_{q'}, \rho_q)$. This information structure makes it possible for the outside option to be exercised in equilibrium. This is a common result in game-theoretic models where certain events such as strikes, wars, or domestic unrest will occur only if there is imperfect information. As before, a player who is recognized in this game will need to take into account the expected utility that the player to whom they are making a proposal could obtain from continuing the game (their continuation value). In addition, however, a proposer will also need to consider whether it is optimal to propose a set of policies that satisfies the minority's reservation payoff (the minimum payoff necessary to avoid it exercising its outside option).

Example 1: One-Dimensional Bargaining. In the one-dimensional case, as previously, players care only about the taxation dimension of policy, and there is a landowning majority. If recognized, players B and C (the landowners) face a choice between proposing $\theta = 1, \tau = 0$ to each other, or alternatively making a "compromise" proposal $\theta - \tau = (\theta_q - \tau_q) + c$ that will satisfy player A's reservation payoff. The existence of the positive cost c, which is borne by all players if the outside option is exercised, allows B or C to satisfy player A's reservation constraint by applying a capital tax rate that is higher than that which A would obtain from exercising an outside option. Expected utility for B and C from not compromising would be $p(2 + (\theta_q - \tau_q) - c) + (1 - p)(3)$. Expected utility for B and C from the "compromise" proposal that provides player A her reservation payoff would be $2 + (\theta_q - \tau_q) + c$. As a consequence, B and C will not compromise and will instead propose $\theta - \tau = 1$ as long as the following inequality is satisfied:[3]

$$p < \frac{(\theta_q - \tau_q) + c - 1}{(\theta_q - \tau_q) - c - 1} \qquad (7.1)$$

When the inequality in Equation 7.1 is satisfied, then players B and C will propose $\theta = 1, \tau = 0$ in equilibrium, and player A will propose a tax rate that satisfies either B's or C's continuation constraint. The implication for democratic stability is that if player A does in fact have an outside option, then he or she will always choose to use it. As long as p is sufficiently low, neither player B nor player C has an incentive to compromise and satisfy player A's reservation constraint. In other words, they find it worthwhile to risk the outside option being used.

Example 2: Two-Dimensional Bargaining. One of the interesting features of bargaining across two dimensions is that because it forces players to compromise in order to satisfy the continuation constraints of other players, it may also simultaneously increase the likelihood that they provide the minority player with at least his or her reservation payoff. In Example 2, if player C offers to player B, as he or she is likely to do in equilibrium, then he or she will need to compromise on religious toleration in order to meet player B's continuation constraint. Given that player A shares the same preference with regard to religious toleration as player B, player C's "compromise" offer may also provide player A with sufficient utility that he or she will not exercise an outside option. Due to the symmetry of the preferences in Example 2, the same conclusion can be drawn for an offer by player A to player B. The end result of this would be that the minority will be less likely to resort to an outside option when political conflict occurs over two dimensions of policy.

It is possible, given the preference distribution in Example 2, to have an equilibrium with the same pattern of offers as in the previous sections and in addition where the outside option is never used in equilibrium.[4] For

---

[3] I do not consider player A's equilibrium offer here, because for most plausible parameter values the continuation values for players B and C actually exceed their reservation payoff. Any offer from A that satisfies the continuation constraint of B or C will not result in an outside option being used.

[4] The pattern of offers is A→B, C→B, and B is indifferent between offering to A or to C. This is similar to the result obtained in two-person alternating-offer bargaining games where the outside option is irrelevant if its value is sufficiently small. See Osborne and Rubinstein (1990). This equilibrium holds as long as the expected value of the outside option for either A or C (depending on who is in the minority)

this equilibrium to exist, the inequality in Equation 7.2 must be satisfied. This presents the conditions under which an offer by player A that meets player B's continuation constraint will also satisfy player C's reservation constraint.[5] The left-hand side of the inequality represents the utility that player C would obtain from player A's equilibrium proposal to player B, while the right-hand side represents the utility that player C would derive from using an outside option. This inequality is more likely to be satisfied when the cost of exercising the outside option, c, is high, and it is less likely to be satisfied when the expected outcome of the outside option is favorable for player C.

$$1 + \frac{9 - 10\delta}{2\delta - 3} > 1 + (\theta_q - \tau_q) - \rho_q - c \qquad (7.2)$$

The above inequality is satisfied for many plausible ranges of parameters for which the inequality in Equation 7.1 is also satisfied. For these combinations of parameters this implies that if the minority has an outside option, it will not use it in equilibrium in the two-dimensional bargaining case, but it will resort to the outside option in the one-dimensional bargaining case. Finally, this same effect would also apply if this game were extended to allow for political parties. Given that a party of A and B will choose a set of policies $\rho_{ab} = 1, 1 \geq (\theta - \tau)_{ab} > (\theta - \tau)_a$, then as long as player A's equilibrium offer in the noncooperative game satisfies the reservation constraint of player C, then the policy adopted by a party of A and B would also satisfy this constraint. In fact, it would satisfy the constraint for a greater range of possible realizations for the cost of the outside option, and for a greater range of possible policies that result from exercising the outside option. In sum, forming a party might further reduce the likelihood that the outside option will be used in equilibrium.

To summarize, my basic argument about party government and credible commitment developed in Chapter 2 can hold even in a situation where players have an option of resorting to extraconstitutional action. In addition, I have argued that the same conditions that increase credibility by leading to more moderate economic policies may also reduce the risk that a legislative minority will resort to extraconstitutional action. When there are multiple cleavages in society, compromises necessary to

---

is less than 2. Otherwise, it is possible that a player might prefer not to be in the majority. This seems an implausible result, however.

[5] Because of the symmetry of the preferences in Example 2, when this inequality is satisfied an analogous inequality regarding player C's offer will also be satisfied.

satisfy members of one's own majority may also push policies closer to the minority's preferred set of policies.

Further Hypotheses

There are a number of additional arguments that have been made about the sources of democratic stability. Here I present two explanations that have been directly applied to the case of Great Britain after 1688.

Mancur Olson (1993, 2000) suggested that democracy results from "accidents of history that leave a balance of power or stalemate – a dispersion of force and resources that makes it impossible for any one leader or group to overpower all of the others."[6] Olson sees English history after 1688 as providing strong confirmation for his hypothesis, based on the claim that after 1688 "[n]one of the victorious leaders, groups, or tendencies was then strong enough to impose its will upon all of the others or to create a new autocracy." The big problem with this interpretation, as I argue below, is that one group *did* eventually establish full control in England. After 1715 the Whigs had command of all government institutions, and they retained this control for a considerable period of time.

Weingast (1997a) adds an additional dimension to the problem of democratic stability. He presents a simple model with a sovereign and two distinct groups of citizens, showing how democratic stability can be undermined if the sovereign pursues a strategy of playing different groups of citizens off against one another. For Weingast, democratic stability depends on the two groups successfully committing to a strategy of opposing any attempts to tread upon the basic rights of any citizens. He argues that one real-world manifestation of such a strategy is an "elite pact," a written commitment between different groups to respect constitutional ground rules. The Revolution Settlement of 1690 in England might be seen as just such an accord between leaders of the Whigs and the Tories, aimed at avoiding the infringements on basic rights suffered under James II. My empirical discussion of democratic stability in England and France considers whether historical evidence supports this interpretation.

---

[6] In the absence of such conditions, he hints that democracy may nonetheless be possible if multiple groups within a country are able to commit to a power-sharing agreement.

3. Explaining British Stability after 1688

After the flight of James II, Britain in 1688 seemed poised for a renewed period of political strife, much like that which had occurred earlier in the seventeenth century. Plumb (1967: 1) argues that "by 1688 conspiracy and rebellion, treason and plot, were a part of the history and experience of at least three generations of Englishmen." The Glorious Revolution did in fact mark the beginning of a new period where opposing factions quarreled, and where parliamentary leaders periodically resorted to measures of dubious legality. There was also significant uncertainty about whether the house of Hanover would control the throne after the death of Queen Anne. What is so surprising given this past history of instability is that after 1715, neither the Whig nor the Tory party leaders opted for armed rebellion, as had been the case in the past.[7] After 1715, democratic stability was secured in Great Britain, as the threat of large-scale rebellion gradually receded. This occurred in a political context where the Whigs held a durable and dominant majority in both the House of Commons and the House of Lords. The Tories, in contrast, were consigned to playing the role of a vocal but powerless minority.

In what follows I review the different factors that historians have seen as leading to the growth of democratic stability in Great Britain. These factors are broadly consistent with the observable implications of my formal model, though they clearly also involve phenomena that my simple bargaining model cannot capture.

Evidence from Historical Debates

Modern discussions of democratic stability in eighteenth-century England often begin by referring to J. H. Plumb's classic study, *The Growth of Political Stability in England: 1675–1725*. Plumb and subsequent authors have highlighted a number of different explanations for the swift movement from instability to stability. These include the arrival of a Whig government, policy compromise, restrictions on civil liberties, and restrictions on political competition. I consider each in turn.

All historical accounts of democratic stability in eighteenth-century England recognize that for much of this period, Great Britain was

---

[7] The main exception here would be Bolingbroke, who left Britain after the Tory defeat of 1715 and took up service with the Pretender in France. There was a Jacobite uprising in 1715 and a more significant one in 1745.

effectively under a regime of one-party rule. Plumb (1967) goes as far as suggesting that stability was not actually achieved until one-party rule was established in 1715. Other authors, such as Holmes (1993), argue that the foundations of stability were actually laid as early as the 1690s. In either case, the reality of one-party rule after 1715 argues against the interpretation by Olson (1993) that democracy emerges when opposing social groups are locked in a stalemate. If so, one would have expected democratic stability to erode in Great Britain after 1715. The length of one-party rule under the Whigs after 1715 raises the question of why the vast majority of Tories were willing to remain in the parliamentary minority rather than resorting to rebellion.

A second factor cited by historians involves political compromise. As described in Chapter 6, after 1722 the Whig leader Robert Walpole pursued compromise policies in order to hold his coalition together, and this had an externality of dissuading all but the most extreme Tories from resorting to rebellion. This explanation falls directly in line with the predictions of the theoretical model developed above. Walpole shifted the burden of taxation by keeping the land tax rate relatively low, and as compensation he significantly increased excise taxes. Speck (1977) emphasizes that this was intended to placate landowning interests within the Whig party.[8] The danger always existed for a Whig government that landowning Whigs might leave the party to form a coalition with the Tories. An additional effect of Walpole's policy of moderate land taxation may have been to dissuade a number of Tories from supporting the Jacobite cause. Though Tories would have still been opposed to most of Walpole's policies, the reduction in land taxation may have been sufficient to deter them from rebelling.

If a number of historians such as Plumb (1967) and Speck (1977) have emphasized that there was a gradual "fusion" of the landowning elite and the monied elite in Great Britain after 1715, this fusion initially reflected this acceptance of Walpole's compromise policies rather than a commonality of interest between landowners and the monied interest. As previously argued, Dickson (1967) has shown that investors in government bonds and other stocks remained almost exclusively London-based until at least 1750. As a result, it may be more accurate to speak of a "quiet symbiosis" between a landed interest and a monied interest that remained quite separate.[9]

---

[8] Schofield (2001a, b) has also focused on the compromise nature of Walpole's policies.
[9] This is the term applied by Stone (1980).

Walpole's strategy of pursuing compromise policies also applied to religion and to foreign policy. For these issues the motivation for compromise seems to have had less to do with maintaining internal party cohesion than with avoiding taking actions that might mobilize the Tories and lead to future electoral losses. Plumb (1967) suggests that Walpole had been strongly influenced by the experience of the Sacheverell trial of 1710, where an attempt by the Whig leadership to prosecute an outspoken Anglican clergyman backfired by contributing to the Tory landslide of 1710. Throughout his period as prime minister, Walpole resisted attempts by the dissenters to increase dramatically the degree of religious toleration in the United Kingdom. He agreed to repealing the Occasional Conformity Act and the Schism Act, two laws passed by the Tories, but he refused to repeal more longstanding requirements for officeholders to demonstrate formal allegiance to the Church of England (Harris 1993). This would have involved moving away from the status quo in which dissent was only tacitly allowed. In the area of foreign policy, Walpole steered even closer to a policy that satisfied the Tories, refusing to become engaged in land wars on the European continent.

In addition to political compromise, a third factor that historians often associate with the emergence of political stability in England involved increased restrictions on political protest. This idea is consistent with the theoretical model presented above, to the extent that such restrictions would increase the cost of exercising an outside option. This of course begs the question of why some governments might pursue this strategy while others would not. As argued in Chapter 5, despite their early emphasis on individual rights, in the wake of their election triumph of 1715, the Whig majority in Parliament took several steps that significantly restricted civil liberties. One move involved temporarily suspending habeas corpus. In addition, the Riot Act of 1715 made it a potentially capital offense for a group of twelve or more individuals to fail to disperse within one hour of being read the Riot Act by a magistrate. Both of these measures were designed to minimize possibilities for anti-Whig popular protest in London, in particular.[10] This serves as an important reminder that the factors that lead to the stability of representative political institutions can involve unreasonable restrictions on basic democratic freedoms. It also leaves open the question of why the Whigs chose to restrict possibilities for protest in this way in 1715, while the sizable Tory majority in power between 1710 and 1715 made no similar attempt.

[10] See Kenyon (1977) and Lease (1950).

A fourth and final factor that may have affected political stability in Great Britain was the Septennial Act of 1716. This was a law passed by a Whig majority that extended the maximum period between parliamentary elections from three years to seven years. While historians have seen the Septennial Act as being crucial to the creation of a stable political order under the Whigs, they do not generally claim that it either increased the likelihood of rebellion or decreased it. The Septennial Act was supported by those who claimed that "a restless and Popish Faction are designing and endeavoring to renew the Rebellion within this Kingdom." By all accounts, however, the true motivation was to preserve a sizable Whig majority in the Commons.[11]

Relations between Crown and Parliament

Aside from asking why representatives from the minority do not resort to violence, another important question for the stability of democratic institutions involves the possibility that a monarch might preserve his or her prerogatives by pitting different legislative factions against each other. This would be a potential problem to the extent that a monarch enjoys significant agenda-setting power within a legislature. While I have not formalized this claim, it is possible to argue that formation of a cohesive majority party will make it more difficult for a monarch to impose his or her preferences on society. To the extent that a monarch could impose his or her preferences by proposing a preferred policy to a divided legislature, then a cohesive majority party would be better able to resist this sort of maneuver. Referring specifically to the example of England after 1688, Schattschneider suggested "that William III and the friends of the old British monarchy did not relish party government is understandable because the parties stripped the monarchy of power and importance" (1942: 3–4).

Schattschneider's observation is firmly supported by historical opinion regarding parties and the monarchy after 1688. As argued in Chapter 6, while William III and Queen Anne were able to rely on the consistent

---

[11] There was much debate whether the Septennial Act violated the Revolution Settlement. The primary text for the Revolution Settlement, the Bill of Rights of 1689, stated that Parliaments should be "held frequently." Whether this requirement was satisfied by having frequent sessions of the same Parliament or whether it necessitated frequent changes of Parliament was ambiguous. This ambiguity was later addressed by the Triennial Act of 1694, which the Septennial Act reversed. On this point, see the discussion in Kemp (1968: 39–50), as well as in Lease (1950).

support of a number of placeholders in Parliament, they could obtain a Commons majority only if they also had the support of either Whig or Tory backbenchers. Initially, William III and Anne both attempted to govern with ministers from both the Whig and the Tory ranks, but in order to obtain Commons support for their bills, each monarch was eventually prompted into governing with ministers drawn principally from either the Tory or the Whig ranks, but not both at the same time. In 1715 it was even more unthinkable for George I to have a mixed government. After all, his very succession to the throne had been dependent on Whig support for the Hanoverian cause.[12]

Weingast (1997a) provides an alternative interpretation of the relationship between monarch and Parliament after 1688, placing his emphasis on the Revolution Settlement as a mechanism through which both Whig and Tory could agree to basic constitutional principles. For Weingast the Revolution Settlement was a compact to resist specific future transgressions by the monarchy. The Bill of Rights did certainly break important constitutional ground by making it illegal for the monarchy to pass laws, levy taxes, or maintain a standing army without consent of Parliament. However, it may be inaccurate to suggest that through the Revolution Settlement both Whig and Tory leaders committed themselves to respect basic constitutional principles. During the period of partisan conflict between 1690 and 1715, it was common for those who found themselves in the opposition to be thrown in prison on dubious legal grounds. Robert Walpole himself spent time in prison under a Tory government before 1715. Another example of this type of behavior occurred when a Tory government in 1701 put several Whig Lords on trial on trumped-up charges.[13]

Summary

Observations by historians about the origins of democratic stability in eighteenth-century England are consistent with the model presented earlier in this chapter. Whig dominance after 1715 did not augur instability as long as Whig majorities avoided voting for extreme policies that would have led to large-scale rebellion. In practice, Robert Walpole during his period in power appears to have avoided extreme policies with regard to land taxation in order to placate part of his own majority. This had a

---

[12] Stone (1980) notes that in 1715, there were over fifty people with a more direct claim to the throne than George I. As a result, the Hanoverian succession increased the dependency of the Crown on parliamentary party support.

[13] See Horwitz (1977) and Plumb (1956).

simultaneous effect of deterring Tories from opting for open revolt. This pattern of behavior derived directly from the cross-cutting character of political cleavages in Great Britain. In addition, Walpole pursued a moderate course with regard to religious toleration so as to avoid mobilizing the Tories. Finally, the Whigs also resorted to less democratic measures by restricting popular protest. This raised the cost of resorting to violence.

4. Explaining Instability in France, 1789–1792

While there were numerous proposals during the eighteenth century to reinvigorate French national representative institutions, it was not until 1789 that the monarchy finally agreed to call the Estates General. In Chapter 6, I argued that rather than representing a rising commercial bourgeoisie as Marxist interpretations of the French Revolution have suggested, the Constituent Assembly of 1789–1791 was split into two polarized camps, with the majority of nobles and clergy on the right and most Third Estate deputies from the professions being situated on the left. Events in France between 1789 and 1792 raise important questions about the foundations of democratic stability. In particular, why did the creation of the Constituent Assembly not result in the sort of stable political order observed in England after 1688? Furet and Richet (1963) suggest that during 1790 and 1791 a number of deputies within the Constituent Assembly sought to consolidate what they saw as the gains of a revolution similar to that which had been achieved in England a hundred years before.

Instead of a consolidation, however, politics became increasingly unstable in France as both left- and right-wing deputies resorted to extraconstitutional action. An increasingly large number of right-wing members withdrew from the assembly altogether. The biggest single exodus occurred in the summer of 1791, when 293 deputies from the right quit the Constituent Assembly in order to protest against a majority vote to suspend the powers of the king. This vote had itself been prompted by the King's attempt to flee France. Upon leaving the Assembly the rightist deputies called openly for foreign intervention to put a halt to the revolution. This was a clear resort to an "outside option." On the left of the assembly, leaders from the Jacobin party in particular resorted increasingly to an outside option by allying themselves with popular protestors in Paris, the *sans-culottes*, in order to ensure their control over affairs.

The question of why the deputies of the Constituent Assembly and Legislative Assembly did not succeed in creating a stable democratic order in France is obviously a very large one, which has preoccupied historians for over two centuries. As with my consideration of England after 1688, I do not pretend here to offer more than a very partial explanation for events in France. I instead limit my effort to examining different historical accounts of legislative politics in France between 1789 to 1792, and I ask whether the potential explanations for the absence of democratic stability are consistent with the formal model presented earlier.

Political Cleavages and Instability

There are three key characteristics of politics in France after 1789 that seem clearly linked to the instability of representative institutions, and each of these is consistent with the formal model developed above. These include the unidimensional character of political conflict combined with a polarization of preferences, the relative weakness of political parties, and the emergence of popular violence that lowered the cost for legislators of resorting to an outside option. At least one crucial factor not captured by the formal model was also present, however. This involves the behavior of Louis XVI, whose actions played a major role in polarizing the political debate during 1791 and 1792.

As argued in Chapter 6, one clear difference between events in England after 1688 and in France after 1789 is that in France the political debate tended to be much more unidimensional. In England the division between landed and monied interest cross-cut other cleavages such as religious opinion. Under these conditions intraparty bargaining within the Whig party pushed toward more "moderate" policies that helped ensure democratic stability. In France divisions over public finance tended to coincide with cleavages over other issues. So, for example, opinions in the debate on whether ecclesiastical lands should be sold tended to coincide with opinions on broader questions of privilege in French society, and with opinions on issues such as religious toleration. Under these conditions there were far fewer opportunities for a French political entrepreneur, in the manner of Robert Walpole, to construct a majority coalition through compromise policies. One would not have expected the unidimensional character of politics to lead to instability in France were it not for the fact that preferences of deputies across this single left-right dimension were also highly polarized. The debates in the Constituent Assembly were polarized between a sizable right-wing group, composed for the most part of members of the clergy and nobility, and a sizable left-wing group, dominated for a good part of the period 1789–92 by the Jacobin Club.

A second potential reason for instability during the Constituent Assembly period may have involved the weakness of party organizations. Soon after its foundation, the Jacobin Club was subject to a split. The centrist Society of 1789 aimed to form a coalition that would consolidate the gains of the Revolution while also establishing a stable constitutional form of government. Ultimately, however, as has been discussed in Chapter 6, the Society of 1789 failed to form a stable majority coalition. A second split occurred in the Jacobin ranks in 1791.[14] The Feuillants had the explicit goal of creating a moderate center party that would exclude both the Jacobins and the extreme right. The Feuillant club initially appeared to have a considerably larger number of deputies than the Jacobins. In the Legislative Assembly that first sat in October 1791, some 260 deputies initially declared themselves as Feuillants, 136 declared themselves as Jacobins, and 300 refused to choose between the two factions (Furet and Richet 1963: 144–45). However, the initial advantage held by the Feuillants was steadily undermined as Jacobin leaders made efforts to win back members.

A further reason for the Feuillants' failure was that they were undermined by popular violence. The ease with which deputies from the Constituent Assembly were able to use popular protest to influence legislative outcomes was a third principal factor that one can see as explaining instability during this period. It is also consistent with the theoretical model. In August of 1792 an insurrection took place that replaced the city government in Paris, and under pressure from rioters, the Legislative Assembly voted to essentially remove Louis XVI from power and to replace him with an executive council. Furet and Richet (1963) suggest that this marked the end of Feuillants' chances of holding power. Parisian popular violence had in fact undermined the stability of representative institutions in France as early as 1789. With the transfer of the Constituent Assembly from Versailles to Paris in the fall of 1789, a large number of right-wing deputies found themselves on occasion being physically intimidated by Parisian demonstrators (Harris 1986). While initially left-wing deputies did not deliberately attempt to profit from these protests, Tackett (1996) reports that over time members of the Jacobin Club began informing popular groups of the locations at which right-wing deputies were meeting so that their preparations for parliamentary sessions might be disrupted. Increasingly, popular protests would be used strategically by the Jacobin

---

[14] Furet and Richet (1963) provide a concise history of the Feuillant Club and its relationship with the Jacobins.

deputies in order to attempt to marginalize their opponents. Subsequently, Jacobin leaders including Marat and Robespierre would form an alliance with the *sans-culottes* in order to increase their grip on affairs.

Relations between Monarch and Legislature

In addition to the features highlighted above, failure to establish a stable political order in France after 1789 also owed a great deal to the actions taken by Louis XVI. One of the curiosities of French legislative politics between 1789 and 1792 was that Louis XVI was unable to profit from the divisions between different parliamentary factions in order to impose a revolutionary settlement to his liking. Given the lack of a cohesive majority party and the fact that ministers of the Crown retained significant agenda-setting power during this period, one might have expected Louis XVI to be able successfully to pursue a strategy of divide and rule. During the early days of the Constituent Assembly in 1789, Louis XVI had been unwilling to exploit the fact that he had potential defenders in the assembly. This was particularly true of the *monarchiens* on the moderate right who sought to institute a constitutional monarchy, perhaps modeled on the English system. By the summer of 1791, the Feuillants similarly favored consolidating the gains of the Revolution within the framework of a constitutional monarchy. With hindsight, this might have provided an opportunity for Louis XVI to retain a significant degree of authority. In practice, any hope of pursuing such a strategy was scuttled by Louis XVI's attempted flight to France's eastern border. It remains something of a curiosity, then, that Louis XVI did not make more of an attempt to profit from the divisions in the Constituent Assembly and its successor, the Legislative Assembly, in order to preserve some of his prerogatives.

5. Summary

This chapter has attempted to demonstrate two things. First, the argument that representative institutions can help promote credible commitment does not necessarily depend on the assumption that political actors must respect any decision made by a legislative assembly. Even in a context where groups have the option of resorting to revolt, credibility for policies can emerge as a byproduct of party formation in a plural society. Thus, the model developed in Chapter 2 is relevant even in contexts such as early eighteenth-century England or eighteenth-century France, where the possibility of revolt was real. The second principal objective of this chapter has been to demonstrate that democratic stability does not necessarily depend on the willingness of all relevant political groups to accept legislative policy decisions. In an environment where revolt is feasible and where individuals do not face higher moral imperatives not to rebel, the process of forming a majority may nonetheless result in a policy outcome sufficiently moderate that in equilibrium no actors rebel. My brief historical discussion has provided evidence to support this basic argument. In England compromise policies designed to hold the Whig coalition together may have also have had the effect of keeping a number of Tories from going into open rebellion after 1715. In France, in contrast, political instability seems to have been linked to the absence of a stable majority based on moderate policies.

8

Conclusion

Credibility of economic policies depends on both the partisan preferences of political actors and on the institutional context within which policy decisions are made. In this study I have attempted to explore the link between one type of institution – representative government – and commitment to repay public debt. I have asked whether and when governments with representative assemblies might find it easier to obtain access to credit at low rates of interest. A look at the development of sovereign borrowing in Europe suggests that in examples as diverse as the medieval Italian city states, the Netherlands in the sixteenth century, and Great Britain after 1688, increased ability to borrow was linked to the development of representative political institutions.

I have considered three features of representative government that may improve policy credibility. For one, credibility may depend on the creation of constitutional checks and balances. These could include a separation of powers between legislature and executive, a bicameral legislature, or, in the language of formal political science, any constitutional provision that increases the number of veto points in a political system. I have argued that checks and balances may improve credibility, but they are neither a necessary nor a sufficient condition for this to occur. A second feature of representative government that may improve credibility involves party formation in a plural society – a society in which there are multiple political cleavages. To the extent this view is accurate, credibility of debt repayment will depend on the emergence of a cohesive majority party that includes those social groups that have an immediate interest in avoiding default. Finally, I have argued that bureaucratic delegation is a feature of representative government that can improve credibility only if interests opposed to default already have political influence in a forum such as a legislative assembly.

In the remainder of this concluding chapter I first review my empirical findings regarding public debt and political representation in Great Britain and France. I then consider the implications of these findings for research on representative democracy and economic performance in other contexts. Finally, I discuss implications for the study of institutions more generally.

1. Review of Empirical Findings

My investigation of debt politics in Great Britain and France suggests that representative institutions can help reduce the risk of default on debt but that the link between representative government and credible commitment is more complex than has been previously emphasized.

In Great Britain, the rehabilitation of Parliament's role in policy making in 1688 did indeed give the Crown greater access to credit at lower rates of interest. The reason this change took place, however, had less to do with a new constitution than with the formation of a new political party, the Whigs, through which government creditors combined with other interests. When the Whigs held power, default premia on British government debt dropped significantly, while whenever the Tories held power, fears of a default resurfaced. Within this context the creation of the Bank of England also helped improve credibility, but it did so only so long as there was a Whig coalition that was ready to defend the bank against political attack.

For the case of France, I have argued that the adoption of British-style institutions would not, in all likelihood, have allowed the monarchy to commit to repaying its debts. In the early eighteenth century when key royal advisors recommended calling the Estates General, they did so precisely because they thought the Estates would choose to default, not because they hoped to emulate the British example. The motivation for calling the Estates would in fact have been to reduce the political influence of government creditors in France. Likewise, when the Constituent National Assembly assumed responsibility for public finance in France in 1789, it is evident that the type of financial interests who had been members of the Whig coalition in the United Kingdom did not participate in a durable majority coalition in the Constituent Assembly. Finally, I considered the repeated attempts by French monarchs throughout the eighteenth century to obtain access to credit by indirect borrowing through royal officials or by establishing a public bank. These bureaucratic innovations did not provide a means for credible commitment, given that the king's creditors lacked political influence within a representative assembly.

2. Representative Democracy and Economic Performance

Studying the role of institutions in European economic development is a subject of considerable historical interest, but it can also help provide insights for current debates about democratic institutions and economic performance. In their 1989 article, North and Weingast make direct reference to the relevance of their work for the dilemmas facing today's developing countries.[1] Subsequently, a number of authors working on the political economy of development have referred to North and Weingast (1989) to suggest that certain features of representative democracy can allow governments to solve commitment problems. When institutions such as "limited government" are absent, they argue, governments will face higher costs of borrowing, private investors will be deterred by risk, and economic performance will stagnate.[2]

The arguments and empirical tests presented in this book have several implications for this literature. First, when considering the link between democratic institutions and economic performance, it is important not to ignore partisan political context. Existing work often portrays commitment problems in the context of a game played between a ruler and a homogeneous population where a ruler has an incentive to act opportunistically by raising taxes, changing regulations, or more generally transgressing property rights. As argued by Weingast (1995), the fundamental problem in this context is that any government strong enough to protect property rights will also have the power to violate them. It is important to recognize, however, that many credibility problems derive from distributional conflicts within society itself. So, for example, commitment problems in government borrowing involve a division between those who own government securities and those who pay the taxes used to service debt. In other contexts commitment problems can emerge as a result of distributional conflicts between owners of labor and owners of capital, between rich and poor, or between groups with different preferences over public spending. The fact that existing discussions of democratic institutions and commitment fail to take into account such distributional conflicts

[1] This is also a theme in North (1990).
[2] See Bates (1996), De Long and Shleifer (1993), Firmin-Sellers (1994), Henisz (2000, 2001), Olson (1993, 2000), and Weingast (1997b).

lends credence to the criticisms made by Elster (2000) and Przeworski and Limongi (1993), who suggest that convincing theories of democratic institutions and commitment need to take account of partisan motivations of actors. What this implies then is that discussions of government commitment need to draw on the numerous political economy models that emphasize distributive conflict. This could include both the formal models reviewed in Drazen (2000) and Persson and Tabellini (2000) as well as classic models developed by political scientists such as Bates (1981) and Frieden (1991).

Constitutional Checks and Balances

Taking distributional politics seriously leads to new predictions about the effect of constitutional checks and balances on commitment. I have argued in this book that while institutional features such as bicameralism may improve opportunities for credible commitment, they are neither a necessary nor a sufficient condition for this to occur. Whether and when checks and balances make a difference depends on the nature of distributional conflicts in society and on the balance of forces between the political parties that form to represent different groups. In some cases checks and balances may be irrelevant, because the majority does not face a credibility problem. This arguably was the case for the Estates of Holland in the sixteenth and seventeenth centuries where government creditors were prominently represented. It was also the case for England after 1715 where political institutions provided for multiple veto points, but where the political influence of government creditors was attributable more directly to the development of the Whig party. Alternatively, in some cases checks and balances may be irrelevant because those opposed to government opportunism would lack veto power even within a system characterized by checks and balances. I have argued that this may have been the case had the French monarchy during the eighteenth century adopted English-style political institutions.

My idea that constitutional checks and balances are neither a necessary nor a sufficient condition for credible commitment is directly relevant to recent cross-country research. Beck et al. (1999) and Henisz (2000) have collected impressive cross-country data sets on political institutions. Using these data, several studies have found that countries in which multiple actors have decision-making power tend to have higher levels of private investment and higher levels of growth.[3] It is critical to note, however, that these studies focus not just on cases where there are multiple veto points but on cases where there are multiple veto points controlled by multiple political parties. For example, in the case where there is a bicameral legislature but both houses are controlled by the same party, the indices of checks and balances developed by Beck et al. (1999) and Henisz (2000) would both code such a country as being identical to a country in which there was a unicameral legislature controlled by a single party. What would be interesting to investigate for future research is whether the correlation between the number of constitutionally determined veto points and the level of private investment or economic growth is weaker than the correlation between levels of private investment and the veto player indices developed by Beck et al. and Henisz. The theory developed in this book suggests that this should be the case, because having constitutional checks and balances does not guarantee that a greater range of social groups will actually have political influence.

It is also possible to indirectly test the argument that constitutional checks and balances are not a necessary condition for credible commitment. In countries where the constitution does not provide for multiple veto points, it is nonetheless possible for credible commitment to occur if the majority of members of a legislature have an interest in opposing actions such as default. In addition, as I have argued, in pluralist societies with multiple political cleavages, policies may be credible even if interests such as government creditors are a small minority. In a separate paper (Stasavage 2002b), I indirectly tested this observable implication using the datasets developed by Beck et al. and Henisz (2000). My results are consistent with other studies in that I find that rates of private investment, on average, are higher in countries where there are multiple veto points controlled by multiple political parties. However, this average masks a more complex reality. I also find that the group of countries in which a single party holds power is exceptionally diverse. Some of these governments have succeeded in attaining very high rates of private investment,

---

[3] Henisz (2000) posits and finds empirical support for a linear relationship between his index *political constraints* and economic growth across countries. In other studies Falaschetti (2001) and Henisz (2001) have identified a positive correlation between the presence of multiple veto players in government and levels of private investment. This is based on the idea that constitutional checks and balances may solve commitment problems not only in the area of government debt, but also with regard to tax and regulatory policies more generally.

while others have failed to do so.[4] One can observe a similar pattern when investigating the relationship between risk ratings on government bonds and checks and balances. This suggests that in a number of cases credible policies emerge even in the absence of constitutional checks and balances.

Multidimensional Politics

The conclusions of this book also have implications regarding the multidimensional character of political bargaining. Existing political economy models of economic policy making generally restrict themselves to considering a single dimension of partisan conflict, such as that between labor and capital. One obvious reason for modeling politics as being unidimensional involves tractability. Specifying additional dimensions of political conflict makes median-voter and related solution concepts inapplicable. Moreover, the salience of different dimensions of conflict is certain to vary considerably from country to country, making generalization difficult. But unidimensional models also have a down side; when applied to cases such as England after 1688, they will produce inaccurate conclusions. My goal in saying this is not to demonstrate that politics is multidimensional; Laver and Hunt (1992) have already argued this convincingly for a set of OECD countries based on expert survey data. Likewise, authors have shown that models with multiple dimensions of political conflict provide a better explanation of U.S. congressional voting patterns than would a unidimensional model.[5] Finally, classic work from political science emphasizes the idea that there are multiple dimensions of political conflict in many societies.[6] Rather than repeating these earlier findings, my objective has instead been to argue that the multidimensional character of politics should be considered more explicitly in political models of economic policy choice.

The other reason for considering multidimensional models is that it is now possible to use noncooperative game theory to make predictions about equilibrium outcomes of multi-issue political competition. The results of the legislative bargaining model I develop in Chapter 2 are not general in that I consider only a three-player game and a limited range of

[4] More formally, in Stasavage (2002b) I show that the conditional variance of private investment as a share of GDP is negatively correlated with the number of veto players in government.
[5] Heckman and Snyder (1996) and Poole and Rosenthal (1991).
[6] See Almond (1956), Lipset (1960), Lipset and Rokkan (1967), and Schattschneider (1942, 1960).

preference profiles, but they nonetheless provide useful predictions and insights. As argued by Baron (1994), under conditions where social choice theories would predict that multidimensional conflict would result in continuous cycling of policies, it is possible, using a noncooperative legislative bargaining model, to obtain equilibrium predictions due to the assumption that bargaining proposals are made in sequence (random or other).[7] Legislative bargaining models in which there are two dimensions of conflict may be useful for considering politics in many societies, both past and present, that are divided along an economic cleavage (such as land vs. capital) as well as along a social cleavage such as religion, foreign policy, or social policy.

Delegation and Commitment

The final implication of this book for the politics of economic performance involves the frequent recommendation that governments solve commitment problems by delegating to an independent agency. The best-known example of this is delegation in monetary policy, where it is argued that a legally independent central bank can help produce lower inflation and higher social welfare. Delegation may also help solve commitment problems in other areas of government action. For example, with utilities regulation, governments seeking to attract investment in utilities may face a significant commitment problem due to the heavy sunk costs involved in such investment (Spiller 1995). Therefore, it has been argued that granting control of regulation for telecommunications, electricity, or some other sector to an independent agency may serve as a form of commitment that leads to increased investment.

The arguments developed in this book and the historical evidence from France and Great Britain suggest that whether delegation does in fact

---

[7] In a recent review essay, Diermeier and Krehbiel (2001) have suggested that noncooperative game theory offers a number of more general possibilities for demonstrating existence of equilibria under conditions where alternative methods might fail to yield results. There are also several formal voting models, which have recently been developed, that can deliver equilibrium predictions even when there are multiple dimensions of political conflict. Besley and Coate (2001) have used the "citizen-candidate" model developed by Osborne and Slivinski (1996) and themselves (Besley and Coate 1997) to consider the implications of issue bundling for regulatory policy. Roemer (2001) has proposed an alternative model that he uses to examine several empirical issues where the multidimensional character of politics has an influence on outcomes. Levy (2001) has considered party competition in a citizen candidate model where there are multiple dimensions of conflict.

improve credibility depends heavily on the partisan composition of government. When an individual or group that suffers from a credibility problem has complete control of all the levers of political power, bureaucratic delegation may be essentially meaningless, because a bureaucratic agency can always be threatened with a revision of its statute. This could apply in the case of an authoritarian or monarchical government where one individual or group has complete control. It could also apply in a democratic context to the extent that a single cohesive party has the ability to pass new legislation. My arguments with regard to delegation and commitment are supported by recent cross-country work with Philip Keefer, which shows that delegating to a legally independent central bank has little actual effect on inflation in countries when a single party holds power.[8]

3. Implications for the Study of Institutions

Apart from its implications for the politics of economic performance, this book also has relevance for the study of institutions more generally. I have already noted that discussions of institutions as constraints have been criticized for ignoring partisan incentives on the part of actors. My analysis has attempted to take this issue seriously. In a broader sense, arguments about institutions as constraints are subject to the observation that they say little about how institutions are chosen or how they are enforced. In the case of constitutions, if they can be easily amended or ignored, then what effect should they be expected to have on policy outcomes? If institutions are endogenous to actor preferences, then, in the extreme case, one could follow Riker's (1980) well-known critique by suggesting that institutional structure will have only a short-run impact on political outcomes.

Institutions as Equilibria

The model of the politics of commitment presented in this book directly confronts the issues of institutional choice and enforcement by showing how one institution that may facilitate commitment to repay debt – a majority political party – can arise within the context of a bargaining game. Several other studies have recently presented models where institutions or norms of behavior are equilibrium outcomes of an underlying

---

[8] See Keefer and Stasavage (2001, 2002). These papers use the indices of political institutions developed by Beck et al. (1999) and Henisz (2000).

game.[9] Bawn (1999) has considered how alternative ideologies, defined as rules about distributing benefits among different groups, can be represented as equilibrium strategy profiles of a bargaining game. Calvert and Fox (2000) have considered how political parties can be modeled as equilibrium outcomes of a legislative bargaining game.[10] Norms of behavior within a legislature have also been modeled as equilibrium outcomes of a noncooperative game by Diermeier (1995), who considers the issue of deference to committees, and Shepsle and Nalebuff (1990), who investigate norms of seniority. Outside the legislative context, Hafer (2001) has investigated the endogenous development of property rights.[11]

The potential contribution of the institutions as equilibria approach is not to demonstrate that institutions are in fact equilibrium outcomes of noncooperative games; this is a postulate rather than a falsifiable hypothesis. The objective is instead to develop propositions about when and where certain types of behavior are more likely to emerge. In this book the goal has been to investigate the conditions under which governments will be committed to repaying their debts. I have suggested that in societies where the majority may suffer from a credibility problem with respect to public debt or any other policy, the process of forming a durable legislative majority may nonetheless lead to the adoption of moderate policies consistent with credible commitment. The game-theoretic model I have used to investigate this possibility delivers several predictions about when this effect is likely to occur. Most importantly, the existence of a second dimension of political conflict increases the possibility that a majority party will refrain from taxing government creditors through default. As I have argued in Chapter 7, it is possible for this effect to operate even under conditions where actors are not bound by parliamentary decisions but instead can exercise an outside option.

Links to Other Traditions

As a final point, I hope that one further contribution of this book will be to show that game-theoretic analysis of institutions can help to improve our

---

[9] The approach of modeling institutions as equilibria of underlying games has been advocated by Calvert (1995a, b). Recently, Diermeier and Krehbiel (2001) have argued in favor of a similar research program.

[10] See also Carruba and Volden (2000).

[11] Greif, Milgrom, and Weingast (1994) and Milgrom, North, and Weingast (1990) have also provided models where actors in a noncooperative game develop complex strategies for enforcing cooperation, and these strategies involve "institutional" features such as centralized communication.

understanding of a number of phenomena that are more often considered by scholars working within the tradition of "comparative historical institutionalism." As such, this study can contribute to the idea that scholars who use rational choice models and scholars in the comparative historical tradition can learn from each other.[12] Work in the field of comparative politics has long emphasized that a focus on the complexity of coalition politics and on the multidimensional nature of political conflict can help us to understand why some economic policies are implemented and why others fail to gain a hearing. Scholars who develop formal models of economic policy making have not been ignorant of this fact, but their work has at times tended to ignore the multidimensional nature of politics in favor of obtaining general theoretical results. I have suggested here that if one accepts restrictions on the generalizability of one's theoretical model, then it is possible to use game theory to consider a phenomenon such as coalition building and its effect on policy. At the same time, the use of game-theoretic tools may help us to make new observations about the effects of coalition building that one might not have otherwise discovered, such as the importance of party formation for credible commitment.

---

[12] This is a point that has been made on several previous occasions, but which is worth reaffirming. See Thelen (1999) for a review.

Appendix

This appendix derives the results of the legislative bargaining model presented in Chapter 2. I deal first with the general case, before then finding equilibria for specific configurations of parameters (Examples 1 to 4). In any subgame perfect equilibrium of the legislative bargaining game, each player will maximize his or her utility subject to the constraint of offering another player at least his or her continuation value, which is the expected utility from voting against a proposal and continuing to the next round. In an equilibrium where player A offers to player B, player C offers to player B, and player B offers to player A, the three continuation constraints A1–A3 would need to be satisfied. These equations represent the continuation constraints for player A's offer to B, player C's offer to B, and player B's offer to A, respectively. For each of the examples considered in this paper, there is a subgame perfect equilibrium with this pattern of offers. In many cases there is also a subgame perfect equilibrium with the following sequence of offers: A→B, C→B, B→C, but as described in the text, in most cases the proposals in this equilibrium are identical to those where C offers to A. Player B makes the same proposal regardless of whether he or she offers to player A or player C, and so I do not consider this possibility here.

$$2 + e_b(\theta - \tau)_a + z_b\rho_a = \frac{\delta}{3}[6 + e_b(\theta - \tau)_a + z_b\rho_a + e_b(\theta - \tau)_b$$
$$+ z_b\rho_b + e_b(\theta - \tau)_c + z_b\rho_c)] \tag{A1}$$

$$2 + e_b(\theta - \tau)_c + z_b\rho_c = \frac{\delta}{3}[6 + e_b(\theta - \tau)_a + z_b\rho_a + e_b(\theta - \tau)_b$$
$$+ z_b\rho_b + e_b(\theta - \tau)_c + z_b\rho_c)] \tag{A2}$$

$$2 + e_a(\theta - \tau)_b + z_a\rho_b = \frac{\delta}{3}[6 + e_a(\theta - \tau)_a + z_a\rho_a + e_a(\theta - \tau)_b$$
$$+ z_a\rho_b + e_a(\theta - \tau)_c + z_a\rho_c)] \tag{A3}$$

Example 1: Single-Issue Bargaining. The single-issue bargaining case is straightforward to evaluate. If $z_a = z_b = z_c = 0$, then in any subgame perfect equilibrium using pure stationary strategies, as long as players B and C have $e > 0$, then B if recognized will propose $\theta - \tau = 1$ to C, and C will make an identical proposal to B. Any proposal made by player A to player B will need to satisfy the following continuation constraint:

$$2 + e_b(\theta - t)_a = \frac{\delta}{3}[6 + e_b(\theta - t)_a + 2e_b] \qquad (A4)$$

which implies the following equilibrium proposal for player A:

$$(\theta - \tau)_a = \frac{6 - 6\delta - 2\delta e_b}{e_b(\delta - 3)} \qquad (A5)$$

Example 2: Effect of a Second Issue on Bargaining. This example considers the effect of a second issue on expected capital taxation. I first demonstrate that if player A owns only capital $e_a = -1$, players B and C own only land $e_b = e_c = 1$, and the three players place equal weight on the religious toleration dimension: $|z_a| = |z_b| = |z_c|$, then there is a subgame perfect equilibrium with the sequence of offers: A→B, C→B, B→A, and in this equilibrium the expected rate of capital taxation is strictly decreasing as the salience of the religious toleration dimension increases $|z| \rightarrow 1$. Given the configuration of preferences assumed in the paper, we can reduce the number of unknown parameters in the above equations by recognizing that players B and A will propose full religious toleration to each other if recognized: $\rho_a = \rho_b = 1$. Likewise, C will propose a capital tax rate of unity and a land tax of 0 to B if recognized: $(\theta - \tau)_c = 1$.

I substitute into Equations A1–A3 for $e_a = -1$, $e_b = 1$, $e_c = 1$, $\rho_a = \rho_b = 1$, $(\theta - \tau)_c = 1$, and $z_a = z_b = z$, $z_c = -z$. The system of equations can then be solved for player A's proposed tax rate: $(\theta - t)_a$, B's proposed tax rate: $(\theta - t)_b$, and C's proposal for religious toleration: ρ_c. However, the solution for $(\theta - t)_b$ is in fact greater than 1 for all $0 < \delta < 1$. This violates the assumption of the model that the maximum desirable tax rate is unity, given the government budget constraint. As a consequence, I substitute $(\theta - t)_b = 1$ into Equations A1 and A2 and then solve for $(\theta - t)_a$ and ρ_c. This results in the set of policy proposals listed in Equations A6–A8. Since $(\theta - t)_a$ is decreasing in z, the salience of the religious toleration dimension, the expected rate of capital taxation (equal to the average of the proposals by A, B, and C) is also decreasing in z:

$$(\theta - t)_a = \frac{6 + 3z - 7\delta - 3\delta z}{2\delta - 3}, \qquad \rho_a = 1 \tag{A6}$$

$$(\theta - t)_b = 1, \qquad \rho_b = 1 \tag{A7}$$

$$(\theta - t)_c = 1, \qquad \rho_c = \frac{9 - 9\delta - \delta z}{z(2\delta - 3)} \tag{A8}$$

For this to be an equilibrium, it needs to be demonstrated that no player would have an incentive to deviate by proposing to a different player when recognized. For B this is trivial, because he or she cannot improve on proposing his or her own ideal point. For A to deviate, two conditions would need to be satisfied. First, he or she would need to propose a set of policies giving him or her greater utility than his or her equilibrium proposal, as in A9. Second, his or her alternative proposal would also need to satisfy the continuation constraint of C, as in A10.

$$2 - (\theta - \tau)_{dev} + z\rho_{dev} > 2 + z - \frac{6 + 3z - 7\delta - 3\delta z}{2\delta - 3} \tag{A9}$$

$$2 + (\theta - \tau)_{dev} - z\rho_{dev} = \frac{\delta}{3}\left[6 + \frac{6 + 3z - 7\delta - 3\delta z}{2\delta - 3}\right.$$
$$\left. + \frac{-9 + 9\delta + \delta z}{(2\delta - 3)}\right] \tag{A10}$$

Using A10 it is possible for substitute for the term $-(\theta - \tau)_{dev} + \rho_{dev}$ in Equation A9 to obtain the following expression:

$$4 - \frac{\delta}{3}\left[6 + \frac{6 + 3z - 7\delta - 3\delta z}{2\delta - 3} + \frac{-9 + 9\delta + \delta z}{(2\delta - 3)}\right]$$
$$> 2 + z - \frac{6 + 3z - 7\delta - 3\delta z}{2\delta - 3} \tag{A11}$$

Player A will only have an incentive to deviate if the inequality in A11 is satisfied. The inequality cannot be satisfied when $z = 1$, and when $z < 1$ it can be satisfied only for very high discount factors. For example, when $z = 0.5$, A will not defect as long as $\delta < 0.95$. Using the same method it can be demonstrated that player C never has an incentive to defect.

Example 3: Effect of Player B Having a Mixed Income. Example 3 considers how the expected rate of capital taxation might be affected if players bargain over two dimensions, but player B derives some income from capital while still earning the majority of his or her income from land. I show here that as the portion of player B's income derived from capital increases $e_b \to 0$, the expected rate of capital taxation falls.

I now assume that $e_a = -1$, $e_c = 1$, and e_b is left as a parameter. In addition, $z_a = z_b = 1$, $z_c = -1$. Given these assumptions, we can substitute for $\rho_a = 1$, $\rho_b = 1$ and $(\theta - \tau)_c = 1$. Solving for the proposals of each player results in the following set of proposals, which hold as long as $e_b > 0.64$. For smaller values of e_b, player B will propose a capital tax rate of less than unity, and the result that expected capital taxation is decreasing in e_b still holds:

$$(\theta - t)_a = \frac{9 - 9\delta - \delta e_b}{e_b(2\delta - 3)}, \qquad \rho_a = 1 \tag{A12}$$

$$(\theta - t)_b = 1, \qquad \rho_b = 1 \tag{A13}$$

$$(\theta - t)_c = 1, \qquad \rho_c = \frac{6 + 3e_b - 7\delta - 3\delta e_b}{2\delta - 3} \tag{A14}$$

Player A would have an incentive to deviate from the above proposal by offering to player C, and C would accept if the following two conditions were satisfied:

$$2 - (\theta - \tau)_{dev} + \rho_{dev} > 3 - \frac{9 - 9\delta + \delta e_b}{e_b(2\delta - 3)} \tag{A15}$$

$$2 + (\theta - \tau)_{dev} - \rho_{dev} = \frac{\delta}{3}\left(6 + \frac{9 - 9\delta + \delta e_b}{e_b(2\delta - 3)}\right.$$
$$\left. - \frac{6 + 3e_b - 7\delta - 3\delta e_b}{2\delta - 3}\right) \tag{A16}$$

As in Example 2, we can use Equation A16 to substitute for the term $-(\theta - \tau)_{dev} + \rho_{dev}$ in A15, which results in the following inequality. The inequality in Equation A17 cannot be satisfied for any $0 < \delta < 1$, and as a result, A will never have an incentive to deviate. A similar exercise shows that player C would never have an incentive to deviate, and it is again trivial to show that player B would not deviate, because he or she cannot improve on proposing his or her own ideal point.

$$4 - \frac{\delta}{3}\left(6 + \frac{9 - 9\delta + \delta e_b}{e_b(2\delta - 3)} - \frac{6 + 3e_b - 7\delta - 3\delta e_b}{2\delta - 3}\right)$$
$$> 3 - \frac{9 - 9\delta + \delta e_b}{e_b(2\delta - 3)} \tag{A17}$$

Example 4: Effect of Religion Being Less Salient for Player A. The final example considers how expected capital taxation changes if player A cares relatively less about religious toleration than do players B and C. After substituting for $\rho_a = \rho_b = 1, (\theta - \tau)_c = 1$, and $e_a = -1, e_b = e_c = 1$, I assume that $z_b = 1, z_c = -1$, and z_a remains a parameter. Solving the system of equations containing the continuation constraints results in the following set of policy proposals. This set of proposals holds for all $z_a > 0.6$. For lower values of z_a, player B will propose a capital tax rate lower than unity, though again the result that expected capital taxation is decreasing in z_a still holds.

$$(\theta - t)_a = \frac{9 - 10\delta}{2\delta - 3}, \qquad \rho_a = 1 \tag{A18}$$

$$(\theta - t)_b = 1, \qquad \rho_b = 1 \tag{A19}$$

$$(\theta - t)_c = 1, \qquad \rho_c = \frac{9 - 10\delta}{2\delta - 3} \tag{A20}$$

A will defect by offering to C, and C will accept if the following two conditions are met:

$$2 - (\theta - \tau)_{dev} + z_a\rho_{dev} > 2 + z_a - \frac{9 - 10\delta}{2\delta - 3} \tag{A21}$$

$$2 + (\theta - \tau)_{dev} - \rho_{dev} = \frac{\delta}{3}\left(6 - \frac{9 - 10\delta}{2\delta - 3} + \frac{9 - 10\delta}{2\delta - 3}\right) \tag{A22}$$

The two conditions above can be met only when there is very little discounting of the future, but when the discount factor is nonetheless less than 1. When $z_a = 0.75$, for example, A would defect by offering to C only if $1 > \delta > 0.975$. A similar result can be shown for an offer by player C. For these very high discount factors it is possible to have mixed strategies, where player A mixes between offering to B and offering to C and where C mixes between offering to A and offering to B.

References

Contemporary Writings and Other Primary Sources

An Impartial View of the Two Late Parliaments (1711). British Library.

Archives Parlémentaires. 1862. 1st series, 1787–99. Paris: Dupont.

Broughton, John (1705). *Remarks upon the Bank of England, with Regard More Especially to Our Trade and Government.* London: A. Baldwin.

Castaing, John (1698–1711). *The Course of the Exchange.* London.

Cocks, Sir Richard (1698–1702). *The Parliamentary Diary of Sir Richard Cocks,* David Hayton, ed. Oxford, 1996.

Condorcet, Marquis de (1789). *Sur la proposition d'acquitter la dette exigible en assignats.* Paris: Imprimerie de l'Assemblée Nationale.

Custine, Comte de (1789). *Réflexions sur la proposition du premier ministre des finances de sanctionner, comme Caisse Nationale, la Caisse d'Escompte appartenant à des capitalistes.* Paris: Imprimerie de l'Assemblée Nationale.

Defoe, Daniel (1701a). *The Freeholders' Plea against Stock-Jobbing Election of Parliament Men.* London.

Defoe, Daniel (1701b). *The Villainy of Stock-Jobbers Detected.* London

Defoe, Daniel (1710a). *An Essay upon Loans.* London.

Defoe, Daniel (1710b). *An Essay upon Publick Credit.* London.

Defoe, Daniel (1710c). *Faults on Both Sides.* London.

Dutot (1738). *Histoire du système de John Law,* Antoin Murphy, ed. Paris: Institut National d'Etudes Demographiques, 2000.

Fénelon, François de Salignac de La Mothe (1692). *Lettre à Louis XIV.* Paris: Séquences, 1994.

Fénelon, François de Salignac de La Mothe (1710a). "Plans de gouvernement." In *Fénelon, ecrits et lettres politiques.* Paris: Editions Bossard, 1920.

Fénelon, François de Salignac de La Mothe (1710b). "Projet d'une assemblée des notables." In *Fénelon, ecrits et lettres politiques.* Paris: Editions Bossard, 1920.

Fénelon, François de Salignac de La Mothe (1711). "Plans de gouvernement, concertés avec le duc de Chevreuse, pour être proposés au duc de Bourgogne." In *Oeuvres de Fénelon,* vol. 22, pp. 575–95. Paris: J.-A. Lebel, 1824.

"Histoire des finances pendant la régence de 1715." Bibliothèque de l'Arsenal, Paris, Ms. 4560.

Hume, David (1742). "Of the Parties of Great Britain." London.

Journal d'Adrien Duquesnoy, Député du Tiers-État de Bar-le-Duc (1894). Paris: Alphonse Picard.

Lavoisier, Antoine (1789). *Réflexions sur les assignats et sur la liquidation de la dette exigible ou arriérée lue à la Société de 1789, le 29 août 1790*. Paris: Société de 1789.

Le Moniteur Universel (various dates 1789–1790).

Paterson, William (1694). *A Brief Account of the Intended Bank of England*. London: Randal Taylor.

Pittis, W. (1711). *The History of the Present Parliament and Convocation*. London.

"Projets de gouvernement résolus par M, le duc de Bourgogne, Dauphin" (attributed to the duc de Saint-Simon). M. P. Mesnard, ed. Bibliothèque de l'Arsenal, Paris.

"Remonstrances faites au Roy par le parlement de Bretagne au sujet de la levée du cinquantième en nature de tous les biens du royaume" (1725). Arsenal Ms. 3890, Paris.

Saint-Simon, Louis de Rouvroy de (1715, 1720). *Mémoires*. Paris: Vols. 5 and 7. Gallimard, 1985.

Société de 1789. *Journal de la Société de 1789*. Paris.

Société de 1789. *Mémoires de la Société de 1789*. Paris.

Swift, Jonathan (1710–11). *The Examiner*. London.

Swift, Jonathan (1711a). *The Conduct of the Allies*. London.

Swift, Jonathan (1711b). *Some Advice to the October Club*. London.

Swift, Jonathan (1712). *A Letter to a Whig Lord*. London.

Secondary Sources

Albertone, Manuela (1990). "Le Débat sur le credit public en France et la naissance des assignats." *Economies et Sociétés*, vol. 24, July–October, pp. 405–29.

Albertone, Manuela (1992). *Moneta e politica in Francia: Dalla cassa di sconto agli assegnati (1776–1792)*. Il Mulino: Bologna.

Albertone, Manuela (1997). "Réferences economiques et pratiques financières: Le Crédit public en France sous l'ancien régime." In *L'Administration des finances sous l'ancien régime*. Paris: Comité pour l'Histoire Economique et Financière de la France.

Aldrich, John (1995). *Why Parties?* University of Chicago Press.

Almond, Gabriel (1956). "Comparative Political Systems." *Journal of Politics*, vol. 18, pp. 391–409.

Althusser, Louis (1959). *Montesquieu, la politique et l'histoire*. Paris: PUF.

Andréades, A. (1909). *History of the Bank of England*. London: Frank Cass.

Applewhite, Harriet (1993). *Political Alignment in the French National Assembly, 1789–1991*. London: Louisiana State University Press.

Ashton, Robert (1960). *The Crown and the Money Market: 1603–1640*. Oxford: Oxford University Press.

Baron, David (1989). "A Non-Cooperative Theory of Legislative Coalitions." *American Journal of Political Science*, vol. 33, pp. 1048–84.

References

Baron, David (1991). "A Spatial Bargaining Theory of Government Formation in Parliamentary Systems." *American Political Science Review*, vol. 85, pp. 137–64.

Baron, David (1994). "A Sequential Choice Theory Perspective on Legislative Organization." *Legislative Studies Quarterly*, vol. 19, pp. 267–96.

Baron, David, and John Ferejohn (1989). "Bargaining in Legislatures." *American Political Science Review*, vol. 89, pp. 1181–206.

Baron, David, and Michael Herron (1999). "A Dynamic Model of Multidimensional Collective Choice." Mimeo, Graduate School of Business, Stanford University.

Bates, Robert (1981). *Markets and States in Tropical Africa*. Berkeley: University of California Press.

Bates, Robert (1996). "Institutions as Investments." Harvard Institute for International Development, Discussion Paper No. 527.

Bates, Robert, and Da-Hsiang Donald Lien (1985). "A Note on Taxation, Development and Representative Government." *Politics and Society*, vol. 14, pp. 53–70.

Bates, Robert, Avner Greif, Margaret Levi, Jean-Laurent Rosenthal, and Barry Weingast (1997). *Analytic Narratives*. Princeton: Princeton University Press.

Bawn, Kathleen (1999). "Constructing 'Us': Ideology, Coalition Politics, and False Consciousness." *American Journal of Political Science*, vol. 43, pp. 303–34.

Beard, Charles (1913). *An Economic Interpretation of the Constitution of the United States*. New York: Macmillan.

Beck, Thorsten, George Clarke, Alberto Groff, Philip Keefer, and Patrick Walsh (1999). "New Tools and New Tests in Comparative Political Economy: The Database of Political Institutions." Mimeo, World Bank.

Beckett, J. V. (1985). "Land Tax or Excise: The Levying of Taxation in Seventeenth and Eighteenth Century England." *English Historical Review*, vol. 100, pp. 285–308.

Beik, William (1985). *Absolutism and Society in Seventeenth Century France: State Power and Provincial Aristocracy in Languedoc*. Cambridge: Cambridge University Press.

Besley, Timothy, and Stephen Coate (1997). "An Economic Model of Representative Democracy." *Quarterly Journal of Economics*, vol. 112, pp. 85–114.

Besley, Timothy, and Stephen Coate (2001). "Issue Unbundling via Citizens' Initiatives." Mimeo, London School of Economics.

Bien, David (1987). "Offices, Corps, and a System of State Credit: The Uses of Privilege under the Ancièn Régime." In Keith Michael Baker, ed., *The French Revolution and the Creation of Modern Political Culture*. Oxford, Pergamon Press.

Bien, David (1989). "Manufacturing Nobles: The Chancelleries in France to 1789." *Journal of Modern History*, vol. 61, pp. 445–86.

Bonney, Richard (1999). "France, 1494–1815." In Richard Bonney, ed., *The Rise of the Fiscal State in Europe: 1200–1815*. Oxford: Oxford University Press, pp. 123–76.

Brewer, John (1989). *The Sinews of Power*. London: Hutchinson.

Broz, J. Lawrence (1998). "The Origins of Central Banking: Solutions to the Free-Rider Problem." *International Organization*, vol. 52, pp. 231–68.

References

Brugière, Michel (1992). "Les Assignats." In Francois Furet and Mona Ozouf, eds., *Dictionnaire critique de la révolution française*. Paris: Flammarion. Pp. 59–72.

Buchanan, James, and Gordon Tullock (1962). *The Calculus of Consent.* Ann Arbor: University of Michigan Press.

Bulow, Jeremy, and Kenneth Rogoff (1989). "Sovereign Debt: Is to Forgive to Forget?" *American Economic Review*, vol. 79, pp. 43–50.

Calvert, Randall (1995a). "Rational Actors, Equilibrium, and Social Institutions." In Jack Knight and Itai Sened, eds., *Explaining Social Institutions*. Ann Arbor: University of Michigan Press. Pp. 57–94.

Calvert, Randall (1995b). "The Rational Choice Theory of Social Institutions." In Jeffrey Banks, ed., *Modern Political Economy*. Cambridge: Cambridge University Press. Pp. 216–68.

Calvert, Randall, and Nathan Dietz (1998). "Legislative Coalitions in a Bargaining Model with Externalities." Wallis Institute of Political Economy Working Paper no. 16.

Calvert, Randall, and Justin Fox (2000). "Effective Parties in a Model of Repeated Legislative Bargaining." Paper presented at the Annual Meeting of the American Political Science Association, Washington, D.C.

Calvert, Randall, and Barry Weingast (1993). "Party Coherence and Cooperation in a Legislature." Paper presented at the American Political Science Association Annual Meeting, Washington, D.C.

Carruba, Clifford, and Craig Volden. 2000. "Coalitional Politics and Logrolling in Legislative Institutions." *American Journal of Political Science*, vol. 44, pp. 255–71.

Carruthers, Bruce (1996). *City of Capital: Politics and Markets in the English Financial Revolution*. Princeton: Princeton University Press.

Carruthers, Bruce (1990), "Politics, Popery, and Property: A Comment on North and Weingast." *Journal of Economic History*, vol. 50, pp. 693–98.

Chandaman, C.D. (1975). *The English Public Revenue: 1660–1688*. Oxford: Oxford University Press.

Chari, Vijay, and Patrick Kehoe (1993). "Sustainable Plans and Mutual Default." *Review of Economic Studies*, vol. 60, pp. 175–96.

Chartier, Roger, and Denis Richet (1982). *Représentation et vouloir politiques: Autour des etats généraux de 1614*. Paris: Editions de l'École des Hautes Études en Sciences Sociales.

Clapham, John (1958). *The Bank of England, a History*. Cambridge: Cambridge University Press.

Clark, Gregory (1996). "The Political Foundations of Modern Economic Growth, England 1540–1800." *Journal of Interdisciplinary History*, vol. 26, pp. 563–88.

Cobban, Alfred (1964). *The Social Interpretation of the French Revolution*. Cambridge: Cambridge University Press.

Collins, James B. (1988). *Fiscal Limits of Absolutism: Direct Taxation in Early Seventeenth-Century France*. Berkeley: University of California Press.

Cox, Gary (1987). *The Efficient Secret: The Cabinet and the Development of Political Parties in Victorian England*. Cambridge: Cambridge University Press.

Cox, Gary (1997). *Making Votes Count: Strategic Coordination in the World's Electoral Systems*. New York: Cambridge University Press.

Cox, Gary, and Mathew McCubbins (1993). *Legislative Leviathan: Party Government in the House*. Berkeley: University of California Press.

Cukierman, A. (1992). *Central Bank Strategy, Credibility, and Independence*. Cambridge: MIT Press.

Davis, Herbert (1951). Introduction to *Jonathan Swift: Political Tracts: 1711–1713*. Oxford: Basil Blackwell.

De Krey, Gary Stuart (1985). *A Fractured Society: The Politics of London in the First Age of Party*. Oxford: Clarendon Press.

De Long, J. Bradford, and Andrei Shleifer (1993). "Princes and Merchants: European City Growth before the Industrial Revolution." NBER Working Paper no. 4274.

Dessert, Daniel (1984). *Argent, pouvoir et société au grand siècle*. Paris: Fayard.

Dickinson, H. T. (1981). "Whiggism in the Eighteenth Century." In John Cannon, ed., *The Whig Ascendancy: Colloquies on Hanoverian England*. London: Edward Arnold. Pp. 28–50.

Dickson, P. G. M. (1967). *The Financial Revolution in England*. London: Macmillan.

Diermeier, Daniel (1995). "Commitment, Deference, and Legislative Institutions." *American Political Science Review*, vol. 89, pp. 344–55.

Diermeier, Daniel, and Timothy Feddersen (1998). "Cohesion in Legislatures and the Vote of Confidence Procedure." *American Political Science Review*, vol. 92, pp. 611–21.

Diermeier, Daniel, and Keith Krehbiel (2001). "Institutionalism as a Methodology." Research Paper no. 1699, Graduate School of Business, Stanford University.

Dixit, Avinash, and John Londregan (2000). "Political Power and the Credibility of Government Debt." *Journal of Economic Theory*, vol. 94, pp. 80–105.

Dixit, Avinash, and Robert Pindyck (1993). *Investment under Uncertainty*. Princeton: Princeton University Press.

Dixit, Avinash, Gene Grossman, and Faruk Gul (2000). "The Dynamics of Political Compromise." *Journal of Political Economy*, vol. 108, no. 3, pp. 531–68.

Doyle, William (1980). *Origins of the French Revolution*. Oxford: Oxford University Press.

Doyle, William (1996). *Venality: The Sale of Offices in Eighteenth Century France*. Oxford: Clarendon Press.

Drazen, Allan (2000). *Political Economy in Macroeconomics*. Princeton: Princeton University Press.

Dunham, William Huse, Jr., and Charles Wood (1976). "The Right to Rule in England: Depositions and the Kingdom's Authority, 1327–1485." *American Historical Review*, vol. 81, pp. 738–61.

Durand, Yves (1996). *Les Fermiers généraux au XVIIIeme siècle*. Paris: Maisonneuve et Larose.

Durkheim, Emile (1938/1895). *The Rules of Sociological Method*. New York: Free Press.

Ehrenberg, Richard (1928). *Capital and Finance in the Age of the Renaissance*. London: Jonathan Cape.

Eisenmann, Charles (1933). *L'Ésprit des lois et la séparation des pouvoirs*. Paris.

Ellis, E. L. (1969). "William III and the Politicians." In Geoffrey Holmes, ed., *Britain after the Glorious Revolution: 1689–1714*. New York: St. Martin's Press. Pp. 115–34.

Ellman, Matthew, and Leonard Wantchekon (2000). "Electoral Competition under the Threat of Political Unrest." *Quarterly Journal of Economics*, vol. 115, pp. 499–531.

Elster, Jon (2000). *Ulysses Unbound*. New York: Cambridge University Press.

Epstein, David, and Sharyn O'Halloran (1999). *Delegating Powers: A Transactions Cost Politics Approach to Policy Making under Separate Powers*. Cambridge: Cambridge University Press.

Erlanger, Philippe (1938). *Le Régent*. Paris: Gallimard.

Ertman, Thomas (1997). *Birth of the Leviathan: Building States and Regimes in Medieval and Early Modern Europe*. Cambridge: Cambridge University Press.

Esteban, Joan (2001). "A Hobbesian Theory of Agreements." Mimeo, Institut d'Analisi Economica, Barcelona.

Fachan, J. M. (1904). *Historique de la rente française et des valeurs du trésor*. Paris: Berger-Levrault.

Falaschetti, Dino (2001). "Credible Commitment and Investment: Do Checks on the Ability or Incentive to Play Opportunistic Actions Matter?" Mimeo, University of Tennessee.

Farrand, Max (1911). *The Records of the Federal Convention of 1787*. New Haven: Yale University Press.

Faure, Edgar (1977). *La Banqueroute de Law*. Paris: Gallimard.

Félix, Joel (1994). "Les Dettes de l'état à la mort de Louis XIV." In *Comité Pour l'Histoire Economique et Financière de la France: Études et Documents*, vol. 6, pp. 603–8.

Firmin-Sellers, Kathryn (1994). "The Politics of Property Rights." *American Political Science Review*, vol. 89, pp. 867–88.

Forbonnais, Véron Duverger de (1758). *Recherches et considérations sur les finances de France depuis l'année 1595 jusqu'à l'année 1721*. Basle: Frères Cramer.

Frieden, Jeffry (1991). "Invested Interests." *International Organization*, vol. 45, no. 4, pp. 425–51.

Frieden, Jeffry (1994). "Making Commitments." In Barry Eichengreen and Jeffry Frieden, eds., *The Political Economy of European Monetary Unification*. Boulder: Westview Press. Pp. 25–46.

Fryde, E. B., and M. M. Fryde (1963). "Public Credit, with Special Reference to North-Western Europe." In M. M. Postan, E. E. Rich, and Edward Miller, eds., *The Cambridge Economic History of Europe*, vol. 3: *Economic Organization and Policies in the Middle Ages*. Cambridge: Cambridge University Press, pp. 430–553.

Furet, François (1988). *La Révolution, I 1770–1814*. Paris: Hachette.

Furet, François, and Denis Richet (1963). *La Révolution française*. Paris: Hachette.

Garber, Peter (2000). *Famous First Bubbles: The Fundamentals of Early Manias*. Cambridge: MIT Press.

Given, James (1990). *State and Society in Medieval Europe: Gwynedd and Languedoc under Outside Rule*. Ithaca: Cornell University Press.

Grandmont, Jean-Michel (1978). "Intermediate Preferences and Majority Rule." *Econometrica*, vol. 46, pp. 317–30.

References

Greif, Avner (1993). "Contract Enforceability and Economic Institutions in Early Trade: the Maghribi Traders' Coalition." *American Economic Review*, vol. 83, no. 3, pp. 525–48.

Greif, Avner, Paul Milgrom, and Barry Weingast (1994). "Coordination, Commitment and Enforcement: The Case of the Merchant Guild." *Journal of Political Economy*, vol. 102, no. 4, pp. 745–76.

Gueniffey, Patrice, and Ran Halévi (1992). "Clubs et Sociétés Populaires." In François Furet and Mouna Ozouf, eds., *Dictionnaire critique de la révolution française*, vol. 2: *Institutions et créations*. Paris: Flammarion, pp. 107–32.

Hafer, Catherine (2001). "The Political Economy of Emerging Property Rights." Unpublished manuscript, New York University.

Hamilton, Earl J. (1936). "Prices and Wages at Paris under John Law's System." *Quarterly Journal of Economics*, vol. 51, pp. 42–70.

Hamilton, Earl J. (1947). "Origin and Growth of the National Debt in Western Europe." *American Economic Review*, vol. 37, pp. 118–30.

Hargreaves, E. L. (1930). *The National Debt*. London: Edward Arnold.

Harris, Robert (1986). *Necker and the French Revolution of 1789*. London: University Press of America.

Harris, Tim (1993). *Politics under the Later Stuarts*. London: Longman.

Harsin, Paul (1933). *Crédit public et banque d'état en France du XVIéme au XVIIIème siècle*. Paris: Librairie E. Droz.

Hayden, J. M. (1974). *France and the Estates General of 1614*. London: Cambridge University Press, London.

Hayton, David (1984). "The 'Country' Interest and the Party System, 1689–c. 1720." In Clyve Jones, ed., *Party and Management in Parliament 1660–1784*. Leicester: Leicester University Press. Pp. 37–85.

Hayton, David (2002). Introductory survey in *The History of Parliament: The House of Commons 1690–1715*. Cambridge: Cambridge University Press.

Hazard, Paul (1961). *La Crise de la conscience européenne*. Paris: Fayard.

Heckman, James, and James M. Snyder (1996). "Linear Probability Models of the Demand for Attributes with an Empirical Application to Estimating the Preferences of Legislators." NBER Working Paper no. 5785.

Helpman, Elhanan, and Torsten Persson (1998). "Lobbying and Legislative Bargaining." NBER Working Paper, no. 6589, June.

Henisz, Witold (2000). "The Institutional Environment for Economic Growth." *Economics and Politics*, vol. 12, pp. 1–31.

Henisz, Witold (2001). "The Institutional Environment for Multinational Investment." *Journal of Law, Economics and Organization*, vol. 16, pp. 334–64.

Hill, B. W. (1976). *The Growth of Parliamentary Parties, 1689–1742*. London: George Allen and Unwin.

Hoffman, Philip (1994). "Early Modern France, 1450–1700." In Philip Hoffman and Kathryn Norberg, eds., *Fiscal Crises, Liberty, and Representative Government, 1450–1789*. Stanford: Stanford University Press. Pp. 226–52.

Hoffman, Philip, and Kathryn Norberg (1994). *Fiscal Crises, Liberty, and Representative Government 1450–1789*. Stanford: Stanford University Press.

Hoffman, Philip, Gilles Postel-Vinay, and Jean-Laurent Rosenthal (1992). "Private Credit Markets in Paris, 1690–1840." *Journal of Economic History*, vol. 52, pp. 293–306.

Hoffman, Philip, Gilles Postel-Vinay, and Jean-Laurent Rosenthal (1995). "Redistribution and Long-Term Private Credit in Paris, 1660–1726." *Journal of Economic History*, vol. 55, pp. 256–84.

Hoffman, Philip, Gilles Postel-Vinay, and Jean-Laurent Rosenthal (2000). *Priceless Markets: The Political Economy of Credit in Paris 1660–1879*. Chicago: University of Chicago Press.

Hofstadter, Richard (1969). *The Idea of a Two Party System: The Rise of Legitimate Opposition in the United States: 1780–1820*. Berkeley: University of California Press.

Holmes, Geoffrey (1967). *British Politics in the Age of Anne*. London: Macmillan.

Holmes, Geoffrey (1976). *The Electorate and the National Will in the First Age of Party*. Lancaster: University of Lancaster Press.

Holmes, Geoffrey (1993). *The Making of a Great Power: Late Stuart and Early Georgian Britain, 1660–1722*. London: Longman.

Holmes, Geoffrey, and W. A. Speck (1967). *The Divided Society: Parties and Politics in England, 1694–1716*. London: Edward Arnold.

Holmes, Geoffrey, and Daniel Szechi (1993). *The Age of Oligarchy*. London: Longman.

Homer, Sidney, and Richard Sylla (1991). *A History of Interest Rates*. New Brunswick: Rutgers University Press.

Horwitz, Henry (1969). "The Structure of Parliamentary Politics." In Geoffrey Holmes, ed., *Britain after the Glorious Revolution: 1689–1714*. New York: St. Martin's Press. Pp. 96–114.

Horwitz, Henry (1977). *Parliament, Policy, and Politics in the Reign of William III*. Manchester: Manchester University Press.

Horwitz, Henry (1987). "Party in a Civic Context: London from the Exclusion Crisis to Fall of Walpole." In Clyve Jones, ed., *Britain in the First Age of Party*. London: Hambleton. Pp. 173–94.

Horwitz, Henry (1996). "The 1690s Revisited: Recent Work on Politics and Political Ideas in the Reign of William III." *Parliamentary History*, vol. 15, pp. 361–77.

Huber, John (1996). "The Vote of Confidence in Parliamentary Democracies." *American Political Science Review*, vol. 90, pp. 269–82.

Humphreys, Macartan (2001). "To Bargain or to Brawl? Politics in Institutionally Weak Environments." Mimeo, Harvard University.

Hyde, J. K. (1973). *Society and Politics in Medieval Italy: The Evolution of Civil Life, 1000–1300*. London: Macmillan.

Israel, Jonathan (1991). *The Anglo-Dutch Moment: Essays on the Glorious Revolution and Its World Impact*. Cambridge: Cambridge University Press.

Israel, Jonathan (1995). *The Dutch Republic: Its Rise, Greatness, and Fall*. Oxford: Oxford University Press.

Jackson, Matthew, and Boaz Moselle (2002). "Coalition and Party Formation in a Legislative Voting Game." *Journal of Economic Theory*, vol. 103, pp. 49–87.

Jones, Clyve (1987). "The House of Lords and the Growth of Parliamentary Stability, 1701–1742." In Clyve Jones, ed., *Britain in the First Age of Party.* London: Hambleton. Pp. 85–110.

Jones, Clyve (1991). "The Parliamentary Organization of the Whig Junto in the Reign of Queen Anne: The Evidence of Lord Ossulton's Diary." *Parliamentary History*, vol. 10, pp. 164–82.

Jones, Clyve (1984). " 'The Scheme Lords, the Necessitous Lords, and the Scots Lords': The Earl of Oxford's Management and the 'Party of the Crown' in the House of Lords, 1711–14." In Clyve Jones, ed., *Party and Management in Parliament 1660–1784.* Leicester: University of Leicester Press.

Jones, Clyve (1997). "The Parliamentary Organization of the Whig Junto in the Reign of Queen Anne: An Additional Note." *Parliamentary History*, vol. 16, pp. 205–12.

Jones, D. W. (1988). *War and Economy in the Age of William III and Marlborough.* Oxford: Basil Blackwell.

Jones, J. R. (1961). *The First Whigs.* London: Oxford University Press.

Jones, J. R. (1978). *Country and Court: England 1658–1714.* London: Edward Arnold.

Jones, J. R. (1994). "Fiscal Policies, Liberties, and Representative Government during the Reigns of the Last Stuarts." In Philip Hoffman and Kathryn Norberg, eds., *Fiscal Crises, Liberty, and Representative Government, 1450–1789.* Stanford: Stanford University Press. Pp. 67–95.

Kaiser, Thomas E. (1991). "Money Despotism, and Public Opinion in Early Eighteenth Century France: John Law and the Debate on Royal Credit." *Journal of Modern History*, vol. 63, pp. 1–28.

Keefer, Philip, and David Stasavage (2001). "Bureaucratic Delegation and Political Institutions: When Are Independent Central Banks Irrelevant? " World Bank Policy Research Working Paper.

Keefer, Philip, and David Stasavage (2002). "Checks and Balances, Private Information, and the Credibility of Monetary Commitments." *International Organization*, Autumn.

Kehoe, Patrick (1989). "Policy Cooperation among Benevolent Governments May Be Undesirable." *Review of Economic Studies*, vol. 56, pp. 289–96.

Kelsen, Hans (1932). *La Démocratie, sa nature, sa valeur.* Paris: Librarie du Recueil Sirey.

Kemp, Betty (1968). *King and Commons, 1660–1832.* London: Macmillan.

Kennedy, Michael (1979). "The Foundation of the Jacobin Clubs and the Development of the Jacobin Club Network, 1789–1791." *Journal of Modern History*, vol. 51, pp. 701–33.

Kennedy, Michael (1982). *The Jacobin Clubs in the French Revolution.* Princeton: Princeton University Press.

Kennedy, Michael (1984). "The Best and the Worst of Times: The Jacobin Club Network from October 1791 to June 2, 1793." *Journal of Modern History*, vol. 56, pp. 635–66.

Kenyon, J. P. (1977). *Revolution Principles: The Politics of Party: 1689–1720.* Cambridge: Cambridge University Press.

Kernell, S. (2001). "Reassessing the Madisonian Model: Factional Competition and Separation of Powers." Mimeo, University of California, San Diego.

Key, V. O. (1964). *Politics, Parties, and Pressure Groups.* New York: Crowell.

Kitschelt, Herbert (1994). *The Transformation of European Social Democracy.* New York: Cambridge University Pres.

Kohn, Meir (1999). "The Capital Market before 1600." Mimeo, Dartmouth College.

Kramnick, Isaac (1968). *Bolingbroke and His Circle: The Politics of Nostalgia in the Age of Walpole.* Cambridge: Harvard University Press.

Krehbiel, Keith (1993). "Where's the Party?" *British Journal of Political Science,* vol. 23, pp. 235–66.

Laprade, William Thomas (1936). *Public Opinion and Politics in Eighteenth Century England.* New York: Macmillan.

Laver, Michael, and W. B. Hunt (1992). *Policy and Party Competition.* New York: Routledge.

Laver, Michael, and Norman Schofield (1990). *Multiparty Government: The Politics of Coalition in Europe.* Oxford: Oxford University Press.

Lease, Owen C. (1950). "The Septennial Act of 1716." *Journal of Modern History,* vol. 22, pp. 42–47.

Legoff, T. J. A. (1997). "Les Caisses d'amortissement in France (1749–1783)." In *L'Administration des finances sous l'ancien régime.* Paris: Comité pour l'Histoire Economique et Financière de la France. Pp. 177–96.

Levi, Margaret (1988). *Of Rule and Revenue.* Berkeley: University of California Press.

Levy, Brian, and Pablo Spiller (1996). *Regulation, Institutions and Commitment: Comparative Studies of Telecommunications.* Cambridge: Cambridge University Press.

Levy, Gilat (2001). "The Role of Parties in Multidimensional Policy Space." Mimeo, London School of Economics.

Ligou, Daniel (1965). "Les Élus généraux de Bourgogne et les charges municipales de 1692 à 1789." *Actes du 90eme Congrès National des Sociétés Savantes,* pp. 95–118.

Lijphart, Arend (1977). *Democracy in Plural Societies.* New Haven: Yale University Press.

Lindblom, Charles (1982). "The Market as Prison." *Journal of Politics,* vol. 44, no. 2, pp. 324–26.

Lipset, Seymour Martin (1960). *Political Man.* Garden City: Doubleday.

Lipset, Seymour Martin, and Stein Rokkan (1967). *Party Systems and Voter Alignments: Cross-National Perspectives.* New York: Free Press.

Londregan, John (2001). "Problem Solving and Partisanship, the Double-Edged Sword of Constitutional Design." Mimeo, University of California, Los Angeles.

Lüthy, Herbert (1959–61). *La Banque protestante en France.* Paris: SEVPEN.

Luzzato, Gino (1963). *Il Debito pubblico della repubblica di Venezia, 1200–1500.* Milan.

Macaulay, T. B. (1861). *The History of England from the Accession of James II,* vol 4. London.

References

Maintenant, Gérard (1984). *Les Jacobins*. Paris: PUF.

Major, J. Russell (1960). *Representative Institutions in Renaissance France*. Madison: University of Wisconsim Press.

Major, J. Russell (1964). "The Crown and the Aristocracy in Renaissance France." *American Historical Review*, vol. 69, pp. 631–45.

Manin, Bernard (1997). *The Principles of Representative Government*. Cambridge: Cambridge University Press.

Marion, Marcel (1919). *Histoire financière de la France depuis 1715*. Paris: Arthur Rousseau, vols. 1 and 2.

Marmontel (1819). *Oeuvres complètes de Marmontel*, vol. 18: *Régence du duc d'Orléans*. Paris: Verdière.

Martin, Lisa (1994). "Heterogeneity, Linkage and Commons Problems." *Journal of Theoretical Politics*, vol. 6, pp. 473–93.

Mathias, Peter, and Patrick O'Brien (1976). "Taxation in Britain and France: 1715–1810." *Journal of European Economic History*, vol. 5, pp. 601–50.

Matthews, George (1958). *The Royal General Farms in Eighteenth Century France*. New York: Columbia University Press.

McCarty, Nolan (2000). "Proposal Rights, Veto Rights, and Political Bargaining." *American Journal of Political Science*, vol. 44, pp. 506–22.

McCubbins, Mathew, Roger Noll, and Barry Weingast (1989). "Structure and Process, Politics, and Policy: Administrative Arrangements and the Political Control of Agencies." *Virginia Law Review*, vol. 75, no. 2, pp. 431–83.

McLean, Iain (2001). "Before and after Publius: The Sources and Influence of Madison's Thought." Mimeo, Oxford University.

Milgrom, Paul, Douglass North, and Barry Weingast (1990), "The Role of Institutions in the Revival of Trade: The Law Merchant, Private Judges, and the Champagne Fairs." *Economics and Politics*, vol. 2, pp. 1–23.

Miller, Nicholas (1984). "Pluralism and Social Choice." *American Political Science Review*, vol. 77, pp. 734–47.

Mitchell, B. R. (1988). *Abstract of British Historical Statistics*. Cambridge: Cambridge University Press.

Montesquieu (1979 [1748]). Charles de Secondat, baron de. *L'Ésprit des Lois*. Paris: Flammarion.

Morgan, William Thomas (1920). *English Political Parties and Leaders in the Reign of Queen Anne: 1702–1710*. New Haven: Yale University Press.

Morgan, William Thomas (1921). "The Ministerial Revolution of 1710 in England." *Political Science Quarterly*, vol. 36, pp. 184–210.

Morgan, William Thomas (1922). "An Eighteenth-Century Election in England." *Political Science Quarterly*, vol. 37, pp. 585–604.

Morgan, William Thomas (1929). "The Origins of the South Sea Company." *Political Science Quarterly*, vol. 44, pp. 16–38.

Morini-Comby, Jean (1925). *Les Assignats: Revolution et inflation*. Paris: Nouvelle Librairie Nationale.

Munro, John (2001). "The Origins of the Modern Financial Revolution: Responses to Impediments from Church and State in Western Europe, 1200–1600." Mimeo, University of Toronto.

Murphy, Antoin (1990). "John Law and the Assignats." *Economies et Sociétés*, vol. 24, pp. 431–48.

Murphy, Antoin (1997). *John Law: Economic Theorist and Policymaker*. Oxford: Clarendon Press.

Murphy, Antoin (2000). "Introduction" to Dutot, *Histoire du système de John Law (1716–1720)*. Paris: Institut National d'Etudes Demographiques.

Neal, Larry (1990). *The Rise of Financial Capitalism*. Cambridge: Cambridge University Press.

Nichols, Glenn (1971). "English Government Borrowing, 1660–1688." *Journal of British Studies*, vol. 10, pp. 83–104.

Norberg, Kathryn (1994). "The French Fiscal Crisis of 1788 and the Financial Origins of the Revolution of 1789." In Philip Hoffman and Kathryn Norberg, eds., *Fiscal Crises, Liberty, and Representative Government, 1450–1789*. Stanford: Stanford University Press. Pp. 253–98.

North, Douglass (1981). *Structure and Change in Economic History*. New York: W. W. Norton.

North, Douglass (1990). *Institutions, Institutional Change, and Economic Performance*. New York: Cambridge University Press.

North, Douglass, and Barry Weingast (1989). "Constitutions and Commitment: The Evolution of Institutions Governing Public Choice in Seventeenth Century England." *Journal of Economic History*, vol. 49, pp. 803–32.

O'Brien, Patrick (1988). "The Political Economy of British Taxation, 1660–1815." *Economic History Review*, vol. 41, pp. 1–32.

O'Brien, Patrick, and Philip Hunt (1999). "England, 1485–1815." In Richard Bonney, ed., *The Rise of the Fiscal State in Europe: 1200–1815*. Oxford: Oxford University Press. Pp. 53–100.

Olson, Mancur (1993). "Dictatorship, Democracy, and Development." *American Political Science Review*, vol. 87, pp. 567–76.

Olson, Mancur (2000). *Power and Prosperity*. New York: Basic Books.

Ormrod, W. M. (1999). "England in the Middle Ages." In Richard Bonney, ed., *The Rise of the Fiscal State in Europe: 1200–1815*. Oxford: Oxford University Press. Pp. 25–52.

Osborne, Martin, and Ariel Rubinstein (1990). *Bargaining and Markets*. London: Academic Press.

Osborne, Martin, and Al Slivinski (1996). "A Model of Political Competition with Citizen-Candidates." *Quarterly Journal of Economics*, vol. III, pp. 65–96.

Persson, Torsten, and Guido Tabellini (1994). "Representative Democracy and Capital Taxation." *Journal of Public Economics*, vol. 55, pp. 53–70.

Persson, Torsten, and Guido Tabellini (2000). *Political Economics: Explaining Economic Policy*. Cambridge: MIT Press.

Plumb, J. H. (1956). *Sir Robert Walpole: The Making of a Statesman*. London: Cresset Press.

Plumb, J. H. (1967). *The Growth of Political Stability in England: 1675–1725*. London: Macmillan.

Poole, Keith, and Howard Rosenthal (1991). "Patterns of Congressional Voting." *American Journal of Political Science*, vol. 35, pp. 228–78.

Potter, Mark (1997), "The Institutions of Absolutism: Politics and Finance in France, 1680–1715." Ph.D. dissertation, UCLA.

Potter, Mark (2000). "Good Offices: Intermediation by Corporate Bodies in Early Modern French Public Finance." *Journal of Economic History*, vol. 60, pp. 599–626.

Potter, Mark, and Jean-Laurent Rosenthal (1997). "Politics and Public Finance in France: the Estates of Burgundy, 1660–1790." *Journal of Interdisciplinary History*, vol. 27, pp. 577–612.

Powell, Robert (1996). "Bargaining in the Shadow of Power." *Games and Economic Behavior*, vol. 15, pp. 255–89.

Powell, Robert (1999). *In the Shadow of Power: States and Strategies in International Politics*. Princeton: Princeton University Press.

Prescott, Edward (1977). "Should Control Theory Be Used for Economic Stabilization?" *Carnegie-Rochester Conference Series on Public Policy*, vol. 7, pp. 13–38.

Przeworski, Adam (1991). *Democracy and the Market*. Cambridge: Cambridge University Press.

Przeworski, Adam, and Fernando Limongi (1993). "Political Regimes and Economic Growth." *Journal of Economic Perspectives*, vol. 7, pp. 51–69.

Przeworski, Adam, and Michael Wallerstein (1988). "Structural Dependence of the State on Capital." *American Political Science Review*, vol. 82, no. 1, pp. 11–29.

Raynaud, Philippe (1993). "L'idée Républicaine et 'Le Fédéraliste.'" In François Furet and Mona Ozouf, eds., *Le Siècle de l'avènement républicain*. Paris: Gallimard. Pp. 57–79.

Rebillon, Armand (1932). *Les Etats de Bretagne de 1661 à 1789*. Paris: Auguste Picard.

Richards, James (1972). *Party Propaganda under Queen Anne*. Athens: University of Georgia Press.

Richet, Denis (1973). *La France moderne: L'Ésprit des institutions*. Paris: Flammarion.

Riker, William (1980). "Implications from the Disequilibrium of Majority Rule for the Study of Institutions." *American Journal of Political Science*, vol. 74, pp. 432–46.

Riley, James (1973). "Dutch Investment in France, 1781–1787." *Journal of Economic History*, vol. 33, pp. 733–57.

Riley, James (1986), *The Seven Years War and the Old Regime in France*. Princeton: Princeton University Press.

Riley, James (1987). "French Public Finances, 1727–1768." *Journal of Modern History*, vol. 59, pp. 209–43.

Robinson, James (1998). "Debt Repudiation and Risk Premia: The North-Weingast Thesis Revisited." Mimeo.

Roche, Daniel (1993). *La France des lumières*. Paris: Fayard.

Roemer, John (1998). "Why the Poor Do Not Expropriate the Rich: An Old Argument in New Garb." *Journal of Public Economics*, vol. 70, pp. 399–424.

Roemer, John (1999). "The Democratic Political Economy of Progressive Income Taxation." *Econometrica*, vol. 67, pp. 1–19.

Roemer, John (2001). *Political Competition: Theory and Applications*. Cambridge: Harvard University Press.

Root, Hilton (1989). "Tying the King's Hands: Credible Commitments and Royal Fiscal Policy during the Old Regime." *Rationality and Society*, vol. 1, no. 2, pp. 240–58.

Root, Hilton (1994). *The Fountain of Privilege*. Berkeley: University of California Press.

Rosenthal, Jean-Laurent (1997). "The Political Economy of Absolutism Reconsidered." In Robert Bates et al., eds., *Analytic Narratives*. Princeton: Princeton University Press. Pp. 65–108.

Roseveare, Henry (1969). *The Treasury: The Evolution of a British Institution*. London: Allen Lane.

Roseveare, Henry (1991). *The Financial Revolution*. London: Longman.

Rousseau, Peter, and Richard Sylla (2001). "Financial Systems, Economic Growth, and Globalization." NBER Working Paper no. 8323.

Rubinstein, Ariel (1982). "Perfect Equilibrium in a Bargaining Model." *Econometrica*, vol. 50, pp. 97–109.

Sargent, Thomas, and François Velde (1995). "Macroeconomic Features of the French Revolution." *Journal of Political Economy*, vol. 103, pp. 474–518.

Saugrain, M. Gaston (1896). *The Decline of the Interest Rate*. Paris.

Say, Jean-Baptiste Léon (1865). *Histoire de la Caisse d'Escompte, 1776 à 1793*. Reims: Imprimerie de P. Régnier.

Schattschneider, E. E. (1942). *Party Government*. New York: Farrar and Rinehart.

Schattschneider, E. E. (1960). *The Semisovereign People*. New York: Harcourt-Brace.

Schofield, Norman (1993). "Political Competition and Multiparty Coalition Governments." *European Journal for Political Research*, vol. 23, pp. 1–33.

Schofield, Norman (2001a). "Power, Prosperity and Social Choice: A Review." Mimeo, Washington University, St. Louis.

Schofield, Norman (2001b). "The Republic of Virtue and the Empire of Liberty." Mimeo, Washington University, St. Louis.

Schultz, Kenneth, and Barry Weingast (1996). "The Democratic Advantage: The Institutional Sources of State Power in International Competition." Hoover Institution Essays in Public Policy.

Schumpeter, Elizabeth (1938). "English Prices and Public Finance, 1660–1822." *Review of Economics and Statistics*, vol. 20, pp. 21–37.

Schwartz, Thomas (1989). "Why Parties." Mimeo, UCLA.

Sedgwick, Romney (1970). *The House of Commons 1715–1754*. History of Parliament Trust.

Shepsle, Kenneth (1979). "Institutional Arrangements and Equilibrium in Multidimensional Voting Models." *American Journal of Political Science*, vol. 23, pp. 27–59.

Shepsle, Kenneth (1991). "Discretion, Institutions, and the Problem of Government Commitment." In Pierre Bourdieu and James Coleman, eds., *Social Theory for a Changing Society*. Boulder: Westview. Pp. 245–60.

Shepsle, Kenneth, and Barry Nalebuff (1990). "The Commitment to Seniority in Self-Governing Groups." *Journal of Law, Economics, and Organization*, vol. 6, pp. 42–72.

Snyder, James, and Michael Ting (2000). "An Informational Rationale for Political Parties." Mimeo, MIT.

Speck, W. A. (1969). "Conflict in Society." In Geoffrey Holmes, ed., *Britain after the Glorious Revolution: 1689–1714*. London: Macmillan. Pp. 135–54.

Speck, W. A. (1970). *Tory and Whig: The Struggle in the Constituencies 1701–1715*. London: Macmillan.

Speck, W. A. (1977). *Stability and Strife: England, 1714–1760*. Cambridge: Harvard University Press.

Speck, W. A. (1981). "Whigs and Tories Dim Their Glories." In John Cannon, ed., *The Whig Ascendancy: Colloquies on Hanoverian England*. London: Edward Arnold. Pp. 51–70.

Spiller, Pablo (1995). "Regulatory Commitment and Utilities Privatization: Implications for Future Comparative Research." In Jeffrey Banks and Eric Hanushek, eds., *Modern Political Economy*. Cambridge: Cambridge University Press. Pp. 63–79.

Stasavage, David (2002a). "Credible Commitment in Early Modern Europe: North and Weingast Revisited." *Journal of Law, Economics, and Organization*, March, pp. 155–86.

Stasavage, David (2002b). "Private Investment and Political Institutions." *Economics and Politics*, March, pp. 41–63.

Stasavage, David, and Dominique Guillaume (2002). "When Are Monetary Institutions Credible: Parallel Agreements and the Sustainability of Currency Unions." *British Journal of Political Science*, vol. 32, pp. 119–46.

Stokes, Susan (1999). "Political Parties and Democracy." *Annual Review of Political Science*, vol. 2, pp. 243–67.

Stone, Bailey (1986). *The French Parlements and the Crisis of the Old Regime*. Chapel Hill: University of North Carolina Press.

Stone, Lawrence (1965). *The Crisis of the Aristocracy: 1558–1641*. Oxford: Oxford University Press.

Stone, Lawrence (1980). "The Results of the English Revolutions of the Seventeenth Century." In J. G. A. Pocock, ed., *Three British Revolutions: 1641, 1688, 1776*. Princeton: Princeton University Press. Pp. 23–108.

Szechi, Daniel (1986). "The Tory Party in the House of Commons 1710–1714: A Case Study in Structural Change and Political Evolution." *Parliamentary History*, vol. 5, pp. 1–15.

Tackett, Timothy (1989). "Nobles and the Third Estate in the Revolutionary Dynamic of the National Assembly: 1789–1790." *American Historical Review*, vol. 94, pp. 271–301.

Tackett, Timothy (1996). *Becoming a Revolutionary: The Deputies of the French National Assembly and the Emergence of a Revolutionary Culture*. Princeton: Princeton University Press.

Taylor, George (1967). "Noncapitalist Wealth and the Origins of the French Revolution." *American Historical Review*, vol. 72, no. 2, pp. 469–96.

t'Hart, Marjolein (1993). *The Making of a Bourgeois State: War, Politics, and Finance during the Dutch Revolt*. Manchester: Manchester University Press.

t'Hart, Marjolein (1997). "The Merits of a Financial Revolution: Public Finance, 1550–1700." In Marjolein t'Hart, Joost Jonker, and Jan Luiten van Zanden, eds., *A Financial History of the Netherlands.* Cambridge: Cambridge University Press. Pp. 11–36.

t'Hart, Marjolein (1999). "The United Provinces, 1579–1806." In Richard Bonney, ed., *The Rise of the Fiscal States in Europe: 1200–1815.* Oxford: Oxford University Press, pp. 309–25.

Thelen, Kathleen (1999). "Historical Institutionalism in Comparative Politics." *Annual Review of Political Science,* vol. 2, pp. 369–404.

Tilly, Charles (1990). *Coercion, Capital, and European States AD 990–1990.* Oxford: Oxford University Press.

Tomz, Michael (1999). "Do Creditors Ignore History?" Mimeo, Harvard University.

Tomz, Michael (2001). "How Do Reputations Form? New and Seasoned Borrowers in International Capital Markets." Mimeo, Stanford University.

Tracy, James (1985). *A Financial Revolution in the Habsburg Netherlands.* Berkeley: University of California Press.

Trevelyan, George M. (1933). *England under the Stuarts.* London: Methuen.

Troper, Michel (1980). *La Séparation des pouvoirs et l'histoire constitutionnelle française.* Paris: Librairie Générale de Droit et de Jurisprudence.

Tsebelis, George (2002). *Veto Players: How Political Institutions Work.* Princeton: Princeton University Press.

Tsebelis, George, and Jeannette Money (1997). *Bicameralism.* Cambridge: Cambridge University Press.

Veenendaal, Augustus (1994). "Fiscal Crises and Constitutional Freedom in the Netherlands, 1450–1795." In Philip Hoffman and Kathryn Norberg, eds., *Fiscal Crises, Liberty, and Representative Government, 1450–1789.* Stanford: Stanford University Press. Pp. 96–139.

Veitch, John (1986). "Repudiations and Confiscations by the Medieval State." *Journal of Economic History,* vol. 46, no. 1, pp. 31–36.

Velde, François, and Thomas Sargent (1990). "The Macroeconomic Causes and Consequences of the French Revolution." Mimeo, Stanford University.

Velde, François, and David Weir (1992). "The Financial Market and Government Debt Policy in France: 1746–1793." *Journal of Economic History,* vol. 52, no. 1, pp. 1–39.

Vovelle, Michel (1972). *La Chute de la monarchie, 1787–1792.* Paris: Seuil.

Walcott, Robert (1956). *English Politics in the Early Eighteenth Century.* Oxford: Oxford University Press.

Waley, Daniel (1989). *The Italian City Republics.* New York: Longman.

Weiller, Kenneth, and Philip Mirowski (1990). "Rates of Interest in 18th Century England." *Explorations in Economic History,* vol. 27, pp. 1–28.

Weingast, Barry (1995), "The Economic Role of Political Institutions: Market Preserving Federalism and Economic Development." *Journal of Law, Economics and Organization,* vol. 11, pp. 1–31.

Weingast, Barry (1997a), "The Political Foundations of Democracy and the Rule of Law." *American Political Science Review,* vol. 91, no. 2, pp. 245–63.

Weingast, Barry (1997b), "The Political Foundations of Limited Government: Parliament and Sovereign Debt in 17th and 18th Century England." In John

Drobak and John Nye, eds., *Frontiers of the New Institutional Economics*. London: Harcourt Brace. Pp. 213–46.

Weingast, Barry, and Mark Moran (1983). "Bureaucratic Discretion or Congressional Control? Regulatory Policymaking by the Federal Trade Commission." *Journal of Political Economy*, vol. 91, no. 5, pp. 765–800.

Weir, David (1989). "Tontines, Public Finance, and Revolution in France and England, 1688–1789." *Journal of Economic History*, vol. 49, pp. 95–124.

Wells, John, and Douglas Wills (2000). "Revolution, Restoration, and Debt Repudiation: The Jacobite Threat to England's Institutions and Economic Growth." *Journal of Economic History*, vol. 60, no. 2, pp. 418–41.

White, Eugene Nelson (1989). "Was There a Solution to the Ancien Règime's Financial Dilemma?" *Journal of Economic History*, vol. 49, pp. 545–68.

White, Eugene Nelson (1990). "The Evolution of Banking Theory during the French Revolution." *Economies et Sociétés*, vol. 24, pp. 451–63.

White, Eugene Nelson (1995). "The French Revolution and the Politics of Government Finance, 1770–1815." *Journal of Economic History*, vol. 55, pp. 227–55.

White, Eugene Nelson (1999). "France and the Failure to Modernize Macroeconomic Institutions." Mimeo, Rutgers University.

Williams, Basil (1939). *The Whig Supremacy*. Oxford: Oxford University Press.

Wolfe, Martin (1972). *The Fiscal System of Renaissance France*. New Haven: Yale University Press.

Index

Act of Settlement (1701), 73, 105
Albertone, Manuela, 148–49
Aldrich, John, 15, 39
Althusser, Louis, 11
Anne (Queen of England): partisan politics during reign, 122–25; political instability during reign, 163, 166–67; succession to the throne, 73, 105
Antwerp, 55
Aristotle, 12
assignats, 8, 132, 145–49
Atterbury plot, 105

Bank of England: establishment, 5–8, 69–70, 74–75, 79, 108, 120; example of delegation, 18–19; inspiration for French reformers, 92, 131–32, 141, 143–44, 149; partisan affiliation of directors, 111; partisan politics, and, 123–25; share prices, 82–84, 100
Banque Royale, 92, 131, 138–42; see also Law, John
Baron, David, 15, 32–34, 38, 179
Bates, Robert, 176
Bawn, Kathleen, 44
Beard, Charles, 11–12
Bien, David, 87, 89
Bill of Rights (1689), 72, 167
Bonney, Richard, 92

borrowing, government, see debt, public
Brewer, John, 60
Bulow, Jeremy, 31

Caisse d'Escompte, 69, 95, 144–45, 148
Calvert, Randall, 15–16, 39, 42–44, 116, 181
capital mobility, effect on commitment, 22
Charles I (of England), 62
Charles II (of England), 62–63, 117, 127
checks and balances: commitment and, 10–14, 23, 173; empirical findings, 176–77; formal model of, 45–47
civil war, English, 62–63
Clapham, John, 123
Clark, Gregory, 84
clubs, political, 114–16; see also Jacobin Club; Society of 1789; Tory party; Whig party
Cobban, Alfred, 146
Cocks, Sir Richard, 122
Compagnie des Indes, 92, 131, 139–40; see also Law, John
Condorcet, Marquis de, 149
Constituent Assembly, France (1789): debate over public finance, 144–46; divisions over issues, 147–51;

Anna L. Harvey, *Votes without Leverage: Women in
American Electoral Politics, 1920–1970*
Murray Horn, *The Political Economy of Public Administration:
Institutional Choice in the Public Sector*
John D. Huber, *Rationalizing Parliament: Legislative Institutions
and Party Politics in France*
Jack Knight, *Institutions and Social Conflict*
Michael Laver and Kenneth Shepsle, eds., *Making and Breaking
Governments*
Michael Laver and Kenneth Shepsle, eds., *Cabinet Ministers
and Parliamentary Government*
Margaret Levi, *Consent, Dissent, and Patriotism*
Brian Levy and Pablo T. Spiller, eds., *Regulations,
Institutions, and Commitment*
Leif Lewin, *Ideology and Strategy: A Century of Swedish Politics*
(English Edition)
Gary Libecap, *Contracting for Property Rights*
John Londregan, *Legislative Institutions and Ideology in Chile*
Arthur Lupia and Mathew D. McCubbins, *The Democratic Dilemma:
Can Citizens Learn What They Really Need to Know?*
C. Mantzavinos, *Individuals, Institutions, and Markets*
Mathew D. McCubbins and Terry Sullivan, eds., *Congress:
Structure and Policy*
Gary J. Miller, *Managerial Dilemmas: The Political
Economy of Hierarchy*
Douglass C. North, *Institutions, Institutional Change, and
Economic Performance*
Elinor Ostrom, *Governing the Commons: The Evolution of
Institutions for Collective Action*
J. Mark Ramseyer, *Odd Markets in Japanese History*
J. Mark Ramseyer and Frances Rosenbluth, *The Politics of
Oligarchy: Institutional Choice in Imperial Japan*
Jean-Laurent Rosenthal, *The Fruits of Revolution: Property Rights,
Litigation, and French Agriculture*
Charles Stewart III, *Budget Reform Politics: The Design of the
Appropriations Process in the House of Representatives, 1865–1921*
George Tsebelis and Jeannette Money, *Bicameralism*
John Waterbury, *Exposed to Innumerable Delusions: Public
Enterprise and State Power in Egypt, India, Mexico, and Turkey*
David L. Weimer, ed., *The Political Economy of Property Rights*